Lecture Notes in Computer Scie

Edited by G. Goos, J. Hartmanis and J. van L

Springer

Berlin
Heidelberg
New York
Barcelona
Budapest
Hong Kong
London
Milan
Paris
Singapore
Tokyo

Sushil Jajodia   M. Tamer Özsu
Asuman Dogac (Eds.)

Advances in Multimedia Information Systems

4th International Workshop, MIS'98
Istanbul, Turkey, September 24-26, 1998
Proceedings

 Springer

Series Editors

Gerhard Goos, Karlsruhe University, Germany
Juris Hartmanis, Cornell University, NY, USA
Jan van Leeuwen, Utrecht University, The Netherlands

Volume Editors

Sushil Jajodia
George Mason University
School of Computer Science and Information Systems
Fairfax, VA 22030-4444, USA
E-mail: jajodia@gmu.edu

M. Tamer Özsu
University of Alberta, Department of Computing Science
Edmonton, Alberta, Canada T6G 2H1
E-mail: ozsu@cs.ualberta.ca

Asuman Dogac
Middle East Technical University
Department of Computer Engineering
Ankara, Turkey
E-mail: asuman@srdc.metu.edu.tr

Cataloging-in-Publication data applied for

Die Deutsche Bibliothek - CIP-Einheitsaufnahme

Advances in multimedia information systems : 4th international workshop ; proceedings / MIS '98, Istanbul, Turkey, September 24 - 26, 1998. Sushil Jajodia (ed.). - Berlin ; Heidelberg ; New York ; Barcelona ; Budapest ; Hong Kong ; London ; Milan ; Paris ; Singapore ; Tokyo : Springer, 1998
 (Lecture notes in computer science ; Vol. 1508)
 ISBN 3-540-65107-1

CR Subject Classification (1991): H.5.1, H.4, H.5, I.7, C.2, I.4

ISSN 0302-9743
ISBN 3-540-65107-1 Springer-Verlag Berlin Heidelberg New York

© Springer-Verlag Berlin Heidelberg 1998
Printed in Germany

Typesetting: Camera-ready by author
SPIN 10692647   06/3142 – 5 4 3 2 1 0   Printed on acid-free paper

Preface

This book constitutes the proceedings of the Fourth International Workshop on Multimedia Information Systems (MIS'98) held in Istanbul, Turkey in September 1998. This workshop builds upon the success of the three previous workshops in this series that were held in Arlington, VA, West Point, NY, and Como, Italy. As in the past, this is a small focused workshop, consisting of participants drawn from a wide variety of disciplines (e.g. theory, algorithms, real-time systems, networks, operating systems, graphics and visualization, databases, artificial intelligence, etc.), all of which focus on research on one or more aspects of multimedia systems.

The workshop program included 19 technical papers, three invited talks, and one panel. Of the technical papers 13 were accepted as regular papers and 6 as short contributions. These papers cover a number of areas including:
- Multimedia storage system design
- Image storage and retrieval systems
- Quality of service considerations
- Networking support for multimedia information systems
- Distributed virtual environments
- Multimedia system architecture issues

The invited talks were given by three experts well-known for their work in this area. Satish K. Tripathi's (University of California, Riverside) talk was on "Quality of Service Support for Multimedia Data on Internet", Paul Emmerman (US Army Research Laboratory) discussed "Visualizing the Digital Battlefield", and Val Tannen (University of Pennsylvania) presented "Heterogeneous Data Integration with Mobile Information Manager". The panel discussion, organized by Chahab Nastar of INRIA, France, addressed "Trends in Visual Information Retrieval."

We believe the workshop program to have been very interesting and to have addressed timely issues. We hope that the attendees enjoyed the presentations and the ensuing discussions. Given the location of the workshop, we hope they will have taken advantage of the social life that Istanbul has to offer. Readers of these proceedings may miss out on the social side of the workshop, but we hope they will at least benefit from the offerings of the technical program.

We wish to express our appreciation to all the authors of the submitted papers, to the program committee members, and to our invited speakers and the panel participants.

Sushil Jajodia
July 1998   M. Tamer Özsu
Asuman Dogac

Acknowledgements

We would like to express our gratitude to the U.S. Army Research Office, which has generously supported this series of workshops since its inception.

We are indebted to the program committee members for their assistance in evaluating the submitted papers. The committee consists of:

Karl Aberer (GMD-IPSI, Germany)
Michel Adiba (University of Grenoble, France)
Peter Buneman (University of Pennsylvania, USA)
K. Selcuk Candan (Arizona State University, USA)
Tiziana Catarci (University of Rome "La Sapienza", Italy)
Stavros Christodoulakis (Technical University of Crete, Greece)
Nicolas D.Georganas (University of Ottawa, Canada)
Leana Golubchik (University of Maryland, USA)
Dave Hislop (US Army Research Office, USA)
Veysi Isler (Middle East Technical University, Turkey)
Xiaobo Li (University of Alberta, Canada)
Richard Muntz (UCLA, USA)
Chahab Nastar (INRIA-Rocquencourt, France)
Shamkant Navathe (Georgia Institute of Technology, USA)
Banu Ozden (Bell Labs, USA)
Meral Ozsoyoglu (Case Western Reserve University, USA)
George A. Papadopoulos (University of Cyprus, Cyprus)
Thomas Rakow (Springer-Verlag, Germany)
V.S. Subrahmanian (University of Maryland, USA)
Satish K. Tripathi (University of California, Riverside, USA)
Philip S. Yu (IBM T.J. Watson Research Center, USA)

Finally, we would like to express our gratitude to the University of Maryland Institute for Advanced Computer Studies; the Center for Secure Information Systems, George Mason University; the Research Institute for Multimedia Systems of the University of Alberta; the Middle East Technical University, Ankara, Turkey; and Bosphorus University, Istanbul, Turkey. In particular, we would like to thank the members of the Software Research and Development Center of the Middle East Technical University for their assistance with many organizational issues.

Table of Contents

Quality of Service Support for Multimedia Data on Internet

Satish K. Tripathi

University of California, Riverside

In order to support mutimedia data transfers, the underlying network should support quality of service (QoS) guarantees. The QoS guarantees by the network and the associated systems (hardware/software) is a complex task. In this talk, I'll outline the various issues related to the QoS in the Internet environment. The notion of QoS routing will be described in detail. Various options for routing and their associated overheads will be presented. Implementation issues will also be discussed.

S. Jajodia, M.T. Özsu, and A. Dogac (Eds.): MIS'98, LNCS 1508, pp. 1–1, 1998.
© Springer-Verlag Berlin Heidelberg 1998

Heterogeneous Data Integration with Mobile Information Managers

Val Tannen

University of Pennsylvania

Genomic and protein sequences, and in general molecular biology data, belongs to a relatively new information medium, with its own specific processing algorithms. Integrating such data from heterogeneous sources presents many of the challenges presented by integrating more common multimedia database integration. In this talk we are discussing solutions built as distributed applications because of the need for information sharing and that are easily scalable and reconfigurable in order to accommodate the frequent changes requested by molecular biology researchers. Specifically, we consider *Mobile Information Managers* (MIMs) which combine a specific approach to generating mediators with some aspects of agent technology, with everything based on a strongly uniform formal foundation.

MIMs are downloadable, networked components that have to a large degree uniform capabilities and can run at any site that implements the execution engine (virtual machine) for them. The basic functionality of a MIM is to implement a data integration and transformation from one or more data sources to one (virtual) data target. This target is therefore an (unmaterialized) view of the sources, and it is offered as yet another data source to the rest of the application. Thus, MIMs communicate with queries flowing in one direction and data returning in the other A MIM will contain a high-level description of the schemas for sources and target and of the integration/transformation that governs its activity. These descriptions, as well as the description of the queries and the data are formalized in the same internal framework.

MIMS are "mobile" because we envision the possibility of the dynamic reconfiguration of the system. A user, aware of a subset of data sources it needs to access, should be able to download an appropriate "client" MIM and join a distributed application in progress. A data provider running, say, an Oracle DB, should be able to join too, by downloading and configuring a generic "server" MIM compatible with Oracle sources. A "MIMSys administrator", might decide to download a new "mediating" MIM in a new intermediate node in order to create a another layer of abstraction and simplify the view that a certain class of clients uses. Later on, when demands have stabilized, a decision could be made to replace the mediating MIM with an actual data warehouse. In that case, the old mediating MIM becomes a client MIM that loads the new data warehouse, and a simple server MIM is added to keep providing the rest of the application with the view that the old mediating MIM offered, We expect such transitions to be done without having to modify the MIMs

S. Jajodia, M.T. Özsu, and A. Dogac (Eds.): MIS'98, LNCS 1508, pp. 2–3, 1998.

running in other nodes. The key to realizing the degree of uniformity required for scalability and reconfigurability is the use of formal high-level descriptions for the schemas, the integration/transformation, the queries, the optimization process, and the query evaluation process.

A Scalable Video-on-Demand Server for a Dynamic Heterogeneous Environment*

Maria Papadopouli** and Leana Golubchik***

Abstract. In this paper, we consider a Video-on-Demand storage server which operates in a *heterogeneous* environment and faces (a) fluctuations in workload, (b) network congestion, and (c) failure of server and/or network components. network). We present scheduling of data retrieval techniques which are capable of dynamically resolving congestion which occurs on the storage subsystem due to expected and unexpected changes in I/O bandwidth demand for a *scalable* video server in a *multi-disk* environment. techniques.

1 Introduction

Recent technological advances in digital signal processing, data compression techniques, and high speed communication networks have made Video-on-Demand (VOD) servers feasible. The design of such large scale systems involves several challenging tasks, including the satisfaction of (a) real-time constraints of continuous delivery of video objects as well as (b) quality of service (QoS) requirements. A great deal of work has been performed in the last few years in the area of VOD server design (see [7] for details).

In this work, we consider the retrieval of variable bit rate (VBR) video streams from a VOD storage-server in a *multi-disk environment*. An attractive feature of the use of VBR video (as opposed to constant bit rate (CBR) video) is the constant quality of video that can be provided throughout the duration of an object's display. However, VBR video exhibits significant variability in required video display rates. This variability can affect resource utilization in the system and complicate scheduling of both transmission of objects over a communication network as well as their retrieval from the storage subsystem. There are several works dealing with the support of VBR video for networking applications [6] some of which can be extended for use in the storage-server domain; however, an essential difference in this case, is that a storage server has *a priori* knowledge of the video traces which can aid in *further* improvements of the design.

In many multimedia systems different levels of quality of service (QoS) can be supported through the use of the multiresolution property of video (and/or images). In this work, we present a *scalable* VOD server for a *heterogeneous*

---

* This work was supported in part by the NSF CAREER grant CCR-96-25013.
** Department of Computer Science, Columbia University.
*** Department of Computer Science, University of Maryland at College Park. This work was partly done while the author was with the Department of Computer Science at Columbia University.

S. Jajodia, M.T. Özsu, and A. Dogac (Eds.): MIS'98, LNCS 1508, pp. 4–17, 1998.
© Springer-Verlag Berlin Heidelberg 1998

environment that provides statistical service guarantees and propose scheduling techniques for retrieval of VBR video that exploit the multiresolution property of compressed video streams. An example of such a system includes a video server delivering videos over the Internet, with users (potentially) requesting service using different types of hosts. In this work, we define the *scalability* characteristic, as it applies to a VOD system, as the capability to adjust to changes in (a) workload and (b) availability of storage and network resources as well as the capability to deliver video data at different levels of QoS guarantees.

In general, the video server faces (a) fluctuations in workload, (b) network congestion, and (c) failure of server and/or network components. At the same time, the users, while being served, are subject to changes in their sustained bandwidth requirements due to either (a) network congestion, (b) failure of network components, or (c) moving to a different environment (i.e., network). We define the *sustained bandwidth* of a user, in a certain time period, as the rate at which he/she is "expected" to effectively receive the data in that time period and which corresponds to a certain video quality profile [1]. The flexibility that scalable compression techniques provide, in adjusting the resolution (or rate) of a video stream at any point **after** the compressed video object has been generated can be of great use in designing scalable video servers. Various video compression schemes, such as subband coding and MPEG-2, provide such a multiresolution property. The multiresolution property has been utilized, for instance, in previous work on dynamic adjustment of resolution of video streams being transmitted through a *communication network* [5] based on available network resources; although this approach has produced good results in utilization of available communication network bandwidth, there are several difficulties with adapting it to solving similar problems with utilization of disk bandwidth resources in a *storage* subsystem. In [16] a framework is proposed for a layered substream abstraction with highly scalable compression algorithms to support this abstraction. Finally, simulations in [3] show that the use of scalable video with Laplacian and Pyramidal coding can greatly increase the I/O bandwidth demand that can be sustained and decrease the waiting time for start of new requests for video objects, as compared to the use of full-resolution non-scalable video.

The focus of this paper is on the scheduling of data retrieval and approaches to resolving disk bandwidth congestion under expected and unexpected changes in I/O bandwidth demand. The work presented here differs from other related works in that the scheduling of the retrieval *adapts* to the availability of the *storage* and *network* resources as well as the *user's* bandwidth requirements (that may change dynamically). It is introduced in a dynamic rate-distortion context for a *multi-disk environment*.

Specifically, we consider techniques which dynamically adjust resolution of video streams in progress, in order to adjust to fluctuations in workload and

---

[1] The changes in the sustained bandwidth of a user might be due, for instance to network congestion. Some of the work on determining the sustained bandwidth is discussed in [14].

resource availability while satisfying given QoS constraints and utilizing system resources efficiently. We propose resolution adjustment and load balancing techniques which address: (a) different causes of fluctuations, which include VBR property of video objects, the use of VCR functionality, as well as failure of system components, (b) the extent and duration of "overflow" of disk bandwidth demand beyond the available resources, (c) predictability of future I/O bandwidth demand, and (d) variations in QoS requirements. The resolution adjustment algorithm deals with short term fluctuations in the workload and takes advantage of the multiresolution property of video by adjusting the resolution of video streams in progress on a per single disk basis. The load balancing algorithm, on the other hand, deals with long term fluctuations in workload as well as extensive overlow of I/O bandwidth demand and "shifts" the load between multiple disks in the system; this algorithm takes advantage of both the multiresolution property of video and replication techniques. Furthermore, it also deals with changes in users' sustained bandwidth requirements [2].

2   System Description and Background

In this section we first briefly review the notion of scheduling of video requests in cycles or groups and then discuss data layout issues. Throughout the paper we use the term *stream* to refer to the delivery of a given video object at a given time.

System Parameters	
Notation	Description
L_d	set streams whose data blocks are stored on disk d
B	effective bandwidth of a single disk
τ_w	size of an interval (in units of time)
T_{cycle}	size of a cycle (in units of time)
$X_{i,d}(c)$	r.v. bandwidth requirement (for full resolution) of stream S_i on disk d during cycle c
$X_{i,d}^k(c)$	r.v. bandwidth requirement of the first k layers of stream S_i on disk d during interval c
$fb_{i,d}(w)$	sustained bandwidth of stream S_i on disk d during interval w.
μ	mean bandwidth requirement (for full resolution) of a stream
μ^L	mean bandwidth requirement that corresponds to retrieval of L multiresolution layers

Table 1. Notation

2.1   Data Retrieval and Corresponding Disk Model

To achieve efficient use of available disk bandwidth, it is common to organize the scheduling of streams into (time) cycles or groups, e.g., as in [2]. In their simplest form, cycle-based schemes deliver in each cycle the data that is read in the previous cycle. During each time period, data for each active stream is read from the disks into main memory while, concurrently, the data read

---

[2] We would like to emphasize that the success of resolution adjustment techniques, in general, depends on the number of resolutions available, the workload on the system, and the variability of the VBR video streams, e.g., in the case of subband coding, a large number of layers can be supported, whereas in MPEG-2, the number of layers is restricted to a maximum of 3.

during the previous cycle is transmitted over the network to display stations. The motivation for this organization is to provide opportunities for seek optimization (see [2] for details) [3].

In the remainder of the paper, we will consider scheduling of data retrieval and overflow management in time intervals composed of an integral number of cycles. This slight generalization will allow us to control the scale on which bandwidth re-allocation is performed. Thus, an interval w starting in cycle c, i.e., $[c, \tau_w + c]$, whose size is τ_w (in *number of cycles*) is composed of consecutive, non-overlapping cycles $(c, c + 1,.., c + \tau_w)$, where continuous playback of a video with quality Q_L can be guaranteed if all blocks corresponding to $\{X_{i,d}^L(j)$, where j is a cycle and $j \in [c, c + \tau_w]\}$ have been retrieved (from disk d) by the end of that interval, where $X_{i,d}^L(j)$ is a random variable that indicates the bandwidth requirement of stream S_i on disk d, during cycle j corresponding to video quality Q_L. Lastly, we define the mean bandwidth requirement of stream S_i on disk d during interval w corresponding to video quality Q_L as follows:

$$\mu_i^L(w) = X_{i,d}^L(w) = \frac{\sum_{j=c}^{c+\tau_w} X_{i,d}^L(j)}{\tau_w} \qquad (1)$$

Disk Model

We now introduce a simple disk model that we use in the remainder of this paper. During each cycle of size T_{cycle} each stream retrieves a variable number of blocks corresponding to its bandwidth requirement for that cycle. Given the cycle based scheduling scheme the amount of time needed to retrieve data blocks corresponding to x streams scheduled during that cycle includes (a) a maximum seek τ_{seek}, which is the time to move the disk head between the extreme inner and outer cylinders of a disk, (b) rotational latency τ_{rot}^{avg}, and (c) the transfer time for each of the x streams that is attributable to reading the necessary number of data blocks, τ_{rot}. Note that the amount of data that has to be retrieved per stream in order to maintain continuity in the data delivery is $T_{cycle} * \mu$, where μ is the *mean* bandwidth requirement of each stream. Then, the time to read this data is $\frac{T_{cycle}*\mu}{B_{track}}\tau_{rot} + \tau_{rot}^{avg}$, where B_{track} is the number of bytes per track, and the constraint that there must be time in a cycle to read that much data for x streams is $\tau_{seek} + x(\frac{T_{cycle}*\mu}{B_{track}}\tau_{rot} + \tau_{rot}^{avg}) \leq T_{cycle}$. In the remainder of the paper we assume that $\tau_{rot}^{avg} = \frac{\tau_{rot}}{2}$, which then gives us a bound on the number of streams that can be serviced in one cycle on one disk[4] : $x \leq \frac{T_{cycle}-\tau_{seek}}{0.5+\frac{T_{cycle}\mu}{B_{track}}}\frac{1}{\tau_{rot}}$.
The effective bandwidth of a disk is then $B = \mu * x$.

---

[3] Note that, our bandwidth reallocation techniques, presented later in the paper, are not restricted to cycle-based scheduling, but are presented in that context for simplicity of exposition.

[4] We have assumed that the data blocks of the same video object that correspond to one retrieval unit are stored contiguously on the disk. Therefore, the rotational latency corresponding to retrieval of the last fraction of the data block, i.e., the one that does not (necessarily) make up an entire track is on the average $\frac{\tau_{rot}}{2}$. We have also assumed that zero latency reads [13] are possible for the full size tracks and that B_{track} is a constant (i.e., we do not consider zones here).

2.2 Data Layout and Partial Replication

In this paper we extend the notion of a traditional replication scheme [1] for use in a multiresolution video server environment to instead support backup copies of videos in a *lower* resolution than the primary copy. That is, a backup copy of a video object is not necessarily identical to its primary copy; however, all resolution layers which are replicated, are identical to their primary copy counterparts and correspond to a predetermined video quality level Q_L; thus, the backup copy is composed of the first L layers of each video segment ($L = 1, .., max$). In the remainder of the paper, we refer to this form of replication as *partial* replication.

In general, replication provides opportunities for better disk bandwidth utilization (as will become more apparent in Section 3), since it provides: (a) flexibility to service a stream by partial simultaneous retrieval of data from multiple disks in the system, when there is not sufficient bandwidth to serve that stream from any one disk, and (b) load-balancing opportunities, i.e., opportunities for "shifting" some of the load from one disk to another. Although much of the discussion on scheduling which follows is not restricted to a particular replication scheme, in Section 4 we present a scheme which is specific to *chained declustering* [9,8]; thus, we describe this particular replication scheme next.

In the traditional chained declustering layout, at any point in time, two physical copies of a data fragment, termed the primary and the backup copy are maintained. If the primary copy of a fragment resides on disk D_i, then the backup copy of that fragment resides on disk D_{i+1} (mod N_d, where N_d is the number of disks in the system). Under dynamic scheduling, a server can choose to retrieve a data block from either of the disks containing a replica of that data block. Thus, in our system, by (re)scheduling some data retrieval from disk D_i to disk D_{i+1}, the server can "create" available bandwidth space on disk D_i, which can be used for retrieval of other blocks corresponding to streams that were originally scheduled for service on either disk D_i or disk D_{i-1} (and consequently can be transferred for service to disk D_i). The provision of a backup copy in a *lower* resolution can also be applied to the chained declustering scheme. Figure 1 illustrates an example system using chained declustering and partial replication.

2.3 Interval-Based Retrieval and Admission Control

Many different approaches to allocating (or reserving) bandwidth, at admission control time, for servicing video streams are possible. And, the scheduling framework described in Sections 3 and 4 are not limited to a specific approach; however, in order to focus the discussion better, we assume the following bandwidth reservation scheme (performed at admission control time) in the remainder of the paper. For each interval, the bandwidth reservation is performed by approximating the bandwidth requirements of the video (during that interval) with its *average* (over that interval), i.e., $\mu_i^L(w)$. The average bit rate reservation can

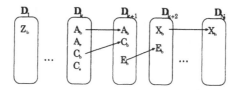

Fig. 1. Chained declustering with partial replication: the segments of the form S_b correspond to the first b resolution layers of a video object and have been replicated. For the S_e segments which compose the remaining or enchanced resolution layers only a single copy is kept. The arrows indicate a potential shift of the retrieval of data blocks from one disk to the next.

utilize resources more efficiently than the peak rate reservation, but leads to potential congestions (due to the variability of the stream bandwidth demand) [5]. One of the foci of this paper is a technique for alleviating these congestions without (significantly) affecting the quality of service provided to the users. In order to limit such congestion (and be able to provide an "acceptable" QoS level), it is necessary to perform some form of admission control.

During *admission control*, it is determined whether there are sufficient available resources for retrieval of a newly requested video stream; this is done by considering $\mu_i^L(w)$ $\forall w$ and determining, on per interval basis, whether there is sufficient bandwidth available in the system for support of this new stream. The reservation of bandwidth resources made during the admission control phase, provides *statistical* guarantees for the retrieval of the streams and only "approximates" the actual retrieval schedule, without preventing potential congestion. Hence, a bandwidth re-allocation mechanism that dynamically alleviates congestions is required. The scheduling techniques presented here are not limited to a specific admission control scheme; thus, in the remainder of this paper, we only make the assumption that the admission control policy results in statistical QoS guarantees as follows — a server can guarantee, to at most n_L users, a video quality of Q_L, with probability P_L, where various methods for determining n_L and P_L can be constructed but are outside the scope of this paper [6].

In this paper, for the sake of simplicity, we assume equal size intervals which are the same for all streams and are equal to an integral number of cycles. In general, we will consider intervals on the order of a few seconds. Of course, in order for continuous playback guarantees to be satisfied, we also need to assume that the user provides a buffer of size $2 * b_{max} * \tau_w * T_{cycle}$, at the user's site, where T_{cycle} is the duration of one cycle, b_{max} is based on the user's video quality requirement and is basically the maximum bandwidth requirement

---

[5] The significance of underutilization of resources due to peak rate reservation in a piecewise (i.e., interval-based) manner, as opposed to average rate reservation with possibility of overflow, depends on the characteristics of the video trace and the size of the intervals.

[6] The discussion on the choice of interval size and the guarantees of the reservation mechanism can be found in [12].

corresponding to the quality of service he/she requests[7]. This buffer space will "mask" the jitter that might otherwise result from altering the data retrieval to be on a per-interval, rather than per-cycle, basis.

3   Scheduling of Data Retrieval

It is the main task of the scheduler to determine the amount of data to be retrieved per stream per cycle and schedule the retrieval for the appropriate cycle and disk. Due to the guarantees made during the admission control phase, the scheduler is ensured that there is available bandwidth somewhere in the system to serve all admitted streams with video quality Q_L with probability P_L (see Section 2.3). However, the scheduler might be required to re-allocated (or shift) part of the workload, due to congestion, across the disks of the system. Recall that, due to replication, some of the data can be retrieved from one of two disks. Furthermore, transferring of some load from one disk to the next one might result in a number of shifts of load between consecutive disks. That is, a video block of stream S_i, of size b_i can be "shifted" from a congested disk D during some time interval T, to disk D' if: (a) a replica of the video block is also stored on disk D' **and** (b) the available bandwidth (that exists or could be "made available") on disk D' during time T *at least* corresponds to the amount needed to retrieve a block of size b_i. Below, we present a general framework for re-allocating bandwidth to streams in cases of fluctuations in order to dynamically exploit the available bandwidth of the system.

3.1   Resolution Adjustment on Multiple Disks

An optimal assignment of data block retrievals to disks, i.e., one that minimizes the amount of data that can *not* be retrieved (due to overflow), can be determined using a "max flow" algorithm [4] [8].
Graph Generation
We begin with the needed generation of an appropriate graph. The construction of this graph and the computation of the corresponding optimum schedule under given constrains requires the knowledge of the amount of bandwidth that was *reserved* at admission control time for retrieval of data blocks corresponding to active streams as well as the amount of bandwidth that is *required* by these streams during the time interval in question. The max flow algorithm is specified on a per-interval basis, i.e., we can determine, on a per-interval basis, whether overflow will occur in that interval and run the max flow algorithm in order to determine a new assignment of streams to disks and the corresponding retrieval schedule which alleviates overflow in an optimal manner (given the optimality criteria stated above), where τ_w is a parameter of the scheduling algorithm. The

---

[7]   Here, we assume double buffering at the user's site, for ease of exposition.

[8]   See [11] for extensions to use with lower bounds on edges.

max flow algorithm will be applied on a graph $G^L(w) = (V, E)$ (e.g., see Figure 2), which can be constructed as follows:

$$G^L(w) = (V, E), \quad V = \{D_1, D_2, \ldots, D_{N_d}\} \cup \{V_1, \ldots, V_n\} \cup \{s\},$$
$$E = \{(s, V_j), \; j = 1, .., n\} \cup \{(V_j, D_i), j \in L_{D_i}, \; i = 1, .., N_d\}$$

where L_{D_i} is the set of streams whose data blocks are stored on disk D_i and where each node D_i has capacity B, which is the effective bandwidth capacity of disk D_i (see Section 2.1). There are n number of nodes V_j, each corresponding to a currently active stream S_j, and each connected to the start node s (an artificial node) with an edge $(s, V_j) \in E$ whose capacity is bound by l_j and u_j, i.e., the flow on this edge, (s, V_j), is $l_j \leq f_j \leq u_j$. If the required bandwidth of stream S_j during interval w, $fb_j(w)$, is less than $X^L_{j,d}(w)$, then $l_j = u_j = fb_j(w)$. Therefore, if the (adjusted) sustained bandwidth of a user is less than or equal to the mean bandwidth that the server has reserved for that user, then the retrieval corresponding to S_j will be at least of size $fb_j(w)$. If, on the other hand, the user's required bandwidth is higher than $X^L_{j,d}(w)$, then $l_j = \mu^L_j(w)$ (refer to Section 2.1) and $u_j = fb_j(w)$. Furthermore, if the first k layers of a stream S_i are stored on disk D_j, then there is an edge (V_i, D_j), with its lower and upper capacity equal to 0 and $\mu^k_i(w)$, respectively. The max flow algorithm will assign a flow to each edge (s, V_i) which represents the bit rate that the server will deliver to S_i during interval w. Note that, a flow > 0 on edges (V_j, D_i) indicates that a fraction of stream S_j will be retrieved from disk D_i.

The max flow algorithm produces one bandwidth allocation (from all possible ones) that retrieves the maximum total amount of data for the active streams with respect to the guarantees of certain quality of service and constraints on the playback rates of the users [9].

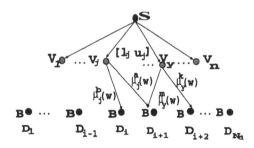

Fig. 2. Graph for the max flow algorithm

Lastly, the time complexity of the max flow algorithm is $O(|V||E|log|V|)$, e.g., the algorithm by Sleator and Tarjan [15] can be used. Then, given that the

---

[9] We should emphasize that the feasibility of a flow on the above graph will depend on the statistical guarantees the server makes at admission control time.

maximum total number of streams in the system is $n_f * N_d$, the time complexity becomes $O((N_d + N_d * n_f + 1) * (3 * n_f * N_d)(log(N_d * n_f + N_d + 1))$ or $O((n_f * N_d)^2(log(max(N_d, n_f))))$. The max flow algorithm can run at the beginning of an interval to compute the optimal bandwidth allocation for the next interval. Of course, the tradeoff here is between having sufficient time to run the max flow algorithm (i.e., making the intervals longer) and the amount of buffer space needed at the user site (which grows with the interval length).

3.2 Resolution Adjustment on Per-Disk Basis

In this section we consider the problem of "per-disk" re-adjustment of the data retrieval schedule. As already mentioned in Section 1, the motivation here is to be able to resolve short term overflow problems relatively quickly and on a per-disk basis.

One of the important requirements of bit rate re-adjustment is to minimize the distortion that the streams will experience as a result of the re-adjustment process. We define the distortion of a stream S_i during time interval t, due to a decrease of information retrieved from $b_i(t)$ to $b_i(t) - \beta_i$ as a non-decreasing (cost) function R_i: $R_i(\beta_i, t) = \tau_i * \Delta_i(\beta_i, t)$, where, $b_i(t)$ corresponds to a (feasible) retrieval schedule[10] of the requested resolution, τ_i is a distortion tolerance factor[11], and $\Delta_i(\beta_i, t)$ is the distortion due to retrieving only $b_i(t) - \beta_i$ instead of $b_i(t)$ amount of data.

Each layer k is associated with a "distortion measure", $\delta_i(b_i^k(t)) = r_k$, where $b_i^k(t)$ corresponds to the amount of data that needs to be retrieved for the kth layer of stream i at time interval t[12]. Therefore, r_k indicates the resolution improvement, if in addition to the first $k - 1$ layers of video retrieval, we also retrieve the k-th layer. When β_i amount of data is not retrieved, the decoder will be able to decode only the first λ_i layers (instead of all λ_{max} layers that compose the requested resolution data blocks), and therefore, the distortion that the user will experience during interval t will be as follows:

$$\Delta_i(\beta_i, t) = \sum_{k=\lambda_i+1}^{\lambda_{max}} \delta_i(b_i^k(t)), \quad where \; \lambda_i = \max_k(\beta_i \leq \sum_{l=k}^{max} b_i^l(t)). \tag{2}$$

Here, the cost function R_i quantifies the QoS of a stream S_i.

The server runs the Resolution Adjustment (RA) algorithm (given below) on a future time interval t after detecting a congestion in that interval in order to determine the proper bandwidth re-allocation. Let us assume that for that

---

[10] A retrieval schedule is feasible when it does not violate the disk bandwidth constraints while it guarantees normal playback at the receiver without discontinuities.

[11] The distortion tolerance factor, τ_i, is a function of: (a) QoS requirements of the user, (b) feedback mechanism, and (c) subjective distortion measures on specific video segments, e.g., the service of streams in FF/REW mode, which can tolerate larger distortions.

[12] Distortion measures may vary from a simple mean squared error (MSE) estimate to more complicated perception-based functions.

interval t, B_{of} is the disk bandwidth overflow on the disk in question, b_i^{max} is the retrieval unit corresponding to requested resolution of the video, and b_i^{base} is the retrieval unit corresponding to some minimum acceptable resolution, as specified by the user[13]. Then, RA can be formulated as follows[14]:

- **Find** β_i $i = 1, \ldots, n$
- **Minimize** $max_i\{R_i(\beta_i)\} - min_i\{R_i(\beta_i)\}$
- **such   that :**
  1. $\sum_i \beta_i = B_{of}$
  2. $0 \leq \beta_i \leq b_i^{max} - b_i^{base}$, **where** β_i **is a non-negative integer,** $i = 1, 2 \ldots, n$, **where** n **is the number of active streams on the disk.**

The RA problem is a "fair resource allocation" problem that can be solved using the FAIR algorithm, as given in [10], of complexity $O(n \log(max(n, B_{of})))$, where n is the number of active streams on a disk and B_{of} is the disk bandwidth overflow. If RA does not have a feasible solution, we can attempt to shift the overflow to the remaining disks in the system (as described above) [15].

4   Application of Max Flow Formulation

In this section we consider sources of congestion due only to changes in sustained bandwidth of users and then evaluate the performance of the resulting server, termed $S_{scalable}$. This evaluation focuses on the retrieval scheduling/overflow management policy which was formulated in Section 3 as a max flow problem. For the purposes of comparison we use a baseline server, termed $S_{independent}$, which does not take advantage of replication (and here specifically chained decluster-ing with partial replication). In $S_{independent}$ all disks are independent, i.e., a retrieval for a particular stream is always scheduled on a specific disk without the flexibility of replication, that exists in $S_{scalable}$, which allows "shifting" of the load across disks. The metric used in evaluating the overflow management policy is the percentage of ("newly available") bandwidth that we are able to utilize (we explain this in more detail below). The results of this evaluation have been obtained through simulation, where we use the disk model given in Section 2.1. The parameters of that model used in this section are as follows: (a) $\tau_{seek} = 30$ msec, (b) $\tau_{rot} = 10$ ms, (c) $B_{track} = 100$ KB, and (d) $T_{cycle} = 530$ msec.

Below we illustrate that, through the use of chained declustering with partial replication, the server is not only capable of resolving overflow due to fluctua-tions, for instance, of VBR video compression, but is also sufficiently flexible and can take advantage of the available bandwidth that results from reductions

---

[13] For instance, in the notation of the previous section, if the required bandwidth of stream S_i during interval t $fb_i(t)$, is higher than $X_{i,d}^L(t)$, then $b_i^{base} = \mu_i^L(t)$ and $b_i^{max} = fb_i(t)$; otherwise $b_i^{base} = b_i^{max} = fb_i(t)$.

[14] In this formulation, we drop the "time dependence" in the notation in order to simplify it.

[15] This approach can result in certain disadvantages, the description of which is left out due to lack of space; see [12] for details.

in the sustained bandwidth of some users. For the purposes of the following discussion, we term the users with decreases in sustained bandwidth requirements in an interval w as "degraded" users; similarly, we term the users with increases in sustained bandwidth requirements in an interval w as "upgraded" users. The simulations described below aim to evaluate the bandwidth re-allocation process of $S_{scalable}$ and $S_{independent}$ by computing the portion of bandwidth (that can be scheduled) that was freed by the "degraded" users that can (potentially) be re-assigned to the "upgraded" users in order to satisfy their requests for increases in bandwidth, in an interval w.

Let us consider some such interval w. In order to focus on the comparison between overflow management of the two servers, we fix the load on each disk of both server to be the same. Specifically, for our simulation we consider a cluster of 45 disks. The load on each disk, i.e., the total amount of bandwidth that is needed during interval w is determined based on a *uniform* distribution with values ranging in [38 Mbps, 60.8 Mbps].

As already mentioned, $S_{scalable}$ uses the max flow algorithm; Figure 3 illustrates the graph for this max flow algorithm that can be created as follows: (a) each disk corresponds to a node and each stream corresponds to an edge, (b) there is an artificial "start" node as well as a "sink" node, (c) for each "upgraded" stream, there is an edge which connects a node corresponding to a disk on which the stream is (at least partially) scheduled with an artificial "start" node, with capacity equal to the *increment* in the bandwidth requirement of that stream, (d) for each "degraded" stream, there is an edge which connects a node corresponding to a disk on which the stream is (at least partially) scheduled with an artificial "sink" node, with capacity equal to the *decrement* in the bandwidth requirement of that stream, (e) for each node that corresponds to a disk there is an edge that connects it to the node that corresponds to the disk on its right[16] (for the last disk, its node is connected with the node of the first disk) — the capacity of this edge is equal to the amount of bandwidth that can be transferred during this interval w from the disk in question to the next disk on its right, which depends on the degree of replication used in the system as well as the bandwidth requirements of streams accessing the disks in that interval.

This graph is somewhat different from the one described in Section 3.1, which is due to the source of change in workload, which in this case is due *only* to the changes in sustained bandwidth of "degraded' and "upgraded" users. In addition, in this case we are considering a specific form of replication, namely that of chained declustering. Moreover, this simplification in the formulation of the max flow algorithm reduces the complexity of the solution to $O((n_f * (N_d)^2)(log N_d))$. The max flow algorithm returns the maximum amount of bandwidth, as a fraction of the total amount of bandwidth that has been "released" by the "degraded" users, which can be re-allocated to the "upgraded" users. Note that, $S_{independent}$ is able to assign additional bandwidth to the "upgraded" users only if the disk on which they are served has some available bandwidth due (in this

---

[16] Recall that in chained declustering, the disk logically to the right of disk i contains copies of data stored on disk i.

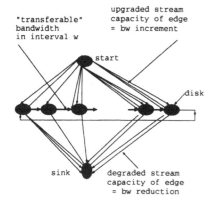

Fig. 3. Graph for the max flow algorithm.

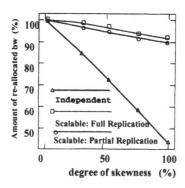

Fig. 4. Amount of bandwidth reallocated to "upgraded" users.

case *only*) to the reduction in the bandwidth requirements of the "degraded" users. Both servers assign to the "degraded" users bandwidth equal to their new reduced bandwidth requirements.

We illustrate in Figure 4 the amount of bandwidth that was "released" by the "degraded" users, which can be re-allocated to the "upgraded" users, as a function of the "skewness" of the changes in users' required bandwidth on the disks. Specifically, the total increment (reduction), $load^d_{increment}$ ($load^d_{reduction}$) in the bandwidth requirements on disk d is given by [17]:

$$load^d_{increment} = \frac{C_{increment}}{\phi(d)^\gamma}, \quad load^d_{reduction} = \frac{C_{reduction}}{f(d)^\gamma} \tag{3}$$

where $C_{increment}$ and $C_{reduction}$ are constants, and $\phi()$ and $f()$ provide a "one-to-one" mapping of the (N_d) disks to the (N_d) different loads (i.e., in Eq. (3) d is in the range 1 to N_d), where N_d is the disk cluster size. As γ increases, the access pattern becomes increasingly skewed. In our simulations we consider the following values of γ: $0.0, 0.25, 0.5, 0.75, 1.0$. Note that the *maximum* total increment (reduction) in bandwidth requirements on a disk is $C_{increment}$ ($C_{reduction}$). In this simulation we consider $C_{increment} = C_{reduction} = 35$ Mbps.

In Figure 4 we illustrate the performance of the two servers, $S_{independent}$ and $S_{scalable}$, with full (100%) and partial replication, where, for simplicity of illustration, we have assumed that the degree of partial replication corresponds to the amount of bandwidth reserved for a stream at admission control time. In the case of partial replication we assume the degree of replication (i.e., percentage of the retrieval unit that is replicated) to be equal with the percentage of bit rate that is reserved during the admission control per stream. As already men-

---

[17] The increment/reduction in sustained bandwidth corresponds to the difference between the current sustained bandwidth requirements and the amount of bandwidth reserved at admission control time.

tioned, the performance metric is the percentage of "released" bandwidth (by the "degraded" users) which can be re-scheduled for use by "upgraded" users.

The performance of both servers degrades as the skewness increases. For example, in the case of $S_{scalable}$ and $\gamma = 0.25$ with 100% replication, 99% of the "released" bandwidth is re-allocated to "upgraded" users, whereas with partial replication 97% of the "released" bandwidth is re-allocated. However, in the case of $\gamma = 1.0$ with 100% replication, 91.6% of the "released" bandwidth is re-allocated, whereas in the case of partial replication 89.8% is re-allocated. Therefore, as expected, the less uniform the change in requested bandwidth, the more difficult it is to re-allocate the bandwidth.

Furthermore, the gap in performance between $S_{scalable}$ and $S_{independent}$ increases as the skewness increases, i.e., even under high skews in changes in bandwidth requirements, $S_{scalable}$ is able to re-allocated a large percentage of the "released" bandwidth by exploiting replication (or specifically chained declustering in this case) and "shifting" the increase in load (due to "upgraded" users) from one disk to another (i.e., one that has the newly available bandwidth due to "degraded" users). For instance, under full replication both servers have the same performance when $\gamma = 0.0$, whereas when $\gamma = 1.0$, the gap in performance between $S_{scalable}$ and $S_{independent}$, is more than 48.5%. Note also that the performance of $S_{independent}$ decreases almost linearly from 100% to 43%, as the skewness increases. This is due to the fact that as the "skew" increases less "good matches" will occur on each disk. By a "good (or perfect) match" we mean the case where the total amount of additional bandwidth that is requested (by the "upgraded" users) to be retrieved from a single disk is approximately the same (or exactly the same) as the total amount of the reduction in requested bandwidth (due to the "degraded" users) on the same disk. In the case of $S_{scalable}$ the higher is the degree of replication, the less the probability of having a "good match" affects the performance of the server. For example, under full replication, the performance of $S_{scalable}$ is 100% (for $\gamma = 0.0$) and is reduced to 91.6% (for $\gamma = 1.0$), whereas under partial replication the performance of $S_{scalable}$ is reduced from 100% (for $\gamma = 0.0$) to 89.8% (for $\gamma = 1.0$). Thus, based on the results depicted in Figure 4, we can conclude that skewness has a greater effect on the performance of $S_{independent}$ than on the performance of $S_{scalable}$.

In summary, due to proper utilization of replicated data, $S_{scalable}$ is more effective at taking advantage of the bandwidth that has been "freed" in an interval w due to "degraded" users and assigning it to the "upgraded" users, and therefore it adapts more effectively to changes in bandwidth requirements or availability of resources. This becomes more critical under higher degrees of skewness, that is, there is a larger improvement in the percentage bandwidth that can be "re-allocated" by $S_{scalable}$ as compared to $S_{independent}$. Finally, the higher is the degree of replication the less skewness affects the performance of $S_{scalable}$. This reduced sensitivity to skewness, of course, is achieved at the cost of additional storage space.

5 Conclusions

In summary, in this paper we consider the problem of delivery of VBR video streams in a VOD server under provisions of statistical quality of service guarantees. We present several techniques for re-scheduling the video streams and adjusting bandwidth allocations for streams in progress when fluctuations in workload as well as changes in availability of resources occur while satisfying QoS constraints and utilizing system resources efficiently.

References

1. D. Bitton and J. Gray. Disk Shadowing. *VLDB*, pages 331–338, 1988.
2. M. Chen, D. Kandlur, and P. Yu. Optimization of the Grouped Sweeping Scheduling (GSS) with Heterogeneous Multimedia Streams. *ACM Multimedia '93*, pages 235–242, 1993.
3. T.C. Chiueh and R. Katz. Multi-resolution video representation for parallel disk arrays. In *Proceedings of ACM Multimedia*, pages 401–409, 1993.
4. T.H. Cormen, C.E. Leiserson, and R.L. Rivest. *Introduction to Algorithms*. The MIT Press, 1989.
5. A. Elefteriadis. *Dynamic Rate Shaping of Compressed Digital Video*. Ph.D. dissertation, Columbia University, 1995. Technical Report CU/CTR/TR 419-95-25.
6. A. Elwalid, D. Heyman, T.V. Lakshman, and D. Mitra. Fundamental Bounds and Approximations for ATM Multiplexers with Applications to Video Teleconferencing. *IEEE Journal on Selected Areas in Communications*, 13(6), August 1995.
7. J. Gemmell, H.M. Vin, D.D Kandlur, and P.V. Rangan. Multimedia storage servers: A tutorial. In *IEEE Computer*, pages 40–49, May 1995.
8. L. Golubchik, J.C.S. Lui, and R.R. Muntz. Chained Declustering: Load Balancing and Robustness to Skew and Failure. *RIDE-TQP Workshop*, February 1992.
9. H. Hsiao and D. J. DeWitt. Chained Declustering: A New Availability Strategy for Multiprocessor Database Machines. In *Proceedings of Data Engineering*, pages 456–465, 1990.
10. T. Ibaraki and N. Katoh. *Resource Allocation Problems*. The MIT Press, 1988.
11. C. Papadimitriou and K. Steiglitz. *Combinatorial Optimization: Algorithms and Complexity*. Prentice-Hall, Inc., 1982.
12. M. Papadopouli and L. Golubchik. A scalable video-on-demand server for a dynamic heterogeneous environment. Technical Report CUCS-013-98, CS dept., Columbia University, 1998.
13. C. Ruemmler and J. Wilkes. An Introduction to Disk Drive Modeling. *IEEE Computer Magazine*, pages 17–28, March 1994.
14. S. Seshan, M. Stemm, and R.H. Katz. Spand: Shared passive network performance discovery. *Proc 1st Usenix Symposium on Internet Technologies and Systems*, December 1997.
15. R.E. Tarjan. *Data Structures and Network Algorithms*. CBMS-NSF Regional Conference Series in Applied Mathematics, 1983.
16. D. Taubman and A. Zakhor. A common framework for rate and distortion based scaling of highly scalable compressed video. *IEEE Transaction on Circuits and Systems for Video Technology*, pages 329–354, 1996.

Dynamic Skyscraper Broadcasts for Video-on-Demand *

Derek L. Eager[1] and Mary K. Vernon[2]

[1] Department of Computer Science
University of Saskatchewan
Saskatoon, SK Canada S7N 5A9
eager@cs.usask.ca
[2] Computer Sciences Department
University of Wisconsin – Madison
Madison, WI 53706
vernon@cs.wisc.edu

Abstract. Skyscraper Broadcasting is a recently proposed statically scheduled broadcast technique for video-on-demand that addresses the network-I/O bottleneck to provide significantly superior performance over previous approaches. This paper defines a scheme for *dynamically* scheduling the objects that are broadcast on the skyscraper channels. The dynamic broadcasting scheme is designed to provide all clients with the precise time at which their requested object will be broadcast, or an upper bound on that time if the delay is small. New segment size progressions are proposed that not only improve dynamic scheduling, but also simplify the server disk layout problem and allow clients with inexpensive (single-tuner, limited storage) settops to receive skyscraper broadcasts. Preliminary simulation results show that the proposed dynamic scheme (1) provides factors of two or more improvement in mean client waiting time, (2) outperforms the static system with respect to variability in client waiting time, and (3) delivers reasonable service to clients with inexpensive settops while providing clients that have more expensive settops with a high level of service that is relatively isolated from detrimental performance impact from the diskless clients.

1 Introduction

An important goal in the design of video-on-demand systems (e.g., Time Warner's test market system in Orlando [11] or Microsoft's prototype Tiger Video File-server [3]) is to reduce the number of channels required to deliver quick response to the end user. To address this issue, a series of recent papers have proposed Pyramid Broadcasting [13,14], Permutation-Based Pyramid Broadcasting [1], and, most notably, Skyscraper Broadcasting [8]. The innovative idea in these

* This research was partially supported by the National Science Foundation under Grant HRD-9896132, and by the Natural Sciences and Engineering Research Council of Canada under Grant OGP-0000264.

S. Jajodia, M.T. Özsu, and A. Dogac (Eds.): MIS'98, LNCS 1508, pp. 18–32, 1998.

schemes is that the data for each object is divided into fragments of increasing size, and these fragments are broadcast during predefined periods on separate channels. The periodic broadcast of the initial smallest fragment is most frequent, allowing new requests to begin playback quickly. Periodic broadcast of each larger fragment is scheduled on a different channel in a manner such that a client can always begin receiving the next larger fragment either during or immediately following the broadcast of a given fragment. Clients must be able to receive on two channels simultaneously and must be able to buffer a fragment that is received earlier than needed for playback. Since multiple broadcasts of a smaller fragment are scheduled for each broadcast of a larger fragment, clients that receive different small segment broadcasts batch together *during playback* (i.e., when they receive the same larger segment broadcast), in addition to batching while they wait for playback as in earlier schemes. Thus, fewer system channels are required to provide a given target client response. Of the three schemes that propose and improve on this idea, the segment size progression in the skyscraper broadcast technique offers the lowest latency while requiring a client buffering capability that is easily satisfied by a single commodity disk.

The skyscraper broadcast scheme divides objects into two categories: *hot* and *cold*. Each hot object is assigned K channels on which its skyscraper segments are periodically broadcast, as described above. The cold objects are broadcast on the remaining channels using a conventional channel allocation algorithm such as first-come first-serve. Batching of requests for cold objects occurs only while the requests are waiting to start playback.

This paper investigates several potential improvements in the skyscraper broadcast scheme proposed by Hua and Sheu. In particular, we

- define a scheme for *dynamically* scheduling the objects broadcast on the skyscraper channels, thus allowing a much larger number of objects to reap the cost/performance benefits of the skyscraper broadcasts; the dynamic scheme provides clients with the precise time at which their broadcast will begin, or an upper bound on that time if the delay is small,
- derive new segment size progressions for the static or dynamic skyscraper channels that simplify the server disk layout problem, allow clients with inexpensive (limited storage) settops to receive the skyscraper broadcasts, and improve dynamic skyscraper system performance, and
- provide a preliminary evaluation of the performance benefit that can be obtained by dynamically scheduling the skyscraper channels.

One motivation for dynamic skyscraper scheduling is that recent evaluation of conventional broadcasting schemes has shown that periodic broadcast of the hot objects on isolated groups of channels is not necessarily superior to dynamically scheduling all objects on all available channels [12]. Another motivation is that there may not be a clear distinction between *hot* and *cold* objects in many video-on-demand systems; furthermore, the particular objects that are most popular may change with the time of day or as new objects are installed. Dynamic scheduling of the skyscraper broadcasts may be beneficial for a potentially large set of *lukewarm* objects on a given server, providing a smooth increase in broadcast frequency as a function of current object popularity as well as being more responsive to dynamically changing object popularity. Finally, the unused small-segment broadcasts for a particular lukewarm or cold object might be reassigned to requests that are waiting to catch up with a different active skyscraper broadcast, further reducing the response time for the more popular objects.

The remainder of the paper is organized as follows. Section 2 reviews the previously proposed static skyscraper broadcast scheme and defines the new dynamically scheduled alternative evaluated in this paper. Section 3 explores the cost/performance trade-offs of new skyscraper segment size progressions. Simulation results that compare the performance of the static and dynamic skyscraper schemes are presented in section 4, and section 5 provides the conclusions of this work.

2   Skyscraper Broadcasts

In section 2.1 we describe more precisely how the skyscraper channels are organized. In section 2.2 we develop a dynamically scheduled skyscraper broadcast scheme that provides clients with precise times at which their requested object will broadcast, or with an upper bound on that time in the case that the delay is small. The notation used in the remainder of this paper is defined in Table 1.

Table 1. Skyscraper Broadcast System Parameters.

Parameter	Definition
n	number of objects that are broadcast on skyscraper channels
C	total number of channels devoted to skyscraper broadcasts
K	number of channels per skyscraper broadcast
P	progression of relative segment sizes on the skyscraper channels
W	the largest segment size in a skyscraper broadcast
N	number of groups of dynamic skyscraper channels
T	total time to play an entire object
T_1	duration of a unit-segment broadcast
L	total size of the object
r	required object playback rate
S	total number of unit-segments in an object playback

2.1   Static Skyscraper Broadcasts

In the skyscraper broadcast scheme [8], K channels are assigned to *each* of the n most popular objects. Each of the K channels repeatedly broadcasts a distinct segment of the object at the required playback rate. The progression of *relative* segments sizes on the channels, $\{1, 2, 2, 5, 5, 12, 12, 25, 25, 52, 52, 105, 105, ...\}$, is bounded by the parameter, W, and padded with W values up to length K, in order to limit the storage capacity required in the client settop. For example,

Figure 1 illustrates the periodic broadcasts that occur on the channels assigned to a given object for $K = 8$ and $W = 12$. Note that repeated broadcast of the first unit-segment occurs on channel 0, repeated broadcast of the next two-unit segment occurs on channel 1, and so forth. (This scheme was named skyscraper broadcasting because when the segment sizes are stacked one above the other, they form the shape of a skyscraper.)

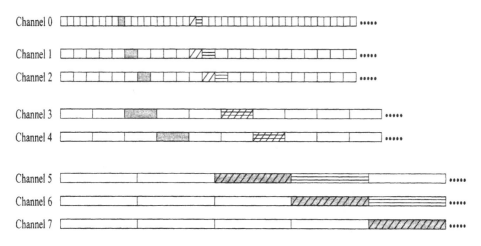

Fig. 1. K Skyscraper Channels for Broadcasting a Single Object. ($K = 8$; $W = 12$)

The gray shading in Figure 1 illustrates the *reception sequence*, or sequence of broadcasts that a client receives, for a client who requests the object just prior to the gray unit-segment broadcast on channel 0. Note that in this reception sequence, four units of data from channel 3 are buffered while the data from channel 1 and 2 are played, and then the buffered data plays while subsequent data is buffered and during the gap between reception on channels 4 and 5.

Two other reception sequences are shown in the figure: one diagonally striped, the other horizontally striped. Note that these two sequences share broadcasts on channels 3 and 4, while the diagonally striped sequence shares broadcasts on channels 5 through 7 with the gray shaded sequence. A total of eleven units of data must be buffered by a client who receives the diagonally striped sequence.

Hua and Sheu show that for the given progression and alignment of relative segment sizes, a client starting in any unit-segment broadcast can receive the necessary sequence of segments without jitter, requiring simultaneous reception on at most two channels by the client. They also show that the storage required in the client settop is equal to $(W - 1) \times L/S$, where L is the total size of the object, and S is the sum of the relative segment sizes that are broadcast on each of the K channels. Note that L/S is the size of a unit-segment.

The duration of each unit-segment broadcast, T_1, is equal to the total object playback time (T) divided by S. For example, if K=8, W=12, and T equals two hours, a new broadcast begins on channel 0 every 2.35 minutes. This can be contrasted with a conventional broadcast system, where each channel broadcasts an entire object. In this case, if 24 channels are assigned to a two-hour object, a playback will begin every 5 minutes.

2.2   Dynamic Scheduling of Skyscraper Broadcasts

In this paper, rather than devoting K channels to a single object, we investigate the performance potential of dynamically changing the object that is broadcast on the skyscraper channels, in response to client requests. A key question is how to identify reception sequences where it is safe to change the object that is broadcast. Below we identify non-overlapping clusters of skyscraper broadcast periods that can be dynamically scheduled, describe the basic dynamic skyscraper scheme, and an optimization of this scheme termed *channel stealing*.

Skyscraper Transmission Clusters Let each non-overlapping transmission cluster *start with* the earliest reception sequence that contains a given broadcast period on channel K. Thus, the gray shaded sequence in Figure 1 starts a new transmission cluster. The horizontally striped sequence starts the next transmission cluster in that figure. The reader can verify that a third cluster begins on channel 0 twelve slots after the horizontally striped period. In fact, each new cluster begins on channel 0 precisely W slots after the previous sequence.

The other reception sequences that belong to a given transmission cluster (for example, the cluster that starts with the gray reception sequence in Figure 1) are all sequences that (1) use the same segment broadcast on channel K, and (2) do not use any broadcast periods on channels 0 through $K - 1$ that are in (the first sequence of) the next transmission cluster. Thus, the cluster that begins with the gray reception sequence includes all of the unmarked segments between the gray shaded segment and the striped segments on channels 0 through 4, plus the diagonally striped segments on channels 1 and 2.

The dynamic system will allow each cluster to broadcast a different object in response to client requests. All sequences in the same cluster will broadcast the same object, allowing client requests to batch together during playback, as in the static skyscraper system. Note that, according to the above definition for non-overlapping transmission clusters, some broadcast periods such as the diagonally striped segment on channel 0 in Figure 1 are not a member of any transmission cluster, and will not be used in a dynamically scheduled system that has the segment size progression defined by Hua and Sheu. We address this issue in section 3.

The Basic Dynamic Scheme Let C channels in the system be allocated to the dynamically scheduled skyscraper broadcasts for objects of a given playback length and rate, and let these channels be organized into N groups of K channels each. C and K are parameters of the configuration. As in the static skyscraper system, each group of K channels has a fixed segment size progression that is upper bounded by the parameter W. For now the reader should assume that the segment size progression is the same as defined by Hua and Sheu and that broadcast periods within a group of channels are aligned as in Figure 1. Thus, each group of K channels broadcasts a sequence of transmission clusters that begin every W slots on channel 0.

The transmission clusters in the different groups of channels are *persistently staggered* such that a new transmission cluster starts on a different group every $\tau = \frac{W \times T_1}{N}$. Each transmission cluster can be scheduled to broadcast any object, in response to client requests. A server disk layout that makes this possible is briefly discussed in section 3.

A new client request is scheduled as follows. First, the client is assigned to the next unit-segment broadcast of a transmission cluster that has already been assigned to that object, if any. Otherwise, the client is assigned to the next unit-segment broadcast of a transmission cluster that has already started but hasn't yet had an object assigned, if any. Finally, the request is scheduled on the next available transmission cluster that will begin broadcasting in the future.

Requests that require a new transmission cluster are scheduled in first-come first-serve (FCFS) order for two reasons. First, recent results show that for fixed length objects, FCFS outperforms other scheduling algorithms such as *maximum queue length first* (MQL) or *maximum factored queue length first* (MFQ) if both the mean and the variability in client waiting time are considered [12]. Second, the broadcast assignment can be done when the request arrives, and thus the system can immediately inform the client when the broadcast will begin.

Temporary Channel Stealing Several optimizations of the above dynamic skyscraper scheme are possible. For example, a unit-segment broadcast period on channel 0 that is not needed to serve new requests for the object can be reassigned to requests that are waiting for a unit-segment broadcast in another active transmission cluster. This is possible because each transmission cluster can serve any object. The clients that can be served by temporary channel 0 reassignments were given a short broadcast delay (i.e., less than T_1), which should be reported as an upper bound rather than a precise delay if channel 0 reassignment is implemented. Note that the requests in an active transmission cluster can only be served early if (1) the two-unit broadcast on channel 1 in their group will begin at the same time as the next unit-segment broadcast in their group, or (2) if channel 1 in the transmission cluster that is doing the stealing is ready to broadcast a two-unit segment and can also be temporarily reassigned. In the case that a channel 1 period is reassigned, the subsequent channel 2 broadcast can also be reassigned, which simplifies the reception sequence for the clients that are served early.

We implement the reassignment of channels 0 and 1/2 described above in the simulator that is used to evaluate the dynamic skyscraper scheme in section 4. When a channel 0 broadcast is reassigned, it is assigned to the eligible request that has been waiting the longest over all other active transmission clusters. This policy turns out to provide noticeably improved performance when temporary channel reassignment is implemented.

It is also possible to temporarily reassign unused broadcast periods on higher numbered channels to requests waiting in another transmission cluster, but this further improvement in stealing is beyond the scope of this paper.

3 Alternative Segment Size Progressions

The segment size progression proposed by Hua and Sheu for statically scheduled skyscraper broadcasts, $\{1, 2, 2, 5, 5, 12, 12, ...\}$, appears to have the maximum possible increases in relative segment size on the K channels, subject to two constraints: (1) for any initial unit-segment broadcast, there must be a sequence of segments that the client can receive that will support continuous playback to the viewer, and (2) clients are required to receive data on no more than two channels simultaneously. Maximum increases in segment size are desirable because this results in smaller unit segments, which in turn increases the frequency at which broadcasts begin on channel 0. On the other hand, the proposed progression of segment sizes is not ideal for the dynamic skyscraper system because particular segment broadcasts can't be used in any transmission cluster.

To address the problem of unused channel bandwidth, we investigate the cost/performance implications of alternative segment size progressions. As will be discussed below, new segment size progressions not only allow all broadcast periods to be used in the dynamic system, but have two further advantages for static as well as dynamic skyscraper systems: (1) they provide service for clients that have settops with a single tuner and very limited storage capacity, and (2) they simplify the server disk layout problem.

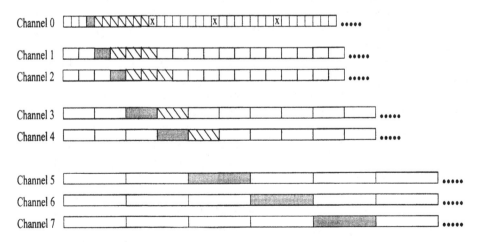

Fig. 2. Segment Size Progression $A = \{1, 2, 2, 4, 4, 8, 8, 16, 16, ...\}$. ($K = 8; W = 8$)

We consider relative segment size progressions of the form $\{1, a, a, b, b, c, c, ...\}$, upper bounded by the parameter W. This is the basic structure of the progression proposed by Hua and Sheu. A key observation is that the width of a transmission cluster on channels 0 and K is equal to W. Thus, to avoid conflicts or holes between transmission clusters the width of the transmission cluster on channels 1 through $K - 1$ must also be equal to W. A necessary condition for transmission group widths equal to W is that *each relative segment size must evenly divide all higher relative segment sizes*. Candidate sequences include: $A = \{1, 2, 2, 4, 4, 8, 8, 16, 16, ...\}$, $B = \{1, 2, 2, 6, 6, 12, 12, 24, 24, ...\}$, and $C = \{1, 2, 2, 6, 6, 12, 12, 36, 36, ...\}$. Progression A is illustrated in Figure 2.

We claim that the following additional requirements guarantee conflict-free transmission clusters as well as jitter-free reception starting from any unit-segment broadcast on channel 0:

- the relative segment size on channels 1 and 2 is two (i.e., $a = 2$),
- the segment size increases by *at most a factor of three* at each other step in the progression, and
- the transmission cluster of width W on a given channel $k > 0$ starts just after channel $k - 1$ broadcasts its first segment of the transmission cluster.

Referring to Figure 2, the argument for the above claim is as follows. Due to the third condition, the first reception sequence in any transmission cluster is jitter-free and requires reception on only one channel at a time. For each other reception sequence in the transmission cluster:

- due to conditions one and three, the reception on channel 1 either directly follows the reception on channel 0 or is overlapped with it,
- due to condition three, for an odd-numbered channel i, the reception on channel $i + 1$ immediately follows the reception on channel i since these two channels have the same segment size,
- for an odd-numbered channel i, if $i + 2$ broadcasts segments twice as large (e.g., progression A), then the broadcast on channel $i + 2$ is either aligned with the end of the broadcast on channel i or the end of the broadcast on channel $i + 1$; if $i + 2$ broadcasts segments three times as large (e.g., channel 3 in progression B or C), the broadcast on $i + 2$ is aligned with the start of the broadcast on channel i, the end of the broadcast on channel i, or the end of the broadcast on channel $i + 1$.

We further claim that progression A is the fastest increasing progression that avoids holes and conflicts between transmission clusters and that also requires simultaneous reception on at most two channels. We claim without further proof that progressions B and C require reception on at most three channels simultaneously.

Note that the storage requirement for the new segment size progressions can be derived by observing that the last unit-segment broadcast in a transmission cluster occurs $W - 1$ time units after the first unit-segment broadcast. Thus, the clients that begin in the last unit-segment broadcast will receive segments $W - 1$

units ahead of their playback time once they batch with the clients that start in the first unit-segment broadcast.

In summary, progression A and the progression defined by Hua and Sheu each require reception on at most two channels, whereas progressions B and C require reception on up to three channels. Progression A has somewhat smaller segment size increases than the progression defined by Hua and Sheu and thus will have slightly higher expected waiting time in a static skyscraper system. Progression A will have better performance than the Hua and Sheu progression in a dynamic skyscraper system because no channel bandwidth is wasted. Progressions B and C have larger segment size increases, and thus would have somewhat better performance than the Hua and Sheu progression in either the static or dynamic system, at the cost of an extra tuner (and some extra storage that can still be easily accommodated by a single commodity disk) in each client settop. Furthermore, each of the new progressions can provide (a lower level of) service to clients with very inexpensive single-tuner settops that can only buffer the frame that is currently being received, by serving requests from such clients in the first reception sequence of a new transmission cluster. This capability is evaluated further in section 4.

The new segment size progressions also simplify the server disk layout problem. A server disk layout that makes dynamic scheduling of the skyscraper channels feasible is omitted due to space constraints, but involves adjusting the optimal stripe unit size so that one transmission cluster of data for each segment of a given object is striped across the available disks an integral number of times.

4   Experimental Results

Models for computing optimal dynamic and static skyscraper system configurations, which would support a fairly complete comparison of these systems over a complex design space, are beyond the scope of this paper. Instead, this section provides some preliminary simulation results to illustrate the potential of the dynamically scheduled skyscraper system. In particular, we provide some initial comparisons of the static and dynamic systems for a few points in the design space, using experimentally determined optimal configurations that satisfy particular constraints. We focus on an aggressive system with 1000 objects, each with a 120 minute playback duration, and Zipf(0) selection frequencies. The results are qualitatively similar for less aggressive systems. The simulation results provided in Figures 3 and 5 for average client waiting time have 95% confidence intervals that are within 10% of the reported values.

4.1   Principal Performance Comparison

We consider systems in which objects are divided two classes: the k most popular *hot* objects and the other $1000 - k$ *cold* objects. Each possible division ($0 \leq k \leq 1000$) is considered, so that our results cover cases of hot sets containing only a few of the very hot objects, as well as hot sets including many *lukewarm* objects. The available channels are statically partitioned between the two classes. We then consider three combinations of broadcast techniques: (1) static skyscraper broadcasts for each object in the hot set and conventional FCFS (with *persistent staggering* of the allocated channels) for the cold objects, (2) dynamic skyscraper broadcasts for the set of hot objects and conventional FCFS for the cold objects, and (3) dynamic skyscraper broadcasts for each set of objects.[1] The relative segment size progression $\{1, 2, 2, 4, 4, 8, 8, 16, 16, ...\}$ is used for the dynamic skyscraper broadcasts, whereas the slightly higher-performance original skyscraper progression, $\{1, 2, 2, 5, 5, 12, 12, 25, 25, ...\}$, is used for the static skyscraper broadcasts.

Performance results are presented for experimentally determined optimal configurations. That is, for each considered division into hot and cold object sets, a search is performed for a channel partitioning that minimizes the overall average client waiting time, under the following constraints. For the static skyscraper scheme, the number of channels allocated to each hot object, K, is equal to the number of channels allocated to the hot set divided by the size of the hot set. The parameter W is selected to be the largest possible given the derived K, so as to provide the most favorable performance data for the static skyscraper system. For the dynamic skyscraper scheme, the only constraint on K is that it evenly divide the number of channels assigned to the hot or cold set. A search is performed for the values of K and W that yield the lowest value for the sum of average client waiting time plus maximum observed client waiting time for the given class of objects. [2]

Figure 3 gives the average client waiting time in each of the three systems, for a system with 1000 objects each with a 120 minute playback duration and Zipf(0) selection frequencies, 1600 total channels, and a client request arrival rate of 40 per minute. For small hot set sizes the overall average client waiting time is very similar in the static skyscraper/FCFS system and the dynamic skyscraper/FCFS system. As the hot set size increases, however, the performance of the static skyscraper/FCFS combination begins to deteriorate, whereas the best performance with the dynamic skyscraper/FCFS combination is achieved in the limiting case when all channels are used for dynamic skyscraper scheduling of all objects.

The use of dynamic skyscraper scheduling on both the hot and cold sets (in general, with different optimal values of K and W for each set), is seen to yield the best mean client waiting time for all of the considered divisions between hot and cold sets; at hot set sizes of five to fifteen, the average client waiting

---

[1] Recall that, among the channel scheduling policies that have been proposed to date for conventional broadcasts, FCFS has the best performance when both mean and variability in client waiting time are considered [12].

[2] Note that using the sum of mean and maximum waiting time as the objective function when searching for the optimal partitioning of channels between the hot and cold classes produced configurations that had significantly lower mean waiting time for cold objects as compared with hot objects, so we simply used mean waiting time as the objective function for determining that configuration parameter.

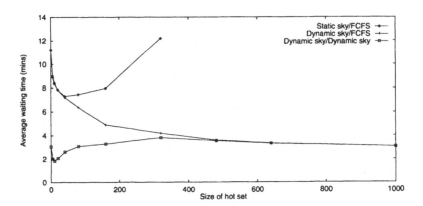

Fig. 3. Average Client Waiting Time vs. Hot Set Size.
(1000 120-minute objects; 1600 channels; $\lambda = 40$)

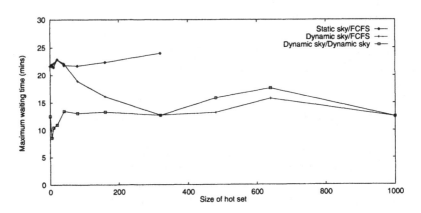

Fig. 4. Maximum Client Waiting Time vs. Hot Set Size.
(1000 120-minute objects; 1600 channels; $\lambda = 40$)

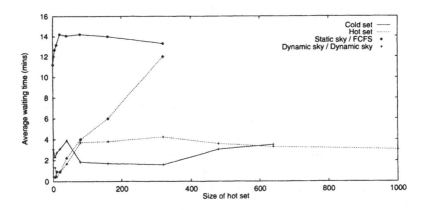

Fig. 5. Average Waiting Time For Hot and Cold Objects vs. Hot Set Size.
(1000 120-minute objects; 1600 channels; $\lambda = 40$)

time is about two thirds of the lowest average waiting time in the dynamic skyscraper/FCFS combination.

Figure 4 shows that the use of dynamic skyscraper scheduling for both the hot and cold sets also yields improved performance with respect to the maximum waiting time observed in the simulations. With a hot set size of five, the maximum waiting time observed when dynamic skyscraper is used on both the hot and cold sets is less than 40% of the lowest maximum waiting time observed in the static skyscraper/FCFS system, and is again about two thirds of the lowest maximum waiting time for the dynamic skyscraper/FCFS system.

Figure 5 gives the average client waiting time for each class of objects in the static skyscraper/FCFS system and in the system where dynamic skyscraper scheduling is used for both the hot and cold sets. Note that the use of dynamic skyscraper scheduling on both the hot and cold sets can offer substantially improved fairness in mean waiting time between the two classes of objects as compared to the static skyscraper/FCFS combination.

4.2 Variability in Client Waiting Time

Measures of the distribution of waiting time for each object, omitted due to space constraints, show the following for the system with dynamic skyscraper broadcasts for both hot and cold object sets, hot set size equal to five, and the experimentally determined optimal configuration of the channels: (1) maximum waiting time for each hot object is roughly twice the mean waiting time for the object (as in the static skyscraper/FCFS system), (2) maximum waiting time for each cold object is significantly (approximately three times) higher than the maximum observed waiting time for each hot object due to the objective function used in the channel partitioning (yet Figure 4 shows that the maximum waiting time for cold objects is still significantly better than in the static skyscraper/FCFS system), (3) the FCFS scheduling of transmission clusters yields reasonable fairness within each class of objects and, considering the inherent randomness of dynamic scheduling, relatively low variance in waiting time for each class; in fact, for the configuration evaluated, the ninetieth percentile waiting time is *less than twice the mean* for each object, hot or cold.

4.3 Heterogeneous Clients

For both static and dynamic skyscraper systems, the new segment size progressions permit a mix of clients with varying storage and reception capabilities. In this section, we consider a scenario in which a fraction of the clients have very limited local storage, and thus must begin reception at the beginning of a transmission cluster.

Dynamic skyscraper scheduling is used for both hot and cold objects, with the number of hot objects equal to five and, as before, the experimentally determined optimal channel configuration. If a request from a client with limited storage arrives during an active transmission cluster for the requested object, the client can only obtain the next available transmission cluster that starts *after* the point in time at which it is no longer possible for any client to batch in with the existing broadcast. Results that are omitted due to space constraints show that this policy is effective in isolating the clients that have settop buffering capabilities from detrimental performance impact owing to the presence of clients without such capabilities. In particular, mean wait for the hot (or cold) objects by clients with settops that have the buffering capability is non-increasing (or slowly increasing) as the fraction of diskless clients increases. Furthermore, the five to ten-fold differential in performance between the two classes of clients is perhaps reasonable given the differential in cost of the settops. Note that clients are informed of the time at which their broadcast will begin, so viewers with inexpensive settops can plan accordingly.

5   Conclusions

As noted in the introduction, the principal contributions of this paper are:

- a dynamically scheduled skyscraper broadcast scheme that provides client requests with the precise time at which their broadcast will begin, or an upper bound on that time if the delay is small,
- new segment size progressions for static or dynamically scheduled skyscraper channels; these progressions improve dynamic scheduling, simplify disk layout, and allow clients with inexpensive settops to receive the skyscraper broadcasts at constrained points in time,
- a preliminary evaluation of the cost/performance benefit that can be derived from dynamically scheduling the skyscraper channels.

Key observations from the preliminary performance study are that dynamic skyscraper systems can significantly outperform static skyscraper systems with respect to overall mean as well as variability in client waiting time. Conversely, the number of channels required for a given target average client waiting time can be significantly lower for the dynamic system. The use of FCFS scheduling of transmission clusters yields reasonable fairness between hot and cold objects and, considering the inherent randomness of dynamic scheduling, relatively low variance in waiting time for each class. In fact, for the representative configuration considered in the preliminary experiments, the ninetieth percentile waiting time is *less than twice the mean* for each object class. We also find that diskless clients can receive a reasonable level of service without a large negative impact on the performance of clients with more expensive settops.

Our on-going and future research plans include (1) developing optimization models for static and dynamic skyscraper configurations and using such configurations to determine the benefit of dynamic scheduling over a greater variety of systems, including systems with multiple length objects and a variety of object popularity distributions, (2) evaluating various policies for reassigning unused skyscraper broadcast periods to waiting requests in other transmission clusters, (3) more detailed exploration of server disk layout strategies for skyscraper broadcasts, (4) the design of skyscraper broadcast systems for variable bit rate transmissions, and (5) the caching of skyscraper segments in widely-distributed VOD servers.

Acknowledgements

The authors wish to acknowledge Li Fan, Arup Guha, Anirban Mahanti, Dan Sorin, Jayakumar Srinivasan, and Thanos Tsiolis for assistance with our simulations and for helpful discussions and comments on this research.

References

1. C. C. Aggarwal, J. L. Wolf and P. S. Yu, "A Permutation Based Pyramid Broadcasting Scheme for Video-on-Demand Systems", *Proceeding of the IEEE International Conference on Multimedia Computing and Systems*, Hiroshima, Japan, June 1996.
2. S. Berson, R. Muntz, S. Ghandeharizadeh and X. Ju, "Staggered Striping in Multimedia Information Systems", *Proceedings of the 1994 ACM SIGMOD Conference*, Minneapolis, MN, May 1994, pp. 79-90.
3. W. J. Bolosky, J. S. Barrera, R. P. Draves, R. P. Fitzgerald, G. A. Gibson, M. B. Jones, S. P. Levi, N. P. Myhrvold and R. F. Rashid, "The Tiger Video Fileserver", *Proceedings of the 6th International Workshop on Network and Operating System Support for Digital Audio and Video (NOSSDAV'96)*, Zushi, Japan, April 1996.
4. A. Dan, P. Shahabuddin, D. Sitaram and D. Towsley, "Channel Allocation under Batching and VCR control in Movie-on-Demand Servers", *Journal of Parallel and Distributed Computing 30*, 2 (November 1995), pp. 168-179.
5. A. Dan and D. Sitaram, "An Online Video Placement Policy based on Bandwidth to Space Ratio", *Proceedings of the 1995 ACM SIGMOD Conference*, San Jose, CA, May 1995, pp. 376-385.
6. A. Dan, D. Sitaram and P. Shahabuddin, "Scheduling Policies for an On-demand Video Server with Batching", *Proceedings of the ACM Multimedia Conference*, San Francisco, CA, October 1994, pp. 15-23.
7. S. Ghandeharizadeh and S. H. Kim, "Striping in Multi-disk Video Servers", *Proceedings of the SPIE High-Density Data Recording and Retrieval Technologies Conference*, October 1995.
8. K. A. Hua and S. Sheu, "Skyscraper Broadcasting: A New Broadcasting Scheme for Metropolitan Video-on-Demand Systems", *Proceedings of the ACM SIGCOMM'97 Conference*, Cannes, France, September 1997, pp. 89-100.
9. E. D. Lazowska, J. Zahorjan, G. S. Graham, and K. C. Sevcik, *Quantitative System Performance*, Prentice Hall, Englewood Cliffs, New Jersey, 1984.
10. B. Ozden, R. Rastogi, and A. Silberschatz, "Disk Striping in Video Server Environments", *Proceeding of the IEEE International Conference on Multimedia Computing and Systems*, Hiroshima, Japan, June 1996, pp. 580-589.
11. T. S. Perry, "The Trials and Travails of Interactive TV", *IEEE Spectrum 33*, 4 (April 1996), pp. 22-28.
12. A. K. Tsiolis and M. K. Vernon, "Group-Guaranteed Channel Capacity in Multimedia Storage Servers", *Proceedings of the 1997 ACM SIGMETRICS Conference on Measurement and Modelling of Computer Systems*, Seattle, WA, June 1997, pp. 285-297.

13. S. Viswanathan and T. Imielinski, "Pyramid Broadcasting for Video-on-Demand Service", *Proceedings of the SPIE Multimedia Computing and Networking Conference*, Vol. 2417, San Jose, CA, February 1995, pp. 66-77.
14. S. Viswanathan and T. Imielinski, "Metropolitan Area Video-on-Demand Service using Pyramid Broadcasting", *Multimedia Systems 4*, 4 (August 1996), pp. 197-208.

Deciding Round Length and Striping Unit Size for Multimedia Servers

KyungOh Lee and Heon Y. Yeom

Dept. of Computer Science, Seoul National University
San 56-1, Sinlim-Dong, Kwanak-Gu,
Seoul,151-742, Korea
{leeko, yeom}@arirang.snu.ac.kr

Abstract. In realtime multimedia storage servers, it is very important to find the optimal values for the round length and the striping unit size since they have strong relation with the throughput. In getting the optimal values, we should not overlook any factor of multimedia servers since this may produce the wrong values far from the optimal. If we use a wrong value, then we may suffer from 2 or 3 times performance degradation. We present a new scheme which considers all possible factors in multimedia servers such as disk properties, buffer space, the characteristics of multimedia objects, and users' trends of requesting. Since we do not use simple peak data rate but the *maximum segment data rate* which is much smaller than the peak data rate, we can use the resources very effectively and still guarantees no starvation and no overflow.

1 Introduction

In recent years, significant advances in computing and networking technologies have made it possible and economically feasible to provide online access to a variety of multimedia data. Multimedia systems like VOD systems require considerable amount of resources and have tight realtime constraints. Data to be sent to clients must be read from disk to memory buffers before actual transmission, and thus the maximum number of clients that the system can support depends upon both disk bandwidth and total buffer size.

As observed in [6], the most natural way to process multiple streams simultaneously is to interleave the readings of the streams in a cyclic fashion. The amount of data that must be read from the disk for each stream within a cycle(or round) should be sufficient for the client for a cycle. Although round length has strong relation with the throughput of multimedia systems, there have been little works about how long the optimal length of the round should be. Striping unit size has also critical influence on the performance of multimedia storage server [3], [4]. Since striping unit size has strong relation with round length [7], we should not consider them separately to maximize the throughput.

We propose a new scheme to find optimal round length and striping unit size considering as many factors(number of disks and their properties, total available buffer size, and characteristics of stored multimedia objects, etc.) as possible.

S. Jajodia, M.T. Özsu, and A. Dogac (Eds.): MIS'98, LNCS 1508, pp. 33–44, 1998.

Since these factors affect the system performance all together, we should not overlook any one of them. For example, if the available buffer space is sufficient but the available disk bandwidth is low, then a long round would show better performance than a short one, while if the available disk bandwidth is sufficient but the available buffer space is low, then a short round would show better performance. Using the proper playback data rate(which is much less than peak data rate and guarantees neither starvation nor overflow) instead of peak data rate, we can reserve the system resources efficiently, and find the optimal value more effectively.

The rest of the paper is organized as follows. Section 2 briefly surveys related works, section 3 describes how we stripe the multimedia objects across the disk array, section 4 explains our new scheme to decide the optimal round length and striping unit size, experimental results are presented in section 5, and finally our conclusions are given in section 6.

2   Related Works

Ozden et al [8] presented schemes(fine-grained schemes as well as coarse-grained schemes) that are based on striping videos across the disks in order to effectively utilize disk bandwidth. For each of the schemes, they computed the optimal amount of data to be retrieved during each disk access so that the number of videos concurrently transmitted can be maximized. For the schemes based on coarse-grained striping, they showed how disk bandwidth can be effectively allocated to requests such that there is no starvation. Finally, through extensive simulations, they compare the performance of the various schemes. Their results show that the scheme based on coarse-grained striping can support the retrieval of more videos than those based on fine-grained striping. However, system resources are wasted since they assume that the display data rates of videos remain the same as the peak data rate.

Vin et al [11] proposed VBR data placement and retrieval techniques. Constant Time Length(CTL) places and retrieves data in blocks corresponding to equal playback duration, Constant Data Length(CDL) places and retrieves constant-sized data blocks. CTL data placement has much lower buffer requirements than CDL but suffers from difficulty during video editing. Therefore, CTL placement policy is attractive for designing multimedia storage server for predominantly read-only environments where storage space management complexity is not an issue(e.g., video-on-demand). However, since the peak data rate is used to calculate the optimal block size, a truly optimized value is not possible.

3   Striping Multimedia Objects

Usually, coarse-grained striping schemes outperform fine-grained schemes, since fine-grained striping schemes waste disk bandwidth because of the excessive number of disk seeks [1], [8]. *Constant Time Length*(CTL) schemes also show better performance than *Constant Data Length*(CDL) schemes [3], [4], since CDL schemes tend to require much more buffer space [5]. Accordingly, we adopted coarse-grained CTL as our basic striping scheme. Reducing the number of seeks required to read the necessary data blocks is much more important in optimizing the throughput than reducing the seek time or the rotational latency. By making it possible for a stream to get enough data for one round from only one access to one disk, we can minimize the frequency of disk seeks.

If we let DT, the playback time of a striping unit, be the same as the round length, T, then each stream needs to access exactly one disk in a round. A CDL striping scheme, however, may require two or more blocks from round to round, even if a similar configuration is adapted. Thus, we divide each multimedia object into segments that have the same playback duration, and these segments are striped along the disks. We apply a staggered striping scheme [2] when placing the first segments of objects, to reduce the possibility of causing load imbalance by storing more segments on one disk than on the others. This striping scheme is illustrated in Fig. 1 and we call the scheme RTL (Round Time Length) striping.

Fig. 1. RTL(Round Time Length) striping

If k active streams are being serviced from disk i at the current service round, then these streams will be serviced from disk $(i + 1)$ *mod* n at the next round where n is the number of data disks in the disk array under the RTL striping model. If we assume that every disk in the disk array is identical [1], then it follows that if we have serviced a set of streams without any problems at round j, then there will be no problems at round $j + 1$.

If the worst case assumption (i.e., that each stream requires peak data rate, all the time) is used to prevent starvation or overflow, then resources can be wasted. Instead of the peak data rate, we use the *maximum segment data rate* ($R(DT)$). (A similar idea was suggested in [5], [9].) Assume that we split a multimedia object i into segments that have equal playback time DT, and let $r_{i,j}$ be the average data rate of the jth segment of object i. We can then define the *maximum segment data rate* of object i, $R_i(DT)$ as follows.

$$R_i(DT) = MAX(r_{i,j}(DT) \text{ for all } j) \tag{1}$$

---

[1] if there are many different kinds of disks, we can assume that every disk has the same characteristics as the slowest disk. Otherwise, we should make several disk arrays that have identical (or similar) disks.

Since each segment is stored contiguously and retrieved segment by segment, there will be neither starvation nor overflow, even though we use $R(DT)$ instead of the peak data rate for resource reservation.

If DT is the same as the playback time of a frame, then $R(DT)$ is the same as the peak data rate, but if DT is the same as the playback time of a whole video object, then $R(DT)$ is the same as the average data rate of that video object. Thus, $R(DT)$ becomes smaller as DT becomes larger, and the following equation holds generally.

$$R(DT_1) < R(DT_2) \text{ if } DT_1 > DT_2 \qquad (2)$$

Figure 2 shows $R(DT)$ of the movies "Terminator" and "The Silence of the Lambs". We can see that $R(DT)$ generally decreases as DT increases. That is, we can say that much resource is wasted, if we reserve resources using the peak data rate. Given this result, we may want to make DT as large as possible, but since every stream reads at least one segment in a round, the larger DT becomes, the more buffer space is required. Therefore, we need to find some optimal value for DT. Intuitively, multiples of GOP display time will be better, since segments with similar characteristics should be formed. We can also see that $R(DT)$ decreases slowly after DT exceeds 1000 ms, but it is still almost 3 times greater than the average data rate.

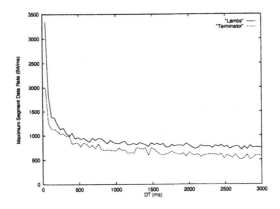

Fig. 2. $R(DT)$ of MPEG-I movie "the Silence of the Lambs" and "Terminator"

4   Deciding Round Length and Striping Unit Size

It is very important to find both the round length and the striping unit size that maximize the throughput. In deciding the round length and the striping unit size, we should consider as many factors (disks, buffers, streams, etc.) as possible to get the optimal solutions. In this section, we present a new scheme that determines the optimal round length and the striping unit size to maximize performance, considering all of the factors in multimedia storage servers.

4.1   Constraints in Admission Control

There are many constraints in admission control, but the buffer constraint (is there sufficient buffer space to store the necessary data, even if a new stream is accepted?) and the disk constraint (is there enough disk bandwidth to read all the necessary data, even if a new stream is accepted?) are the most important for a multimedia storage server. Since they are strongly related to round length, we consider these two constraints first.

Buffer Constraint We need to store retrieved data in a buffer before sending it to clients. Let m be the number of streams to be serviced, $Avail\_Buf$ be the total buffer size, and DT be the playback time of a segment. To accept a new stream, the following constraint should hold.

$$Total\ Amount\ of\ Data\ to\ be\ Stored \le Available\ Buffer\ Size$$

$$2 \cdot \sum_{i=1}^{m} R_i(DT) \cdot T \le Avail\_Buf$$

$$2 \cdot \sum_{i=1}^{m} R_i(DT) \cdot DT \le Avail\_Buf \tag{3}$$

If we assume $R_i(DT)$ to be the same as R(say, constant) for all streams, then we can simplify (3) as follows.

$$2 \cdot m \cdot R \cdot DT \le Avail\_Buf \tag{4}$$

In (4), we can easily see that m is inversely proportional to DT. However, since $R_i(DT)$ is a function of DT as in (2), we cannot simplify $R_i(DT)$ as a constant to get the correct solution, but we can still guess that m is generally in inverse proportion to DT in (3).

Figure 3 shows that this intuition is true. In this figure, we use the MPEG-I trace of "The Silence of the Lambs", and we vary DT from 50 ms to 3000 ms. The upper line shows the maximum number of acceptable streams with a 1 gigabyte buffer, and the lower line shows the maximum number of acceptable streams with a 200 megabyte buffer. Here, the *maximum number of acceptable streams* means the maximum number of streams acceptable when we admit streams while considering only the buffer constraint(i.e., if we assume that there is no limit on disk bandwidth). We can accept about 9,000 streams with 500 ms for DT, but 5,000 streams with 1000 ms in the case of a 1 GB buffer space.

Disk Bandwidth Constraint Disk service time consists of the seek time, the rotational latency, the transfer time of data, and other latencies [10]. Let d be the number of disks in the array, m be the number of streams to be serviced, and k be the number of segments to be retrieved from the most heavily loaded disk. If there are many active streams and many disks in the array, then we can approximate $k \simeq \lceil \frac{m}{d} \rceil$. Provided that the service time to read k blocks from a

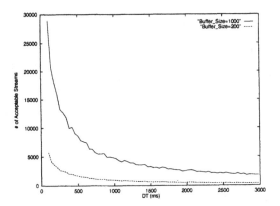

Fig. 3. Number of acceptable streams by the buffer constraint - the case of MPEG-I movie "The Silence of the Lambs"

disk is shorter than a round, we can service m streams without any starvation. That is, if the following equation holds, there will be no problem.

$$Seek\_Time + Transfer\_Time + Rotational\_Latency \leq T$$

$$Seek(k) + \sum_{i=1}^{k} (\frac{R_i(DT) \cdot DT}{Tranfer\_Rate} + Rotation\_Time) \leq DT \qquad (5)$$

In this equation, we can see that k is generally proportional to DT. Since m is proportional to k, we can say that m is generally proportional to DT. Figure 4 shows the maximum number of acceptable streams according to a given DT if we consider only the disk bandwidth constraint. The upper line corresponds to the use of 100 disks and the lower line to the use of 20 disks.

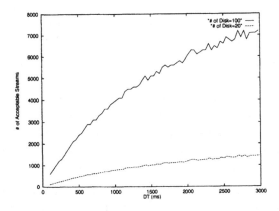

Fig. 4. Number of acceptable streams considering the disk constraint - the case of MPEG-I movie "the Silence of the Lambs"

4.2   Determining the Optimal *DT*

Let B be the total buffer size, D be the number of disks and their properties, M be characteristics of multimedia objects (such as frame size, display rate, GOP, peak data rate, etc.), P be the set of requesting probabilities to each object, and DT be the playback time of a segment. The function that seeks the maximum number of acceptable streams m can then be defined as follows.

$$m = f(B, D, M, P, DT)$$

We can express the function f as follows.

$f(B,D,M,P,DT)=min(Maximum\ Acceptable\ Number\ of\ Streams\ By\ Buffer,\ Maximum\ Number\ of\ Acceptable\ Streams\ By\ Disk)$

With given B, D, M, P, it is our goal to find the DT that maximizes $f()$ (and, hence, m). If DT is large, the value of f is restricted by the buffer constraint, but if DT is small, it is restricted by the disk constraint. Let us therefore define an algorithm to obtain the DT that maximizes $f()$ as $Get\_Max\_f(B, D, M, P)$ given below.

```
Get_Max_f(B,D,M,P)
1: Δ = playback time of a frame;
2: DT=0;
3: DT= DT+Δ;
4: m1=get_Max_By_Buffer_Constraint();
5: m2=get_Max_By_Disk_Constraint();
6: if (m1 > m2) go to 3;
7: return DT;
```

Fig. 5. Algorithm for finding optimal DT

In this algorithm, the function $get\_Max\_By\_Buffer\_Constraint()$ produces the maximum number of acceptable streams considering only the buffer constraint (say, by (3)), and the function $get\_Max\_By\_Disk\_Constraint()$ produces the maximum number of acceptable streams considering only the disk constraint (say, by (5)). Since $m1$ decreases from infinity to 0, while $m2$ increases from 0 to infinity as DT increases, they should cross at least once. If we run $Get\_Max\_f()$ with DT from 0 to the largest playback time among the stored objects, then we can find a solution. In our experiments, we needed to calculate $m1$ and $m2$ less than 30 times in most cases, and even in the worst case 80 calculations was sufficient.

5   Experimental Results

To show the value of DT obtained from $Get\_MAX\_f()$ is optimal, extensive simulations have been performed, using 20 MPEG-I traces from [12].

Since multimedia servers may support homogeneous streams with similar characteristics(say, homogeneous servers) or heterogeneous streams which have very different characteristics such as peak playback data rate or average data rate(say, heterogeneous servers), we conduct experiments with the two cases - homogeneous case and heterogeneous case.

In homogeneous servers, if all requests are for one object, then the skewness of optimal DT may be severe. At first, we compare the difference of the optimal DTs between the following two cases - 100 % of requests are for "the Silence of the Lambs" and 100 % of requests are for "Terminator". A new stream is accepted if this does not break buffer constraints or disk bandwidth constraints. We run the simulation for 1 million seconds. As shown in Fig. 6, the optimal DTs are 1100 ms, and 1200 ms respectively, and we have observed $Get\_MAX\_f()$ produce the same values -1100 and 1200 ms. In the simulation we assume the server has 1G byte buffer and 100 IBM-HDD3200 disks in the array. Although experiments with more than 20 different traces are conducted, the differences among the optimal DTs are less than 100 ms in most cases, and the differences between simulations and the algorithm are negligibly small. From these results, we can see the request frequency to stored multimedia objects is not critical in determining the optimal DT for homogeneous case.

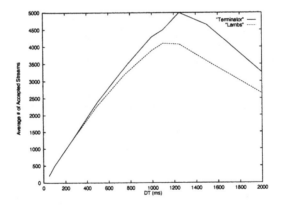

Fig. 6. Number of accepted streams by simulation (100 disks, 1 G byte buffer)

In many situation, multimedia servers support several kinds of heterogeneous streams such as HDTV quality video, NTSC quality video, or CD quality audio, etc. which have greatly different characteristics, and in this case, the request probability has very important implication. To make an environment of servicing heterogeneous streams (the difference of data rates among streams are non-negligibly large), we multiply 10 to original traces. We assume the server has 40 video objects(20 objects are of high data rate videos and the other 20 are of low data rate objects), and the experiments are conducted on the following 4 cases.

1. 100% of requests are for high data rate objects
2. 50% of requests are for high data rate objects and the other requests are for low data rate ones.
3. 25% of requests are for high data rate objects and the other requests are for low data rate ones.
4. 100% of requests are for low data rate objects.

In the simulation we assume the server has 1G byte buffer and 100 IBM-HDD3200 disks in the array. As we can see in Fig. 7, in the 4th case, maximum number(about 2500) of streams are accepted when DT is about 850 ms, but only about 1500 streams are accepted if DT is 400 ms or 1600 ms. This means if we take some wrong value far from the optimal, then the performance goes down significantly. Disk bandwidth constraint makes throughput bad when DT is 400 ms, and Buffer constraint becomes the bottleneck of the throughput when DT is 1600 ms. The optimal values in the 1st, 2nd and 3rd case from extensive simulation are 550 ms, 600 ms and 680 ms respectively. By this simulation, we can see that the optimal value of DT decreases as the ratio of high data rate streams increases. This is natural, since buffer constraint becomes bottleneck of throughput to high data rate streams, but disk bandwidth constraint becomes bottleneck to low data rate streams.

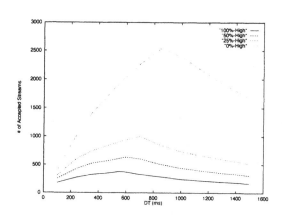

Fig. 7. Number of accepted streams by simulation - heterogeneous server(100 disks, 1000 G byte buffer)

The results from algorithm $Get\_Max\_f()$ are given in Fig. 8, 9, 10 and 11. These figures show that the optimal values for the 4 cases are 560 ms, 600 ms, 700 ms and 840 ms respectively. This clearly shows that $Get\_MAX\_f()$ can find the optimal value for DT, since the results from the algorithm and extensive simulations have little difference.

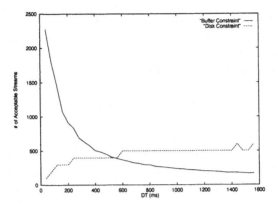

Fig. 8. The result of Get_MAX_f() when 100% of streams are of high data rate(100 disks, 1000 G byte buffer)

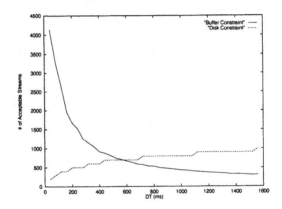

Fig. 9. The result of Get_MAX_f() when 50% of streams are of high data rate(100 disks, 1000 G byte buffer)

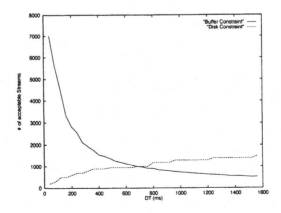

Fig. 10. The result of Get_MAX_f() when 25% of streams are of high data rate(100 disks, 1000 G byte buffer)

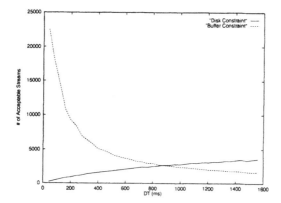

Fig. 11. The result of Get_MAX_f() when 100% of streams are of low data rate(100 disks, 1000 G byte buffer)

6   Conclusion

What value we should use as the round length and by how large size we should stripe multimedia objects across the disks are critical problems in maximizing the performance of multimedia servers. We present a new mechanism to get the optimal round length and the optimal striping unit size considering the all possible factors of multimedia servers such as disk conditions, buffer space, characteristics of multimedia objects and users' trends of requesting.

Our striping scheme uses coarse-grained and CTL(Constant Time Length) striping schemes which are known to be superior to others, and the disk overhead is minimized by making each stream get enough data for a round with only one access to a disk. Also we do not use simple peak data rate but the *maximum segment data rate* which is much smaller than peak data rate. Using this *maximum segment data rate*, we can reserve the resource two or three times effectively but still guarantees no starvation and no overflow.

We show the correctness of our scheme by comparing the results from extensive simulations with those from our algorithm. Since the differences are very small, we can use this scheme to find the optimal round length and the optimal striping unit size at multimedia server design time or re-configuration time.

We use request probability to multimedia objects to get solutions, but since users' trends may change from time to time, optimal value might be different from the original. This error would make little difference in performance in the servers that service homogeneous streams(say, all objects are MPEG-I video), but in the servers that service heterogeneous streams(say, some of streams are MPEG-I and the others are HDTV streams) this causes significant degradation of throughput. But if we do not use the estimated users' trends at all, the error will make even greater degradation of performance. To solve this problem , we need to contrive a scheme which can still guarantee the high throughput even if the users' trends are changing dynamically.

References

[1] Scott A. Barnett and Gary J. Anido. Performability of disk-array-based video servers. *ACM Multimedia Systems Journal*, 6(1):60–74, January 1998.

[2] S. Berson, S. Ghandeharizadeh, R. Muntz, and X. Ju. Staggered striping in multimedia information systems. In *Proc. of ACM SIGMOD*, pages 79–90, Minnesota, USA, June 1994.

[3] E. Chang and A. Zakhor. Admission control and data placement for vbr video servers. In *Proc. of IEEE Int'l conference on Image Processing*, pages 278–282, Austin, June 1994.

[4] E. Chang and A. Zakhor. Cost analysis for vbr video servers. In *IS&T/SPIE Int'l Symposium on Electronic Imaging: Science and Technology*, pages 29–31, California, January 1996.

[5] J. Dangler, E. Biersack, and C. Bernhart. Deterministic admission control strategies in video servers with variable bit rate. In *Proc. of International Workshop on Interactive Distributed Multimedia Systems and Telecommunication Services*, pages 164–171, Hiroshima, Japan, June 1996.

[6] J. Gemmell and S. Christodoulakis. Principles of delay-sensitve multimedia data storage and retrieval. *ACM Trans. of Information Systems*, 10(1):51–90, January 1992.

[7] T. Raymond Ng and Jinhai Yang. An analysis of buffer sharing and prefetching techniques for multimedia systems. *ACM Multimedia Systems*, 4(2):55–69, April 1996.

[8] B. Ozden, R. Rastogi, and A. Silberschatz. Disk striping in video server environments. In *Proc. of IEEE Internation Conference on Multimedia Computing and Systems*, pages 580–589, Hiroshima, Japan, June 1996.

[9] Huanxu Pan, Lek Heng Ngoh, and Aurel A. Lazar. A buffer-inventory-based dynamic scheduling algorithm for multimedia-on-demand servers. *ACM Multimedia Systems Journal*, 6(2):125–136, March 1998.

[10] C. Ruemmler and J. Wilkes. An introduction to disk drive modeling. *IEEE Computer*, 27(3):17–28, March 1994.

[11] H. M. Vin, Sriram S. Rao, and Pawan Goyal. Optimizing the placement of multimedia objects on disk arrays. In *Proc. of IEEE Internation Conference on Multimedia Computing and Systems*, pages 158–165, Washington, USA, May 1995.

[12] Infomatik MPEG-I frame size traces. ftp://ftp-inof3.informatik.uni-wuerzburg.de/pub/MPEG.

Management and Rendering of Multimedia Views *

K. Selçuk Candan[1], Eric Lemar[2], and V.S. Subrahmanian[2]

[1] Computer Science and Engineering Department,
Arizona State University,
Tempe, AZ 85287-5406.
Phone: (602) 965-2770. Fax: (602) 965-5142. candan@asu.edu
[2] Department of Computer Science,
Institute
for Advanced Computer Studies &
Institute for Systems Research,
University of Maryland,
College Park, Maryland 20742.
Phone: (301) 405-2711. Fax: (301) 405-6707. {elemar,vs}@cs.umd.edu

Abstract. Though there has been extensive work on multimedia databases in the last few years, there is no prevailing notion of a multimedia view, nor there are techniques to create, manage, and maintain such views. In this paper, we present a formal definition of a multimedia view definition (MVD). Materializing an MVD corresponds to assembling and delivering an interactive multimedia presentation in accordance with the specification. We develop a probabilistic model of interactive multimedia presentations where the probabilities reflect the likelihood of certain user interactions. Based on this probabilistic model, we develop a prefetching algorithm that anticipate how users will interact with the presentation. These prefetch algorithms allow efficient delivery of these multimedia presentations in accordance with the underlying specification. We have built a prototype system that incorporates these algorithms. We report on the results of experiments conducted on top of this implementation.

1   Introduction

Over the last few years, there has been considerable interest in multimedia databases – most such research has been devoted to content management [29,25], [15], design of hierarchical media storage servers [27,21], and networked media servers [28,30]. Excellent work on querying media databases has been done – ranging from querying image data [26,24,5,15,19], video data [26,2], audio data [34] and mixes of all the above [22,31]. However, there is no prevailing

---

* This work was supported by the Army Research Office under Grants DAAH-04-95-10174, DAAH-04-96-10297, DAAH04-96-1-0398 and DAAG559710047, by the Army Research Laboratory under contract number DAAL01-97-K0135, by an NSF Young Investigator award IRI-93-57756, and by an ASU-FGIA Grant F-014-98

S. Jajodia, M.T. Özsu, and A. Dogac (Eds.): MIS'98, LNCS 1508, pp. 45–56, 1998.
© Springer-Verlag Berlin Heidelberg 1998

notion of a *multimedia view*. In [32], Sheth and Kashyap discuss a declarative view management notion for multimedia information; yet, there is no research in the literature on how such views can be created, managed, and maintained. In contrast, in the setting of relational databases, view management techniques have been widely studied [6,13], as well as in the case of file systems [1], object databases [14], and distributed mediated systems [3]. The benefits that views bring to query processing and optimization in databases are widely known [23]. The primary aim of this paper is to define a notion of *view* for multimedia databases, together with a notion of *materialization* (or rendering) the view. Such a notion would bring to the domain of multimedia databases, the ability to utilize views to enhance efficiency.

In this paper, we start by defining the concept of a multimedia view definition (MVD). MVDs consist of two parts:

- A specification stating what media objects are included in the view.
- A specification describing how these media objects will be presented to the user. *In other words, the results of a multimedia view materialization is an interactive media presentation that is delivered to the user.*

Informally, an MVD is a *declarative* specification of what is to be shown. In classical view materialization, once a view is materialized, *showing* the results is trivial. In contrast, in a multimedia view management system, this is not the case. Presenting the results of materializing an MVD is not trivial, and needs to take into account, the locations of the objects, the bandwidth offered by the network, the load on different servers, the buffer space offered, etc.

Finally, we will report on our **MediaView** system for the management of such multimedia views, and will include experimental results on the benefits of our probabilistic scheduling algorithms.

2   Multimedia View Definitions

A multimedia view contains not just a specification of the objects, but also a description of how these objects are presented to the user. James F. Allen proposed a formalism based on intervals [4]. Many researchers including [33,20] use intervals for the scheduling of multimedia documents. Several other researchers, including Candan et.al. [10,11], Buchanan and Zellweger [7,8,9], and Kim and Song [17,18], on the other hand, proposed the use of a highly-structured class of linear constraints called *difference constraints* for this purpose. In this paper, we will use the framework introduced by Candan et.al. in [10,11] as *it can handle inconsistencies in the specifications*. Note that in the absence of disjunctions, this framework is capable of expressing the thirteen temporal relationships introduced by Allen. Furthermore, unlike Allen's framework, it is capable to represent quantitative information.

Let MDB be any multimedia database, and let QL be any query language for querying this database. A *content framework*, CF, is a pair, (MDB, QL).

Definition 1 (Multimedia View Definition (MVD)). A *multimedia view definition (MVD)* consists of two parts:

- An content specification, CS, based on a content framework CF is a relation having the schema (Num,ObjId,Type,Query,Constraint), where
  - Num is either a non-negative integer, or the string all,
  - ObjId is a unique string that cannot be the same for two different tuples in CSP, unless the Condition fields of those two tuples are jointly inconsistent,
  - Type is either i (for action object) or q (for query object),
  - Query is a query in QL which returns only a set of media objects as output, and
  - Constraint is a set presentation constraints satisfying the following conditions: Given a row t of relation CF,
    1. if $t.Num \neq$ all and $t.ObjId = o_i$, then $t.Constraint$ is a set of constraints over objects $\{o_{i,1}, \ldots, o_{i,t.Num}\}$ and other objects(including start, end\}).
    2. if $t.Num =$ all, then:
       (a) $t.Constraint$ contains a special constraint of the form $cnum = c$ for some constant integer $c > 0$ and
       (b) all other constraints in $t.Constraint$ are over objects $\{o_{i,1}, \ldots, o_{i,h}\}$ and other objects (including two special objects, start, end\}). Here, $h = \lceil \frac{k}{cnum} \rceil$, where k is the total number of answers to $t.Query$. $o_{i,j}$ refers to the $((cnum \times (j-1)) + 1)$'th object in the answer through the $(cnum \times j)$'th object of the answer to the query. We use specialized techniques to handle the case where $o_{i,j}$ does not exist.
  - An action relation specifying, for each action object a_i, four sets: (ObjId, InObjects, OutObjects, InConstraints, OutConstraints). This relation describes the objects and presentation specifications associated with each object. ∅

Example 1. An example content specification is now given below.

Num	ObjId	Type	Query	Constraint
all	o_1	q	SELECT Map FROM Public_WeatherDB WHERE date = Today AND place = N.Korea.	cnum = 3
1	o_2	i	-	cnum = 3
1	o_3	q	SELECT Video-clip FROM Public_WeatherVideos WHERE date = Today AND place = N.Korea.	
1	o_4	q	-	-
1	o_5	q	-	-

A quick explanation of this table is in order.

- The first tuple describes the nature of object o_1.
- The second tuple says that object o_2 is an interaction object.
- The third tuple shows how a video object o_3 is instantiated.
- Objects o_4 and o_5 are explicitly specified objects.

The constraint fields associated with objects o_1 and o_2 set to cnum $= 3$. What this means is that the result of the query defining object o_1 will be grouped into three groups g_1, g_2, g_3.   ∅

The following is an example action relation:

ActId	InObjects	OutObjects	InConstraints	OutConstraints
a_1	$\{o_5\}$	$\{o_{20}, o_{21}\}$	C_{in}	C_{out}

Here, the sets C_{in} and C_{out} describe the sets of constraints that are inserted to and removed from the original presentation constraints.

3   Interactive Media Presentation Specification

Suppose CSP is a content specification, and $\mathcal{O}_i$ is the set of all interaction objects occurring in the ObjId field of CSP, while $\mathcal{O}_p^\star = \{o_1, \ldots, o_n\}$ is the set of all presentation objects (i.e. objects that are not interaction objects) occurring in the ObjId field of CSP. We define $\mathcal{O}_p = \mathcal{O}_p^\star \cup \{start, end\}$ where start and end are special objects denoting the start and end of the presentation. $\mathcal{O}_p$ is the set of all objects to be shown to the user, based on the content specification, CSP. The reader is reminded that the o_i's may themselves be sets of objects (e.g. the answers to a query). A qo-subset, $\mathcal{QO}(\mathcal{O}_p)$, is any subset of $\mathcal{O}_p$. Let $\mathcal{Q}$ be the power set of $\mathcal{O}_p$.

Presentation and retrieval schedule generation for non-interactive presentations has already been studied in [10] and [16]. Section 4.2 will include a host of *Probabilistic Prefetching and Scheduling Methods* that will support distributed interactive multimedia presentations, building on top of the previous two bodies of work.

Definition 2 (Interactive Multimedia Presentation (IMP) Space). The *Interactive Multimedia Presentation (IMP) Space* w.r.t. a content specification CSP involving objects $\{o_1, \ldots, o_n\}$ (together with start and end), consists of a labeled tree Υ where

- Each node N is labeled by a triple $(\mathcal{QO}_N, \mathcal{CONS}_N, \mathcal{ACT}_N)$, where $\mathcal{QO} \in \mathcal{Q}$, $\mathcal{CONS}_n$ is a set of *presentation* constraints (to be described below) on the objects in $\mathcal{QO}_i$, and $\mathcal{ACT}_N$ is a set of interaction objects.
- The root of Υ; is labeled by $(\{start\}, \emptyset, \emptyset)$ (and no other node in Υ is labeled by $(\{start\}, \emptyset, \emptyset)$;
- Each leaf in Υ is labeled by the triple $(\{end\}, \emptyset, \emptyset)$;
- Each edge (from node N to node N') in Υ is labeled by a seven-tuple $(a, \mathcal{QO}^+, \mathcal{QO}^-, \mathcal{CONS}^+, \mathcal{CONS}^-, \mathcal{ACT}^+, \mathcal{ACT}^-)$, where $\mathcal{QO}^+$ and $\mathcal{QO}^-$ are sets of objects, $\mathcal{CONS}^+$ and $\mathcal{CONS}^-$ are sets of constraints (to be described below) on the objects in $\mathcal{QO}_N \cup \mathcal{QO}^+$, $\mathcal{ACT}^+$ and $\mathcal{ACT}^-$ are sets of action objects, and a is an interaction object or $\perp$. If a is an action object, then
  - $\mathcal{QO}_{N'} = (\mathcal{QO}_N \cup \mathcal{QO}^+) - \mathcal{QO}^-$,
  - $\mathcal{CONS}_{N'} = (\mathcal{CONS}_N \cup \mathcal{CONS}^+) - \mathcal{CONS}^-$, and
  - $\mathcal{ACT}_{N'} = (\mathcal{ACT}_N \cup \mathcal{ACT}^+) - \mathcal{ACT}^-$.

If, on the other hand, a is $\perp$, then
- $\mathcal{QO}_{N'} = \mathcal{QO}_N$,
- $\mathcal{CONS}_{N'} = \mathcal{CONS}_N$, and
- $\mathcal{ACT}_{N'} = (\mathcal{ACT}_N \bigcup \mathcal{ACT}^+) - \mathcal{ACT}^-$.   ∅

Intuitively, each node in the IMP-space specifies a *non-interactive* presentation that is delivered to the user. The transitions between nodes occur if there is a user interaction or if the action objects on the screen are modified without the user action. If N is a node labeled by the triple $(\mathcal{QO}_N, \mathcal{CONS}_N, \mathcal{ACT}_N)$, then this node presents all objects in $\mathcal{QO}_N$ by generating a presentation schedule using constraints $\mathcal{CONS}_N$,

Given any IMP-Space, when the presentation is viewed by a specific user, s/he follows one path in the IMP-Space from the root to a leaf. This is termed an interactive multimedia presentation (IMP) path, and is described below.

Definition 3 (Interactive Multimedia Presentation (IMP) Path). An *Interactive Multimedia Presentation (IMP) Path* w.r.t. a content specification CSP involving objects $\{o_1, \ldots, o_n\}$ (together with **start** and **end**) is a finite path from the root of the IMP-Space (i.e., $(\{start\}, \emptyset, \emptyset)$) to a leaf node (i.e., $(\{end\}, \emptyset, \emptyset)$).   ∅

Note that IMP-spaces may be infinite. For example, the bold-dotted line in Fig. 1(a) shows an infinite sequence of nodes in the IMP-space.

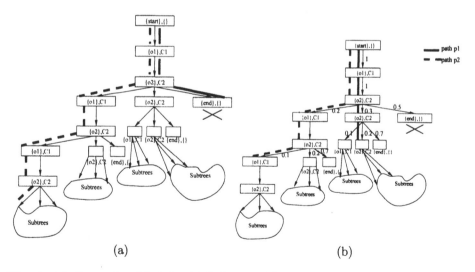

(a)   (b)

Fig. 1. (a) Example of infinite IMP-Space; (b) example of probabilistic IMP-Space

Suppose now that we consider a specific MVD μ. μ can easily be seen to generate an IMP-Space. This is because given μ, we can construct an IMP-space by taking the root of the IMP-space to be $(\{start\}, \emptyset, \emptyset,)$. If we have a partially constructed IMP-space Γ, we can expand any leaf in it (which is not labeled with $(\{\mathbf{end}\}, \emptyset, , \emptyset)$) by finding all actions that are *applicable* in it. The applicable actions can be readily found from a multimedia view definition. Each of those actions is used to generate a new child node IMP-state. This process is repeated till all leaves are labeled with $(\{\mathbf{end}\}, \emptyset, , \emptyset)$ and the expansion is no longer possible.

4   Rendering and Delivering Multimedia Views

In classical relational databases, views define "derived" relations that are computed from underlying "base" relations and stored. The resulting "materialized" views are then often used to rewrite queries, resulting in optimized execution times. In the case of an MVD, this task is much more complex. A materialized view in relational DBMSs is static. In contrast, an MVD must be *presented* to the user and the user has the opportunity to interact with the presentation, making choices on what he wants to see. In this section, we will provide an object-based approach to prefetching objects so as to facilitate the delivery of interactive multimedia presentations generated by a multimedia view.

4.1   Probabilistic Spaces

The prefetch approach depend upon a concept called a *probabilistic IMP-space*.

Definition 4 (Probabilistic IMP-Spaces). Suppose we consider an IMP-space Υ. A *probabilistic extension of* Υ is a pair $(\Upsilon, \wp)$ where $\wp$ is a mapping that takes edges in Υ as input and produces real numbers in the $[0, 1]$ interval as output such that for each non-leaf node N in Υ,

$$\sum_{N' \text{ is a child of } N} \wp(N, N') = 1.$$

$\emptyset$

Intuitively, whenever the user is presented with an interactive option, he chooses at most one of the options. $\wp$ measures the probability of these choices. For example, Fig. 1(b) provides an example of how the IMP-space of Fig. 1(a) can be extended to a probabilistic IMP-space.

Definition 5 (Path Probabilities in Probabilistic IMP-Spaces). Suppose $(\Upsilon, \wp)$ is a probabilistic IMP-space, and N is a node in Υ. Let Υ_N^k denote the subtree rooted at node N k levels down. For any path p in this subtree consisting of at most k edges $(N_0, N_1), (N_1, N_2), \ldots, (N_{k-1}, N_k)$ where $N_0 = N$, the *probability of path p being taken, given that node N has been reached in the playout* is given by $\mathbf{P}(p \mid N) = \Pi_{i=0}^{k-1} \wp(N_i, N_{i+1})$.

$\emptyset$

The above probability is a *conditional probability* that assumes that node N has been achieved via the playout described by the path from the root to node N. This definition associates a probability with each path of length k. As we will see in Section 5, choosing a large k causes the probabilities of most paths to become very small, making it difficult to identify "highly" likely paths. Choosing a k that is too small is not helpful either, it provides few opportunities for prefetching.

Definition 6 (j-bounded Object Appearance Probability). Suppose $PS = (\Upsilon, \wp)$ is a probabilistic IMP-space, N is a node in Υ, Υ_N^j denotes the subtree rooted at node N, j levels down and o is an object in the presentation. Then, the *j-bounded appearance probability of o given* $Hist(t)$ is

$$\mathbf{P}_{j-bounded}(o, N) = \sum_{0 \leq i \leq j} \sum_{\forall path_m \in \Upsilon_N^i \text{ with } o \text{ in it}} \mathbf{P}(path_m).$$

$\varnothing$

Intuitively, $\mathbf{P}_{j-bounded}(o, N))$, describes the probability of object o's occurrence within the presentation subtree of depth j with root N. If we "look ahead" j levels in the tree, then the probability that object o is needed in those j levels is the sum of the probabilities of the paths containing j. We will use this to prefetch objects for efficient materialization.

4.2   Object-Based Prefetching Strategy

Suppose now that our prefetch buffer is of size B bytes. In this strategy, we fill the prefetch buffer by first inserting the most probable object, then the second most probable object, and so on till the buffer is filled. This strategy requires an efficient way of identifying the most probably needed objects in decreasing order of probabilities.

Definition 7 (j-bounded Object Retrieval Profit). Suppose $PS = (\Upsilon, \wp)$ is a probabilistic IMP-space, N is a node in Υ, and o is an object in the presentation. Then, the *j-bounded object retrieval profit* of o is $profit_{j-bounded}(o, N) = \mathbf{P}_{j-bounded}(o, N) \times gain(o, N) - cost(o, N)$,   where $gain$ is a function which evaluates how much system gains by retrieving object o at time t (considering only the next j units of time), and $cost$ is a function which evaluates the cost of the retrieval of the object at node N – and hence at the time node N was reached in the playout.

$\varnothing$

Note that $\mathbf{P}_{j-bounded}(o, N) \times gain(o, N)$ is the expected gain of the system from the retrieval of object o at the time node N is reached. Hence, the term $profit_{j-bounded}(o, N)$ describes how desirable is the retrieval of object o at node N if one considers a future of j time units.

Definition 8. Suppose $PS = (\Upsilon, \wp)$ is a probabilistic IMP-space, N is a node in Υ, and o is an object in the presentation. Then, a *(k,j,c)-retrieval policy* (w.r.t. N) is a set O of objects, such that

---

Algorithm 1. (Object retrieval-caching algorithm ($ORCA$))
Input:

- A probabilistic IMP-space, PS,
- A presentation state, N,
- A set of objects OBJ,
- A $(k, j, c) - retrieval$ policy,
- A bound j on the future.

1. For each object $o_i \in OBJ$, calculate $gain(o_i, N)$ and $cost(o_i, N)$.
2. For each object $o_i \in OBJ$, calculate (incrementally) $\mathbf{P}_{j-bounded}(o, N)$.
3. For each object $o_i \in OBJ$, calculate $profit_{j-bounded}(o_i, N)$, eliminate all objects whose profits are smaller than k,
4. Solve the *0-1 knapsack algorithm* with the knapsack size c, object weights $cost(o_i, N)$, and object values $profit_{j-bounded}(o_i, N)$).
5. Return the set of objects returned by the *0-1 knapsack algorithm*

Fig. 2. Object Retrieval-Caching Algorithm ($ORCA$)

- $\forall_{o_i \in O}(profit_{j-bounded}(o_i, N) \geq k)$.
- $\sum_{o_i \in O}(cost(o, N)) \leq c$. $\qquad\qquad\qquad\qquad\qquad\qquad \emptyset$

Intuitively, a (k,j,c)-retrieval policy dictates that the system chooses (after considering a future of j time units) to retrieve a set of objects such that (1) each of these objects has a profit greater than or equal to k, and (2) the sum of the retrieval costs of these objects is less than or equal to c.

Figure 2 shows the object retrieval-caching algorithm which uses the *optimal (k,j,c)-retrieval policy*. Since, object caching algorithm is expensive ($O(2^j + c \times number\_of\_objects)$), in Fig. 3, we present a heuristic which prunes tree, reducing the execution cost to $O(number\_of\_objects \times c + number\_of\_actionobjects^s)$.

Theorem 1. Let $m = number\_of\_actionobjects$ and let s be an integer such that $0 < s << j$). The total number of nodes created by the heuristic is

$$\sum_{i=1}^{s}(\frac{s!}{(s-i)!} \times m^i + \frac{s!}{(s-i+1)!} \times m^{i-1} \times 2)$$

or, equivalently, it is $O(m^s)$.

5   Implementation and Experiments

We implemented *MediaView*, a multimedia view management system, based on the algorithms described in this paper.

We implemented the object-based prefetching algorithm described in this paper using C on Unix/Solaris platform. We have also implemented a view-definition/case generator to create the view definitions on which these object

---

Algorithm 2. (Tree Creation Algorithm (*TCA*))
Input:

- A probabilistic IMP-space, *PS*,
- A presentation node, *N*,
- A set of objects,
- A bound, *j*, on the future,
- A limit, *s*, on the time points per action object.

1. If $s = 0$ then stop
2. At node N (and current time t) calculate the *j-bounded future* (assuming no user interaction).
3. For each action object a_i, where $t < et(a_i) \leq t + j$, choose s time points $t_{i,b}$, where $1 \leq b \leq s$, $t < t_{i,b} < t_{i+1,b} < t + j + 1$), and $t_{a,b} \neq t_{c,d}$ if $a \neq c$ or $b \neq d$. Here, $et(a_i)$ denotes the end time of action object a_i.
4. Let $t_{\perp,\perp}$ correspond to time t and let $t_{\top,\top}$ correspond to time $t + j + 1$.
5. Let the probability that object a_i is chosen at time $t_{i,b}$ be equal to

$$p(t_{i,b}) = \sum_{t'=t_{i,b}}^{t_{i+1,b}} (\mathbf{P}(a_i, t' | Hist(t_{i,b})))$$

   Let also $p(t_{\perp,\perp})$ be 1.
6. For each pair of time points $(t_{a,b} < t_{c,d})$ such that there exists no other time point $t_{e,f}$ satisfying $t_{a,b} < t_{e,f} < t_{c,d}$, create an edge with probability $1 - p(t_{a,b})$.

7. For each time point $t_{a,b}$ (not $\in \{t, t + j\}$) execute this algorithm recursively (with initial time set to $t_{a,b}$, the bound, j, set to $t + j - t_{a,b}$, and the limit set to $s - 1$) to get a tree $T_{a,b}$. Connect $t_{a,b}$ with the root of $T_{a,b}$ with an edge of probability $p(t_{a,b})$.

Fig. 3. Tree creation algorithm (*TCA*)

prefetching algorithms will be used. The view-definition/case generator uses 2000 objects of varying size (approximately 50% of the objects average 500,000 bytes each, 30% of the objects average 5 MBs each, and the rest average 12 MBs each) to create a document, where there are at most 50 objects visible at a time and there are at most 10 choices that a user can have at a time. The document/case generator also generates user profiles to attach probabilities to each choice.

In addition to the view-definition/case generator, we developed a viewer/case generator which uses document information and user profiles to generate a walk-through (i.e., presentation realization) of the document. The walk-through uses a parameter called *randomness* to decide how much it follows the profiles. If this parameter is equal to 0.0, then the viewer is assumed to follow the user profiles, whereas, if the randomness value is equal to 1.0, then the user behaves completely randomly.

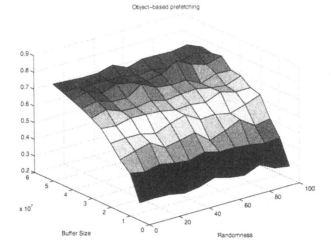

Fig. 4. *Hit-ratio* of object-based prefetching algorithm

We varied the local buffer size between 5MBs and 50MBs and the randomness between 0.0 and 1.0. In each execution, we looked 5 steps ahead for prefetching. We ran each experiment 80 times.

Effectiveness of the Prefetch Strategy (Hit-Ratios): Figure 4 shows the results of the experiments we ran to evaluate the effectiveness of object-based prefetching algorithm. The algorithm proved to be robust against user randomness. It showed an increase in the hit ratio as the local buffer size is increased and reached a plateau around 70%.

Execution Times: Last, we report on the execution times of the prefetch algorithm. For the configuration described above, the object-based algorithm (without the use of the TCA heuristic) takes approximately half a second to execute. This suggests that, despite of its advantages, unless a heuristic (such as TCA) is used to reduce the number of nodes on the tree or the incremental algorithms are used, the object-based algorithm may be too costly to use for larger prefetch depths.

6   Conclusions

Though multimedia database systems have been extensively developed over the last few years, the concept of a multimedia view has remained undeveloped. In this paper, we have taken the first steps towards the development of the concept of *view* for multimedia database systems. We have stated that a multimedia view definition consists of a content specification, specified through queries, and a presentation component, that specifies in what form the results of materialization are to be presented. The crux of our idea is that multimedia views must produce multimedia presentations when they are materialized.

Presenting the results of materializing a multimedia view is not trivial, and it needs to take into account the compute and communication resources. We have presented an object-based prefetching technique that minimize the response time of interactive materialization.

We have implemented *MediaView* based on the algorithm described in this paper. The experiments we ran using this system showed that the prefetching algorithm can be effectively used in improving the efficiency of rendering of multimedia views. Our results show that the strategy may be efficiently implemented in large scale systems, and that on the average, they achieve about 63% correctness in their guess.

References

1. S. Abiteboul, S. Cluet, and T. Milo. (1993) *Querying and Updating the File.* Proc. Int. Conf. on Very Large Data Bases (VLDB), pp. 73-84, 1993.
2. S. Adali, K.S. Candan, S.-S. Chen, K. Erol, and V.S.Subrahmanian. (1996) *Advanced Video Information Systems,* ACM Multimedia Systems Journal, 4, pps 172–186, 1996.
3. S. Adali, K.S.Candan, Y. Papakonstantinou and V.S.Subrahmanian. (1996) *Query Processing in Distributed Mediated Systems, Proc. 1996 ACM SIGMOD Conf.,* Montreal, Canada, June 1996.
4. J.F. Allen (1983) *Maintaining Knowledge about Temporal Intervals,* Communications of the ACM, vol. 26, no. 11, pp. 832-843, November 1983.
5. M. Arya, W. Cody, C. Faloutsos, J. Richardson and A. Toga. (1995) *Design and Implementation of QBISM, a 3D Medical Image Database System,* in: (V.S. Subrahmanian and S. Jajodia, eds.) "Multimedia Database Systems: Issues and Research Directions", Springer 1995.
6. J. Blakeley, N. Coburn, and P.-A. Larson. (1989) *Updating Derived Relations: DEtecting Irrelevant and Autonomously Computable Updates. ACM Trans. on Database Systems,* 14(3):369–400, 1989.
7. M.C. Buchanan and P.T. Zellweger (1993) *Automatic Temporal Layout Mechanisms* ACM Multimedia 93, pp. 341-350, 1993.
8. M.C. Buchanan and P.T. Zellweger (1993) *Scheduling Multimedia Documents Using Temporal Constraints,* Network and Operating System Support for Digital Audio and Video, P. Venkat Rangan (ed.), Springer-Verlag, Berlin Heidelberg New York, pp. 237-249, 1993.
9. M.C. Buchanan and P.T. Zellweger (1993) *Automatically Generating Consistent Schedules for Multimedia Documents,* ACM/Springer-Verlag Journal of Multimedia Systems, vol. 1, no. 2, 1993.
10. K.S. Candan, B. Prabhakaran and V.S. Subrahmanian. (1996) *CHIMP: A Framework for Supporting Multimedia Document Authoring and Presentation,* Proc. 1996 ACM Multimedia 1996 Conference, Boston, MA, Nov. 1996.
11. K.S. Candan, B. Prabhakaran, and V.S. Subrahmanian (1996) *Retrieval Schedules Based on Resource Availability and Flexible Presentation Specifications,* Accepted for publication in ACM-Springer Multimedia Systems Journal.
12. K.S. Candan (1997) *A Framework for Distributed Multimedia Collaborations.* Ph.D. Thesis, University of Maryland at College Park, College Park, Maryland, 1997.
13. Stefano Ceri and Jennifer Widom. Deriving Production Rules for Incremental View Maintenance. In *17th VLDB,* 1991.
14. U. Dayal. Queries and views in a object-oriented databases. In *Int. Workshop on Database Programming Languages,* 1989.

15. C. Faloutsos. (1996) *Searching Multimedia Databases by Content*, Kluwer Academic Publishers.
16. E. Hwang, B. Prabhakaran and V.S.Subrahmanian. (1998) *Distributed Video Presentations.* accepted for publication in IEEE intl. Conf. on Data Engineering'98.
17. M.Y. Kim and J. Song (1993) *Hyperstories: Combining Time, Space and Asynchrony in Multimedia Documents*, RC19277(83726) (revised 1995) IBM Computer Science/Mathematics Research Report, 1993.
18. M.Y. Kim and J. Song (1995) *Multimedia Documents with Elastic Time*, ACM Multimedia Conference '95, 1995.
19. W.-S. Li and K.S. Candan. (1998) *SEMCOG: A Hybrid Object-based Image Database System and Its Modeling, Language, and Query Processin* to appear in Proceedings of The 14th International Conference on Data Engineering, Orlando, Florida, USA, February 23 - 27, 1998.
20. T.D.C. Little and A. Ghafoor (1990) *Synchronization and Storage Models for Multimedia Objects*, IEEE J. on Selected Areas of Communications, vol. 8, no. 3, April 1990, pp. 413-427. April 1990.
21. D. Makaroff and R. T. Ng. (1994) *Schemes for Implementing Buffer Sharing in Continuous Media Systems*, Information Systems, 19, 4, pps 33–54.
22. S. Marcus and V.S. Subrahmanian. *Foundations of Multimedia Database Systems*, Journal of the ACM, Vol. 43, 3, pps 474–523, 1996.
23. I. S. Mumick. (1991) *Query Optimization in Deductive and Relational Databases.* Ph.D. Thesis, Stanford University, CA 94305, 1991.
24. W. Niblack, et. al. (1993) *The QBIC Project: Querying Images by Content Using Color, Texture and Shape*, IBM Research Report, Feb. 1993.
25. V.E. Ogle and M. Stonebraker. (1995) *Chabot: Retrieval from a Relational Database of Images*, IEEE Computer, Sep. 1995.
26. E. Oomoto and K. Tanaka. (1993) *OVID: Design and Implementation of a Video-Object Database System*, IEEE Trans. on Knowledge and Data Engineering, 5, 4, pps 629–643.
27. B. Ozden, R. Rastogi and A. Silberschatz. (1995) *Research Issues in Multimedia Storage Servers*, CM Computing Surveys , December 1995.
28. S.V. Raghavan, B. Prabhakaran and Satish K. Tripathi (1994) *Synchronization Representation and Traffic Source Modeling in Orchestrated Presentation*, Special issue on Multimedia Synchronization, IEEE Journal on Selected Areas in Communication, January 1995.
29. P. Venkat Rangan and H. Vin. (1991) *Designing File Systems for Digital Audio and Video*, Proc, 13th ACM Symp. on Operation Systems Principles, pps 69–79.
30. P. Venkat Rangan, H. Vin and S. Ramanathan. (1992) *Designing an On-Demand Multimedia Service*, IEEE Communications Magazine, pps 56–64, July 1992.
31. V.S. Subrahmanian. (1997) *Principles of Multimedia Database Systems*, Morgan Kaufman Press, Dec. 1997.
32. A. Sheth and V. Kashya. (1996) *Media-independent Correlation of Information: What? How?* Proceedings of First IEEE Metadata Conference, April 1996.
33. T.K. Shih, S.K.C. Lo, S.-J. Fu, and J.B. Chang (1996) *Using Interval Logic and Inference Rules for the Automatic Generation of Multimedia Presentations*, IEEE International Conference on Multimedia Computing and Systems '96, pp. 425-428, Hiroshima, June 1996.
34. E. Wold, T. Blum, D. Keislar, and J. Wheaton. (1996) *Content-based Classification, Search, and Retrieval of Audio*, IEEE Multimedia Magazine 1996.

NETCICATS: Network-Conscious Image Compression and Transmission System*

Sami Iren[1], Paul D. Amer[1], and Phillip T. Conrad[2]

[1] Department of Computer and Information Sciences
University of Delaware, Newark, DE 19716 USA
{iren,amer}@cis.udel.edu
[2] Department of Computer and Information Sciences
Temple University , Philadelphia, PA 19122 USA
conrad@acm.org

Abstract. NETCICATS is a software system for empirically evaluating *network-conscious image compression*, an approach that does not simply optimize compression, but which optimizes overall performance when compressed images are transmitted over a lossy packet-switched network such as the Internet. Based on Application Level Framing, an image is compressed into path-MTU-size Application Data Units (ADUs) at the application layer. Each ADU contains enough information to be processed independently of all other ADUs. Each ADU can be delivered to the receiving application out-of-order, thereby enabling faster progressive display of images. NETCICATS allows the empirical investigation of the combination of transport protocol features and compression algorithms that perform best over a lossy packet-switched network. It includes software components from the network layer (e.g., lossy router), transport layer (e.g., innovative transport protocols), and application layer (e.g., compression algorithms, browsers, etc.). We describe each component of the system and explain how the whole system is used. This paper also presents two network-conscious image compression algorithms: network-conscious GIF and wavelet zerotree encoding.

1   Introduction

For many years, developments in image compression had one primary objective: obtaining the minimum image size. We argue that image compression algorithms should take into account that those images are likely to be transmitted over networks that will lose and reorder packets. Therefore, compression algorithms should not focus solely on achieving minimum image size; algorithms should be optimized to give the best performance when image data is lost or arrives out-of-order.

* Prepared through collaborative participation in the Advanced Telecommunications/ Info Distribution Research Program (ATIRP) Consortium sponsored by the U. S. Army Research Laboratory under the Fed Lab Program, Agreement DAAL01-96-2-0002. This work also supported, in part, by ARO (DAAH04-94-G-0093).

S. Jajodia, M.T. Özsu, and A. Dogac (Eds.): MIS'98, LNCS 1508, pp. 57–68, 1998.
© Springer-Verlag Berlin Heidelberg 1998

We apply the concept of *network-consciousness* [8] to *image compression*, an approach that takes network Quality of Service (QoS) into consideration when designing image compression. Network-conscious image compression is based on the philosophy of Application Level Framing (ALF) [2]. An image is divided into path-MTU-size[1] pieces, called *Application Data Units* (ADUs), at the application layer. Each ADU contains enough semantic information to be processed independently of all other ADUs. As a result, each ADU then can be delivered to the receiving application immediately, without regard to order, thereby potentially enabling faster progressive display of images.

Our approach to testing the network-conscious image compression hypothesis consists of two phases. In phase one, we developed Network-Conscious Image Compression and Transmission System (NETCICATS) to observe the relation between compression algorithms and transport protocols over network with varying characteristics. We want to see how different compression techniques behave when combined with different transport QoS at different loss rates. In phase two of our research, we modified two popular image compression techniques, namely GIF89a[2] and SPIHT [15] (wavelet zerotree encoding), to make them network-conscious.

Our research demonstrates that with a combination of innovative transport protocols and only a small penalty in compression ratio, today's standard compression algorithms can be modified to provide significantly better progressive display of images, and hence performance, in the Internet and wireless environments. In this paper, we describe the tools we have developed to investigate this approach, and present some experimental results gathered using these tools.

Section 2 describes network-conscious image compression and the motivation for it. Section 3 introduces NETCICATS. Sections 4 and 5 summarize two prototype implementations of our approach: network-conscious GIF and network-conscious wavelet zerotree encoding, respectively. Section 6 concludes the paper with a summary.

2   Network-Conscious Image Compression

A network-conscious compressed image is one that is encoded *not* simply to give the *smallest size* for a specified image quality, but to give the *best (i.e., smallest) response time - image quality* combination to an end user retrieving the image over a packet-switched network [10,11]. The basic characteristics of a network-conscious compressed image are: (1) application level framing, (2) progressive display (preferably multi-layered), and (3) robustness and adaptiveness to different user needs and various networking conditions.

The key feature of network-conscious image compression is that it produces path-MTU-size self-contained blocks (ADUs) that can be decompressed indepen-

---

[1] MTU (Maximum Transmission Unit) is the maximum frame size that a link layer can carry. A path-MTU-size ADU is one that can be transmitted from source to destination without the need for IP layer fragmentation and reassembly.

[2] GIF89a is a Service Mark of CompuServe, Inc., Columbus, OH.

dently of each other. When these blocks are transmitted over a lossy network, they can be received and processed out-of-order, thereby permitting better progressive display. ADUs permit the use of a more efficient transport protocol that does not need to preserve order. Having simpler transport protocols is especially important for wireless environments because of their hosts' limited power supply [11].

Assuming some loss, the expected buffer requirements at the transport receiver for an unordered protocol are always less than the buffer requirements for ordered protocols [13]. Furthermore, out-of-order delivery of ADUs reduces the jitter at the receiving application. In ordered transport protocols, ADUs that are received out-of-order are kept in the buffers. When missing ADUs finally arrive, ADUs waiting in the buffer are delivered as a group to the application. This approach makes the delivery of ADUs to the application more bursty. The burstiness may result in bottlenecks at the receiving application [9].

Another advantage of compressing an image into ADUs is that their transmission can be tailored to each ADU characteristic. Not all parts of image data are uniform and require the same QoS. For example, low frequency coefficients (i.e., important data) of a wavelet image require a reliable service. On the other hand, high frequency coefficients (i.e., less important details) can tolerate a certain level of loss. Independent ADUs enable the use of different QoS such as reliability and priority for each ADU type.

Network-conscious compressed images are robust and can also adapt to different networking conditions easily. A lost or bit-errored packet will not destroy an entire image. A network-conscious compressed image can be transmitted over a very low bandwidth lossy network as well as a high bandwidth reliable network. The same compressed image can even be used, without any modifications, in a multipoint communication, where each participant has different requirements.

3   NETCICATS

NETCICATS allows us to empirically investigate the combination of transport protocol features and compression algorithms that perform best over a lossy packet-switched network. NETCICATS was flexibly designed for testing network-conscious image compression with several compression algorithms, a wide range of transport layer services, and on a variety of network conditions with different loss rates and bandwidths.

Since wavelet-based image and video coding has become popular, we based our compression algorithms on wavelet transformation. Recently, several wavelet-based encoding schemes have been developed which outperform DCT-based algorithms in terms of both objective criteria (bit rate versus distortion) and subjective criteria [6]. As Shapiro reports, "the main contribution of wavelet theory and multiresolution analysis is that it provides an elegant framework in which both anomalies and trends can be analyzed on an equal footing." This framework is important in image processing because, "edges, which can be thought of as anomalies in the spatial domain, represent extremely important information despite the fact that they are represented in only a tiny fraction of the image samples" [16].

Figure 1 depicts NETCICATS components to transmit wavelet-encoded images over a lossy, low-bandwidth network. Main components are (1) an image sender, (2) an image receiver, (3) a lossy router, and (4) a reflector.

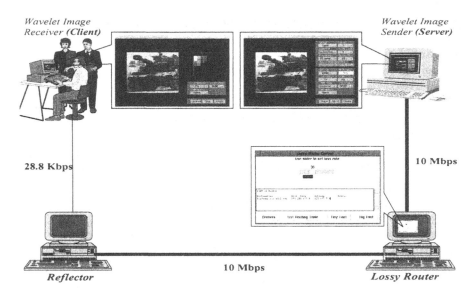

Fig. 1. Network-Conscious Image Compression and Transmission System

The *image sender* allows a user to flexibly control an image's quality and size, and the transport QoS between server and client. The image quality and size are controlled by user-adjustable parameters such as thresholding level (i.e., percentage of wavelet coefficients that are set to zero), quantization level (i.e., number of bits used for quantization), type of mother wavelet (e.g., Daubechies, Haar, Coiflet, etc.), levels of decomposition, and encoding method. The image quality can be measured both subjectively by visualizing the image, and objectively by using its PSNR.

The *image receiver* progressively displays image data as it arrives. In addition to the progressive image, a separate array of grids is updated as each ADU arrives. This grid identifies which wavelet coefficients are currently being displayed, and is especially useful to observe the effects of missing coefficients at different resolutions. A "stop" button allows a user at the image receiver to cancel the transmission of all additional ADUs without severing the transport connection. This saves network bandwidth when an image has progressed sufficiently for the receiver to make a decision (e.g., for tele-medicine—"transport patient vs. do-not-transport", or in situational awareness— "friend vs. foe", "target vs. non-target"). Halting transmission mid-way is made possible by the

ADN-Cancel feature of certain innovative transport protocols being developed by the authors. This feature allows cancellation of messages that have already been submitted to the transport layer. The application specifies an Application Data Name (ADN) for each message, and can cancel the transmission of any message (or group of messages) by specifying its (their) ADN [4]. ADN-cancel is a service that is not supported by either TCP or UDP.

In the University of Delaware Protocol Engineering Lab (PEL), the image sender and image receiver run on two different stations on the same Ethernet. To simulate packet loss on the Internet, routing tables direct all client/server traffic through a special *Lossy Router (LR)*. This LR allows experimenting with different levels of packet loss between the server and client. The LR is intended to run on a machine serving as an IP gateway. All of the normal routing functions of that host are replaced by this software. This way, any communications between two hosts which route their data through the LR will be affected. The current LR simulates any of three loss models: Bernoulli, deterministic, or 2-Step Markov. When forwarding each IP packet, the LR deliberately drops the specified percentage of packets according to the specific loss model. In the Bernoulli model, the given percentage of packets are dropped randomly. In the deterministic model, every k^{th} packet is dopped, where k is a user-controlled parameter. In the 2-Step Markov model (also called Gilbert loss model), there are two states, and losses only occur in the "loss" state (see Figure 2). The average loss rate, L, is defined by $L = p/(p + q)$. This model represents losses with burstiness.

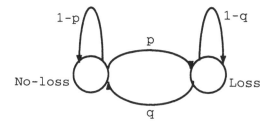

Fig. 2. 2-Step Markov Loss Model

The LR is controlled with an FTP-like protocol called the Simple Lossy Router Protocol (SLRP). This is a simple text-based control protocol that provides the communication between the LR user and the LR software. The LR user can set the loss rate and loss model, list and update the routing table on the lossy router, and collect statistics. A user-friendly interface, called the lossy router control client, hides the details of this protocol from users.

The *Reflector* functions in a similar manner to the LR, except that instead of dropping IP packets, the Reflector delays their forwarding to simulate a lower bandwidth link. This software is useful when an actual lower bandwidth link (such as a PPP link) is not available. Recently, we have replaced this component with U.S. Army SINCGARS combat net radios (see Figure 5).

Three different encoding methods have been implemented: run-length encoding based on path-MTU-size blocks, LZW encoding based on path-MTU-size blocks, and LZW encoding based on an entire image. The path-MTU is another user-defined parameter provided to test the effects of segmentation/reassembly on image data. In the first two encoding methods, each ADU contains enough information to be decoded and located in the receiver's progressive display (i.e., network-conscious compressed image). The authors recognize that these encoding methods may not be optimal methods for encoding wavelet coefficients. NET-CICATS is designed to easily integrate future encoding methods for evaluation. Section 5 discusses one potential better encoding technique to encode wavelet coefficients.

Once an image's quality and size are decided, the NETCICATS' user selects among several different transport protocols and QoS via the Universal Transport Library (UTL), a library of transport protocols that provides application programmers the ability to write to a single Application Programming Interface, then test their application with many different transport protocols [4]. UTL is a library of C functions that a programmer can link with an application. The application can then vary the transport protocol used by altering a single parameter on the "listen" call (passive open) or the "connect" call (active open). By allowing flexible experimentation with different transport protocols, the experimenter can isolate particular aspects of transport services to better understand each one's effects. Figure 3 illustrates how UTL is used by client/server applications. The services currently available to applications via the UTL API are presented in Figure 4.

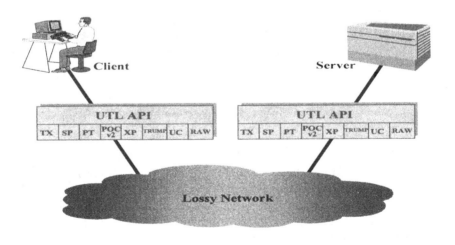

Fig. 3. How UTL is Used in Client/Server Applications

Since wavelet transformation provides a multiresolution representation (information at several levels of importance), NETCICATS allows the use of different QoS paramenters for different resolutions, such as using a specific degree of partial reliability for each layer of information.

UTL API								
TX	SP	PT	POCv2	XP	TRUMP	UC	RAW
•Ordered •Reliable	•Ordered •Reliable •Access to buffered data	•Partially ordered •Reliable •Sync support	•Partially ordered •Partially reliable •Sync support •Access to buffered data	•Unordered •Partially reliable	•Unordered •Partially reliable (time-based; application provides staleness time for each message)	•Unordered •Unreliable	•Pass-thru service

Fig. 4. Services Available to Applications via UTL

Recently, we have added some new components to NETCICATS: three U.S. Army SINCGARS combat net radios for doing experiments in a wireless, low-bandwidth environment. Although the signaling rate of these radios is 16 Kbps, the effective throughput is less than 2 Kbps. We have also added a browser, much like a conventional web browser, for experimenting with the two modified network-conscious image compression algorithms (see Sections 4 and 5). This new environment is shown in Figure 5.

One of the authors' motivations when designing NETCICATS was to develop a system for a hypothetical military communications system for transmitting images of either (1) wounded soldiers for telemedicine, or (2) images of equipment such as tanks, airplanes, etc. for intelligence gathering [3]. Therefore, we have run experiments primarily with military-related images such as tanks, airplanes, missiles, etc.

Here are some of the author's initial observations on using NETCICATS. These observations support our hypothesis on network-conscious image compression.

- Eliminating the ordered delivery requirement of compressed image data certainly provides faster progressive display.
- Transmitting wavelet coefficients that affect the image quality most (i.e., low frequency wavelet coefficients) as early as possible improves progressive display.
- Some applications may tolerate loss of ADUs that carry low-level detail information (i.e., high frequency wavelet coefficients) as these ADUs have little

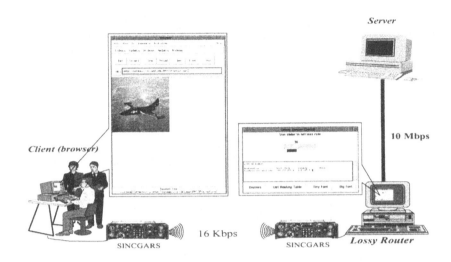

Fig. 5. NETCICATS with SINCGARS Radios and Browser

effect on the final image quality. However, loss of a higher level information severely affects the image quality.

The next step is to modify one or more of the traditional image compression algorithms to make them network-conscious, and compare their performance over a lossy packet-switched network. Sections 4 and 5 talk about two such algorithms.

4 Network-Conscious GIF

We have modified the GIF89a standard to make it network-conscious. The result, called GIFNCa [1], removes the ordered delivery requirement (and for some applications the reliability requirement) of GIF89a by framing image data at the compression phase (i.e., application level).

The tradeoff between GIFNCa and GIF89a is one of compression vs. progressive display performance. GIF89a's advantage is its expected better compression. GIFNCa's advantage is its expected *faster progressive display* at the receiver when transmitted over an unreliable packet-switched network such as the Internet.

We ran a set of experiments comparing (1) GIF89a over a reliable, ordered transport protocol called *Sequenced Protocol (SP)* vs. (2) GIFNCa over a reliable unordered protocol called *Xport Protocol (XP)*. SP and XP were both developed at University of Delaware's PEL as part of the UTL. Both SP and XP are implemented at the user-level over UDP, and use the same code for all functions (including connection establishment/teardown, round-trip-time estimation, retransmission timeout, acknowledgments, etc.); the only exception is that SP provides packet resequencing (i.e., ordered service) at the receiver, while XP does not.

The testing environment is quite similar to Figure 5 except that instead of SINCGARS radios, the Reflector was used to simulate a 28.8 Kbps link. This link is more than ten times greater bandwidth than that expected with the SINCGARS radios. Compressed images are stored on a server, and accessed by a client with an interface similar to familiar web browsers. The packets are routed through the Lossy Router and the Reflector to simulate loss and low bandwidth, respectively. Each experiment downloads a compressed image from server to client through the Lossy Router and Reflector.

The average percentages of image data being displayed at various points in time for 5%, 10%, and 15% IP packet loss rates are graphed in Figure 6. These graphs show that while both GIFNCa and GIF89a take longer to display the image as the loss rate increases, the GIFNCa performance does not degrade as quickly, i.e., it improves *relative to* GIF89a. This result is intuitive. As the loss rate increases, so does the number of buffered out-of-order packets at the receiving transport layer. These buffered packets are waiting for missing packets (in the case of GIF89a over ordered transport protocol). On the other hand, an unordered transport protocol (in the case of GIFNCa) delivers these out-of-order packets to the application (browser) as soon as possible after they arrive; no buffering for reordering purposes is needed.

While more serious and exhaustive empirical study is currently underway, these initial results highlight the potential benefit of using GIFNCa over GIF89a under lossy network conditions.

5   Network-Conscious Wavelet Zerotree Encoding

Wavelet zerotree encoding is based on the hypothesis that, at a given threshold level, if a wavelet coefficient at a coarse scale is insignificant, then all wavelet coefficients of the same orientation in the same spatial location at finer scales are likely to be insignificant [16]. The embedded zerotree (EZW) encoding, originally introduced by Shapiro [16], has been proven to be a very efficient yet not complex encoding scheme. The embedded nature of the algorithm, a representation in which a high resolution image contains all coarser resolutions, effectively sorts bits in order of importance, thus yielding an effective progressive display when transmitted over low-bandwidth networks. Using this embedded coding method, an encoder can stop encoding at any point to meet a target rate. Furthermore, a decoder can stop decoding at any point in the bit stream, and still produce exactly the same image that would have been encoded at the bit rate corresponding to the truncated bit rate.

Set Partitioning in Hierarchical Trees (SPIHT), introduced by Said and Pearlman [15] as a refinement to EZW, differs from EZW in the way subsets of coefficients are partitioned and in the way significance information is conveyed.

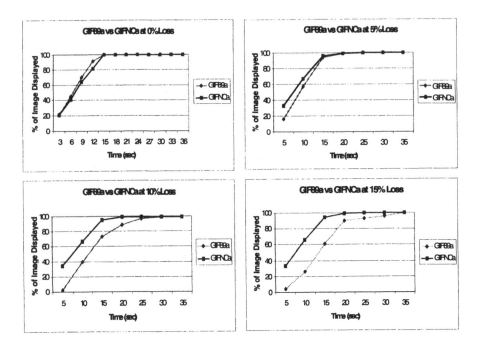

Fig. 6. Comparison of GIF89a and GIFNCa at Various Loss Rates

SPIHT is so effective that even binary uncoded transmission achieves about the same or better performance than EZW [15].

Both EZW and SPIHT are highly state-dependent, and therefore susceptible to bit errors. Even a single bit error ruins the decoding process thereby destroying an entire image. Recent studies concentrate on composing noise-robust zerotree encoders. Most of these studies are based on the idea of dividing the bitstream into several sub-streams each of which receive different amounts of error protection based on their noise sensitivity [12], or interleaving separately encoded substreams in so that any single bit error will corrupt only one substream [5,6].

Recently, Rogers and Cosman [14] introduced a packetized zerotree encoding method on still images that produces fixed 53-byte packets and is robust against packet erasure. A similar study by Crump and Fischer [7] produced variable-length independent packets for video transmission.

Our algorithm differs since these previous studies do not consider progressive display. They solely optimize for robustness, and only the final image quality is a concern. Robustness is one of the primary features of network-conscious compression approach. Therefore, by applying network-consciousness to zerotree encoding we solve that problem by default. Our concern also considers how to modify these algorithms so that they provide a better progressive display under lossy network conditions.

We have modified the SPIHT algorithm for this purpose. Our method produces path-MTU-size, independent packets which are optimized to provide better progressive display. The algorithm is currently in its experimental phase.

6 Conclusion and Future Work

Traditional image compression algorithms are not designed for lossy packet-switched networks and heterogeneous environments with wired and wireless links; they are optimized to minimize image size only. However, minimum image size does not necessarily provide the best performance when those images are transmitted over lossy networks, and used by the receiver for real-time decision making. The ordered-delivery requirement of these algorithms cause unnecessary delays at the receiving end.

This research investigates the relationship between compression algorithms and transport QoS parameters. Our results propose applying network-consciousness to image compression so that the compression algorithms will not be optimized only to give the minimum image size; they will be optimized to give the best performance when transmitted over lossy networks. We have developed NETCICATS to empirically evaluate network-conscious image compression, and two compression algorithms that utilize this approach: network-conscious GIF, and network-conscious zerotree encoding. Initial experiments for network-conscious image transmission are promising.

Our future study includes running experiments in the NETCICATS environment to collect and analyze extensive empirical data on network-conscious GIF and network-conscious zerotree encoding.

References

1. P. Amer, S. Iren, G. Sezen, P. Conrad, M. Taube, and A. Caro. Network-conscious GIF image transmission over the Internet. In *4th International Workshop on High Performance Protocol Architectures (HIPPARCH'98)*, June 1998.
2. D. Clark and D. Tennenhouse. Architectural considerations for a new generation of protocols. In *ACM SIGCOMM '90*, pages 200–208, Philadelphia, PA, September 1990.
3. P. Conrad, P. Amer, E. Golden, S. Iren, R. Marasli, and A. Caro. Transport qos over unreliable networks: No guarantees, no free lunch! In Nahrstedt Campbell, editor, *Building QoS into Distributed Systems*. Chapman and Hall, 1998. www.cis.udel.edu/~amer/PEL/poc/postscript/iwqos97.ps.
4. P. Conrad, P. Amer, M. Taube, G. Sezen, S. Iren, and A. Caro. Testing environment for innovative transport protocols. In *MILCOM '98*, Bedford, MA, October 1998. (To appear).
5. C.D. Creusere. A family of image compression algorithms wich are robust to transmission errors. In *IS&T/SPIE Wavelet Applications in Signal and Image Processing IV*, volume 2825, pages 890–900, August 1996.
6. C.D. Creusere. Image coding using parallel implementations of the embedded zerotree wavelet algorithm. In *IS&T/SPIE Symposium on Electronic Imaging*, volume 2668, San Jose, CA, 1996.

7. V.J. Crump and T.R. Fischer. Intraframe low bitrate video coding robust to packet erasure. In *DCC '97*, Snowbird, Utah, 1997. IEEE.

8. W. Dabbous and C. Diot. High performance protocol architecture. In *IFIP Performance of Computer Networks Conference (PCN '95)*, Istanbul, Turkey, October 1995. IFIP.

9. C. Diot and F. Gagnon. Impact of out-of-sequence processing on data transmission performance. Technical Report Project RODEO RR-3216, INRIA - Sophia Antipolis, France, July 1997. `ftp://www.inria.fr/rodeo/diot/rr-oos.ps.gz`.

10. S. Iren. Network-conscious image compression. PhD Dissertation, CIS Dept., University of Delaware, (in progress).

11. S. Iren, P. Amer, and P. Conrad. Network-conscious compressed images over wireless networks. In *5th International Workshop on Interactive Distributed Multimedia Systems and Telecommu nication Services (IDMS'98)*, Oslo, Norway, September 1998.

12. S.H. Man and F. Kossentini. Robust EZW image coding for noisy channels. *IEEE Signal Processing Letters*, 4(8):227–229, August 1997.

13. R. Marasli, P. Amer, and P. Conrad. An analytic model of partially ordered transport service. *Computer Networks and ISDN Systems*, 29(6):675–699, May 1997.

14. J. Rogers and P. Cosman. Robust wavelet zerotree image compression with fixed-length packetization. In *Data Compression Conference (DCC'98)*, March 1998.

15. A. Said and W.A. Pearlman. A new, fast, and efficient image codec based on set partitioning in hierarchical trees. 6(3), June 1996.

16. J. Shapiro. Embedded image coding using zerotrees of wavelet coefficients. *IEEE Transactions on Image Processing*, 41(12):3445–3462, December 1993.

ABR Service in ATM Networks: Performance Comparison Between BECN and Adaptive Stochastic Congestion Control Schemes with Guaranteed Minimum Cell Rate

Slobodan S. Petrovic

Department of Electrical Engineering J03
University of Sydney
Sydney, NSW 2006, Australia
Email: ssp@ee.usyd.edu.au
Fax: +61.2. 9351.3847
Phone: +61.2.9351.2842

Abstract. Two rate-based feedback schemes for congestion control in ATM networks: Backward Explicit Congestion Notification (BECN) and proposed Adaptive Stochastic (AS) are compared under heavy load conditions. Neither of the schemes dictates a particular switch architecture. The requirements tested include: utilization, queuing delay, queuing delay variance and queue size. The controllable sources' allowed cell rates (ACR) have been dynamically shaped by the feedback messages based on the instantaneous queue size in the ATM switch output buffer. The results of a simulation study are presented which suggest that AS scheme, while retaining practically the same link utilization, can provide for higher priority traffic considerably shorter average queuing delay, queuing delay variance, maximum and average queue size in the switch output buffer, particularly on longer network segments between terminals generating traffic and the switch.

1 Introduction

It is now widely assumed that the future ATM networks will be dominated by bursty traffic. Regarding the traffic control policies for ATM networks, the preventive congestion control implemented by a conjunction of connection admission control (CAC) and usage parameter control (UPC) is not sufficient. Unpredictable statistical fluctuations and burstiness of traffic sources make it difficult to guarantee quality of service and high utilization of the network resources using source traffic parameters declared by the users, such as average rate and burst duration. Traffic management and its most essential aspect - congestion control, in ATM networks should be, therefore, accomplished in a reactive manner in conjunction with a preventive manner. If a truly integrated transport network for all services is wanted, an unpredictable load pattern is inevitable. Therefore, no prediction algorithm is

S. Jajodia, M.T. Özsu, and A. Dogac (Eds.): MIS'98, LNCS 1508, pp. 69–81, 1998.

incorporated in the scheme and it is left to future considerations. A number of congestion control schemes for ATM networks have been developed [1] - [11].

The remainder of the paper is organized as follows: in Section 2 the assumed network structure and how it operates is described; in Section 3 the design of both control algorithms is outlined; in Section 4 the simulation models and obtained results are reported and in Section 5 conclusion remarks are made.

2 The Assumed Network Structure

It is assumed that two types of traffic share the ATM network resources. The first type consists of Variable Bit Rate (VBR) traffic which is delay sensitive i.e. which has stringent delay requirements and is not subjected to any control and hence is uncontrollable. The second type of traffic requires good loss performance, but agrees to have its bit rate controlled when necessary, thus accepting the possibility of longer mean delays during periods of high demand, i.e. cell loss is avoided at the expense of delay and hence is controllable. All delay insensitive Available Bit Rate (ABR) traffic can join this category which is designed for normal data traffic such as file transfer and email. In these experiments delay sensitive traffic was given a higher priority. A simple network topology involves an ATM switching node which is modeled as a single server queuing system fed by a number of highly bursty traffic sources (Fig. 1). The ACRs of the ABR traffic sources take the values being conveyed by the feedback messages which are carried from the switch to the sources' terminals through backward Resource Management (RM) cells. Each source could also be a switch acting as a virtual source and generating RM cells periodically as if it was a source. The switch acts as a virtual destination and returns all RM cells received from the source as if the switch was the destination. In this study RM cells are in-rate since they are counted toward the ACR, what means that the total rate of data and RM cells should not exceed the ACR of the source. During idle periods a source does not generate RM cells. A RM cell is always sent as the first cell after and idle period for the source. In the compared schemes each individual lower priority (controllable) traffic virtual channel (VC) is guaranteed by the network only a minimum bandwidth of a minimum cell rate (MCR), agreed during the connection setup. However, it is allowed to dynamically share the available resources left over from the higher priority (uncontrollable) traffic i.e. the lower priority traffic grabs whatever remains of the network resources (bandwidth and buffer space) after the higher priority traffic is served. Thus the ABR capacity is not fixed, but varies according to the VBR load. Switch complexity does not depend on the number of VCs since there is no per VC queuing. In the switch, output buffering is used, which means that the queuing happens at the output port. The cells of both traffic classes are treated in the switch output buffer, by equal priority and are served with FIFO discipline. The same service discipline applies also to all sources' queues. In order to support the feedback control scheme a simple CAC policy ensures that the peak cell rate of the total higher priority (VBR) traffic is within the ATM switch server capacity in every moment and that the long term mean rate of all the traffic (higher and lower priority together) is within the

ATM switch server capacity. Both AS and BECN schemes operate at the ATM switch output queuing point. Large buffers are assumed and the effect of cell losses is not modeled. Neither packet discarding, nor packet retransmission mechanisms are included.

3 Description of the Compared Schemes

3.1 Adaptive Stochastic (AS) Scheme

The traffic flowing from the sources to the ATM switch is assumed to be a process which takes place in random environment. The design of the control algorithm has been based upon input-output model of the process which allows analysis over the transfer function and realization of the control algorithm with minimal a priori knowledge about the dynamics and parameters of the process. The transfer function is defined as

$$y(k)u^{-1}(k) = B(z^{-1})A^{-1}(z^{-1}) . \tag{1}$$

where z^{-1} is delay operator meaning

$$z^{-1}y(k) = y(k-1), \quad z^{-1}u(k) = u(k-1) . \tag{2}$$

and integer k is the control interval's time index. Since the process is modeled here as the first order linear dynamical system where

$$A(z^{-1}) = 1 + a(k)z^{-1}, \quad B(z^{-1}) = b(k)z^{-1} . \tag{3}$$

it is described by the stochastic difference equation

$$y(k+1) = -a(k)y(k) + b(k)u(k). \tag{4}$$

y(k) is the output equal to instantaneous queue length minus the reference level (threshold). The scalar u(k) is the control input generated by the algorithm. It is a function of the queue size measurement and is used for identification of parameters and for attaining the desired system response. u(k) determines the ACRs of the ABR traffic sources with the goal to maintain the ATM switch output buffer occupancy as close as possible to a certain reference level. u(k) is partitioned among active ABR traffic sources accordingly. ABR traffic sources seen by the switch as inactive are allocated MCR only. An active ABR traffic source's ACR is then formed as the sum of the source's long term mean cell rate and its share of u(k). In proportion to its absolute value, a negative u(k) reduces and a positive u(k) increases the ABR sources' ACRs. Hence, the ACRs fluctuations are dictated by u(k) but can not go below the MCR or above the link rate. The unknown parameters are a(k) and b(k). Their actual values are random and time varying. The uncertainty in b(k) corresponds to uncertainty in the system gain while the uncertainty in a(k) corresponds to uncertainty in the system time constant. Not knowing a(k) exactly is equivalent to not knowing the pole location of the system function. Since the system is operating in a stochastic environment, both y(k) and u(k) are random sequences. The objective of the problem is to find in each control interval the optimal control input that minimizes the scalar real-valued cost functional i.e. the performance criterion

$$J(u) = E\{qy^2(k+1) + ru^2(k) + qy^2(k)\} \quad k = 0, 1, \dots . \tag{5}$$

where E denotes expected value. q and r are positive scalars (weighting factors). As the only information about the process comes from the observation of the queue size, since the queue size is the only directly measurable quantity at the switch, the optimal control policy can be interpreted as follows: at the end of the k-th control interval an optimal control input $u^o(k|k)$ (superscript o stands for 'optimal') is generated, based on the current queue length measurement. k on the left side of | denotes the control interval itself and k on the right side of | means that measurement/observation of the queue length was taken during the control interval k. The next control input $u^o(k+1|k+1)$ is again computed, but based on the information about the queue size available at the control interval k + 1. Thus, the optimal deterministic control shall be recomputed after new information becomes available at each control interval. The switch gives only one feedback value in a single control interval which is equal to the round-trip delay because there is little point in sending further control feedbacks to the sources until previous feedback has had time to take effect. The overall adaptive controller can be viewed as combined of an identifier and a zero-memory controller in the feedback loop. The former is the learning device where the estimates of the parameters are generated in real time and can be designed independently of the controller objectives. The later computes the on-line optimal control for a deterministic system and is parameter adaptive. Accordingly, as this adaptive control problem involves nonlinear parameter estimation, the extended Kalman filter is used to generate the approximate conditional means and the associated error covariances of the unknown parameters. This approach led to the design of a simple proportional controller that has the desired adaptive properties. The closed loop feedback optimal control is given by

$$u^o(k|k) = -g(k)y(k) \qquad k = 0, 1, \dots . \tag{6}$$

The adaptive feedback gain g(k) depends not only on parameters a(k) and b(k) estimates ($a^{est}(k|k)$ and $b^{est}(k|k)$ resp.), but also on conditional error covariances

$$e_a(k|k) = a^{est}(k|k) - a(k) . \tag{7}$$

$$e_b(k|k) = b^{est}(k|k) - b(k) . \tag{8}$$

i.e. it is modulated by the current parameters uncertainty (vectors and matrices are denoted in bold letters, superscript T stands for 'transposed')

$$g(k) = -\{[R(k|k) + \mathbf{b}^T(k|k)\mathbf{Q}\mathbf{b}(k|k)]^{-1}\mathbf{b}^T(k|k)\mathbf{Q}\mathbf{\Phi}(k|k) + R^{-1}(k|k)\mathbf{d}^T(k+1|k)\}[1,0,0]^T . \tag{9}$$

$$\mathbf{b}^T(k|k) = [b^{est}(k|k), S_{bb}(k|k), S_{ab}(k|k)] . \tag{10}$$

$$\mathbf{d}^T(k+1|k) = [qS_{ab}(k|k), qa^{est}(k|k), 0] . \tag{11}$$

$$\Phi(k|k) = \mathbf{F}(k|k) - \mathbf{b}(k|k)R^{-1}(k|k)\mathbf{d}^T(k+1|k) . \tag{12}$$

$$F(k\,|\,k) = \begin{bmatrix} a^{est}(k\,|\,k) & 0 & 0 \\ S_{ab}(k\,|\,k) & a^{est}(k\,|\,k) & 0 \\ S_{aa}(k\,|\,k) & 0 & a^{est}(k\,|\,k) \end{bmatrix} \tag{13}$$

$$R(k|k) = r + qS_{bb}(k|k) . \tag{14}$$

$$\mathbf{Q} = \begin{bmatrix} q & 0 & 0 \\ 0 & 0 & 0 \\ 0 & 0 & 0 \end{bmatrix} \tag{15}$$

$$S_{aa}(k|k) = e_a^2(k|k) . \tag{16}$$

$$S_{bb}(k|k) = e_b^2(k|k) . \tag{17}$$

$$S_{ab}(k|k) = S_{ba}(k|k) = e_a(k|k)e_b(k|k) . \tag{18}$$

The parameters estimates are generated via the equations

$$\mathbf{p}^{est}(i+1|i+1) = \mathbf{p}^{est}(i|i) + \mathbf{G}(i+1)[y(i+1) - \mathbf{c}^T(i)\mathbf{p}^{est}(i|i)] . \tag{19}$$

where $\qquad \mathbf{p}^{est,T}(i|i) = [a^{est}(i|i), b^{est}(i|i)] . \tag{20}$

$$\mathbf{c}^T(i) = [-y(i), u(i)] . \tag{21}$$

The filter gain matrix $\mathbf{G}(i+1)$ satisfies the relation

$$\mathbf{G}(i+1) = \mathbf{S}(i|i)\mathbf{c}(i)[\mathbf{c}^T(i)\mathbf{S}(i|i)\mathbf{c}(i)]^{-1} \quad i = 0, 1, ... , k-1 . \tag{22}$$

$$\mathbf{S}(i+1|i+1) = [\mathbf{S}(i|i) - \mathbf{G}(i+1)\mathbf{c}^T(i)\mathbf{S}(i|i)] / ff . \tag{23}$$

$$S(i\,|\,i) = \begin{bmatrix} S_{aa}(i\,|\,i) & S_{ab}(i\,|\,i) \\ S_{ba}(i\,|\,i) & S_{bb}(i\,|\,i) \end{bmatrix} . \tag{24}$$

with the initial estimates given by

$$\mathbf{p}^{est,T}(0|0) = [a_0, b_0] . \tag{25}$$

$$S(0 \mid 0) = \begin{bmatrix} S_{a0} & 0 \\ 0 & S_{b0} \end{bmatrix} . \tag{26}$$

The AS control algorithm expresses its dual nature by simultaneously performing two functions: perpetual parameters estimation i.e. "learning" and process control. The forgetting factor 'ff' allows the controller's capacity for adaptation on changes in the system parameters to be preserved, by preventing error covariance matrices to become approximately equal to zero. Estimating of parameters could continue only if the matrices are different from zero, i.e. if some level of parameters uncertainty remained. Owing to the forgetting factor, the identification of parameters even if they for some time remain constant, will never be completed. Fortunately, the exact identification of the unknown parameters is not necessary for good control. Through the parameters uncertainty the controller expresses its "cautiousness".

3.2 Backward Explicit Congestion Notification (BECN) Scheme

When the queue length in an ATM switch output buffer exceeds a threshold, the feedback controller will send backward RM cells to the ABR sources currently submitting traffic. Backward RM cells are subject to the same transmission delay as cells in the forward direction. Initially the sources transmit at their peak cell rates (PCR). When a transmitter receives a RM cell it reduces its cell transmission rate to one half of the current rate. Successive RM cells will cause a transmitter to reduce its cell transmission rate to 1/2, 1/4, 1/8, 1/16, 1/32, 1/64 of its PCR after which a further RM cell will cause it to transmit at MCR, because sources are not expected to reduce their ACR to less than MCR. ABR sources seen by the switch as inactive are allocated also MCR only. If no RM cells are received within a recovery time period, the current transmission rate for that source will be doubled, i.e. restored to the previous level once each recovery time period, until it reaches its original PCR. The source recovery period is proportional to the source current transmission rate so that the lower the transmission rate the shorter the source recovery period. The feedback controller transmits no more than a single RM cell to each active source during each control period. To allow the previous RM cell to take effect, the control period is equal to the round-trip delay.

4 Simulation Model and Results

Both flow control algorithms were tested and compared on the same network simulation model (Fig.1), with the same MCRs, the same control threshold and the same time control units. The major shortcoming of BECN scheme - its unfairness in multi-hop networks causing the "beat down problem" did not disadvantage the scheme in these experiments as the simulated network was single-hop. Each source S generates cells that are queued for transmission by the transmitter T.   Each of the transmitters T independently removes cells from its source queue and   transmits them to the receiver R. R is a point of congestion somewhere in the network, e.g. an output buffer on an ATM switch. The ABR traffic sources Ts transmit at the ACRs, as dictated by the feedback. The VBR traffic sources Ts transmit at the PCR. There is a transmission delay between each transmitter transmitting a cell and the cell being received at the receiver. The transmission delay represents the combination of the propagation delay and the switching delay from the source to the point of congestion. For simplicity all the sources are equidistant to the ATM switch and hence the propagation delay is the same between the ATM switch and all the sources. AS scheme's and BECN scheme's control intervals were equal to the round trip delay, i.e. the control rate was matched to the feedback rate. This illustrates a fundamental principle in control theory, which says that the system is unstable when the control is faster than feedback. But the system is unresponsive if the control is slower than feedback.

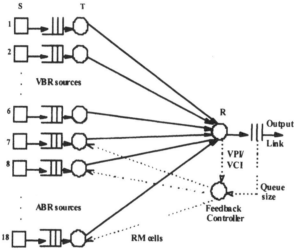

Fig. 1. The simulation model

The performance of the model was examined over source - switch distances (link lengths): 1 km, 10 km, 100 km and 1000 km, with corresponding control intervals 10 µsec, 100 µsec, 1 msec and 10 msec resp. (1 km implies 5 µsec propagation delay). The terminals are connected to the switch through links running at 155 Mbps (365566 cells/s). The switch receives traffic from terminals that are attached to its input ports. All input ports have traffic flowing to a common output port operating at 155 Mbps. The input to the ATM switch is a superposition of streams from 18 (12 ABR and 6 VBR) different ON/OFF sources, also referred to as Interrupted Bernoulli Process (IBP) which alternate active periods, transmitting at their peak cell rate (PCR) and idle periods, transmitting at zero bit rate. Both periods of burst and silence are exponentially distributed with constant average lengths during a simulation. Each burst in average contained 100 cells. The switch server rate is assumed to have a fixed ratio with respect to the long term mean arrival rate. The switch target utilization parameter was set at 0.95 where ABR traffic sources were given 60% and VBR traffic sources 35% bandwidth. In order to have more than a million cells generated, a simulation run time was 3 seconds. The higher priority (VBR) traffic was generated by the sources 1, 2, 3, 4, 5, 6 with PCR 50 Mbps, 40 Mbps, 30 Mbps, 20 Mbps, 10 Mbps, 5 Mbps resp., totally 155 Mbps , therefore equal to the switch server rate and with source utilizations 0.4, 0.5, 0.2, 0.2, 0.3, 0.25 resp.. The lower priority (ABR) traffic was generated by the sources 7, 8, ..., 18 with PCR 155 Mbps each, what means that each ABR source was capable of filling the entire server capacity of the switch. The ABR sources' utilization was 0.10 for sources 7 and 13, 0.08 for sources 8 and 14, 0.05 for sources 9 and 15, 0.04 for sources 10 and 16, 0.02 for sources 11 and 17, 0.01 for sources 12 and 18. The aggregate peak rate of the total traffic thus was 2015 Mbps. The purpose of the experiment was to examine how successfully the two compared schemes can cope with such stressful conditions when arrival rate to the switch output buffer can exceed 13 times the server capacity, while preserving the design goals. The output buffer threshold value employed by both schemes was 50 cells. Opposite to the initial CAC setup where the MCR was specified as zero, two MCR > 0 values were used: PCR/100 (1% link bandwidth) and PCR/1000 (0.1% link bandwidth) - in practice, it is desirable to allow some minimum capacity for processing aggregate ABR traffic when there is contention. As all ABR sources had the same PCR = 155 Mbps, in AS scheme experiments each of the active ABR traffic sources received periodically the same amount of the feedback equal to u(k)/(number of currently active ABR traffic sources). In the case of different PCRs, the formula above could be easily adjusted. In AS scheme as well as in BECN scheme experiments, inactive ABR traffic sources were allocated MCR only, for two reasons mainly: in order to drain out their queues and because of the transmission delay the sources which may seem as inactive, could be in fact, active. The forgetting factor equal to 0.96 was used in examining AS scheme; initial estimates were $S_{a0} = S_{b0} = 1$ and $a_0 = b_0 = 0.1$.

Performance evaluation of the schemes showed that AS scheme achieved average utilization (Fig. 8) for MCR = PCR/100 on 1 km link 0.86% lower, on 10 km link 1.9% higher, on 100 km link 1.7% lower, on 1000 km link equal and for MCR= PCR/1000 on 1 km link 8.4 % lower, on 10 km link 16.8% higher, on 100 km link 2.4% higher, on 1000 km link 0.75% higher. However, the utilization metric gives only a partial picture of efficiency. Ideally, an efficient scheme should also control queuing delays within acceptable limits. The delay varies according to load, but there is always a non-zero queuing delay. AS scheme achieved shorter mean queuing delay in the switch output buffer (Fig. 2) - from 1.5 times (1 km link) to 55 times (1000 km link) when MCR = PCR/100 and from 3.3 times (1 km link) to 80 times (1000 km link) when MCR = PCR/1000. In other words, for the higher MCR the difference between BECN scheme's and AS scheme's mean queuing delay in the switch output buffer, on 1 km link was 46.5μs what equals 9.3 km propagation delay and on 1000 km link 20 ms what equals 4000 km propagation delay. For the lower MCR that difference on 1 km link was 73.5 μs what equals 14.7 km propagation delay and on 1000 km link 28.4 ms what equals 5700 km propagation delay. Queuing delay variance disproportions (Fig. 3) between the two schemes were even larger - from 2.1 times (1 km link) to 327 times (1000 km link) when MCR = PCR/100 and from 1.9

times (1 km link) to 665 times (1000 km link) when MCR = PCR/1000. AS scheme's maximum queue length in the switch output buffer (Fig. 4) was also much smaller - from 4.1 times (10 km link) to 7.9 times (100 km link) when MCR = PCR/100 and 3.9 times (1 km link) to 12 times (100 km link) when MCR = PCR/1000. Comments are not made here on mean queue lengths (Fig. 5) because results correspond to those for mean queuing delays. On the other hand, mean queuing delay, queuing delay variance, maximum and mean queue size in the buffers of sources generating ABR traffic increased as expected, but on much smaller scale (due to limited space these simulation results are not displayed here). An interesting effect was noticed in AS scheme and BECN scheme alike: the smaller of the two MCRs (PCR/1000) created a bottleneck what caused larger queues in ABR traffic sources' buffers and lower utilization due to lower ABR utilization (Fig. 6). The number of VBR traffic cells received (Fig. 7) for both schemes was almost identical, excepting BECN scheme's worse performance on 1000 km link with MCR = PCR/1000. As any MCR > 0 contradicts the initial stipulation that VBR traffic can take the entire server capacity whenever it needs it, both MCRs employed in this experiment caused conflicting demands by VBR and ABR traffic classes, as VBR traffic class, albeit able to fill the entire server capacity (if all VBR traffic sources are simultaneously transmitting), was guaranteed only 98.8% (when MCR = PCR/1000) or only 88% of it (when MCR = PCR/100). The competition between the two traffic classes using the higher MCR brought about the higher utilization. Obviously, although the MCR was guaranteed to all 12 ABR traffic sources, due to their bursty nature they did not use it all the time and not all of them at the same time what allowed the VBR traffic to have enough bandwidth to flow smoothly and unabatedly. Therefore, MCR = PCR/100 should be recommended and MCR = PCR/1000 should be dropped. With the sort and configuration of traffic generators employed throughout these experiments the ABR service class whose capacity and demand thus varied dynamically, was always in a transient state. For such a case there is currently no known model for quantifying fairness. Hence the issue of fairness could not be addressed in this study and for the issues that were addressed, the simple network model (Fig. 1) was appropriate. It should be pointed out that the above cited fundamental principle in control theory is not practically applicable on 1 km link, because 10 μs control interval means that RM cells' share in the total number of generated cells (data and RM cells together) is 27.4% whereby data cells utilization of the server and output link falls to about 70 %. Therefore, in order to prevent such huge number of RM cells being generated, a sort of trade-off should be made by replacing the 10 μs interval with a longer one, e.g. 50 μs or 100 μs (as it is on 10 km link) with RM cells' share in the total number of generated cells 5.4% and 2.7% resp.. The total numbers of ABR and VBR cells received as well as the server/output link utilization would be lower, but the numbers of ABR and VBR data cells much higher and data cells utilization of the server and output link could reach and even exceed 90%.

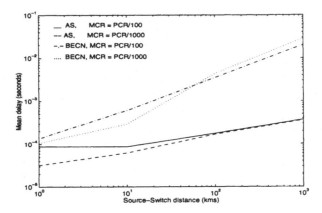

Fig. 2. Mean queuing delay in the ATM switch output buffer

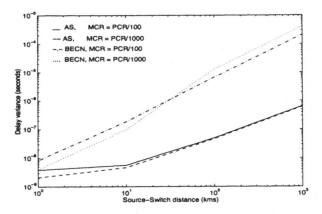

Fig. 3. Queuing delay variance in the ATM switch output buffer

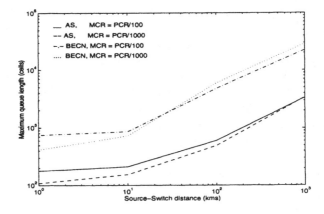

Fig. 4. Maximum queue length in the ATM switch output buffer

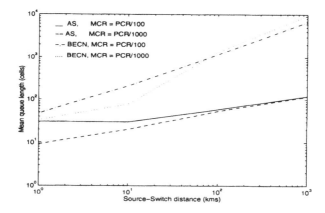

Fig. 5. Mean queue length in the ATM switch output buffer

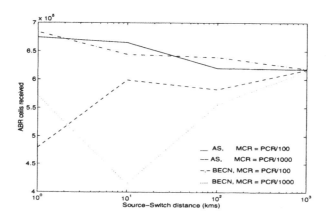

Fig. 6. Number of ABR traffic cells received

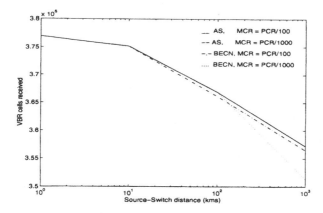

Fig. 7. Number of VBR traffic cells received

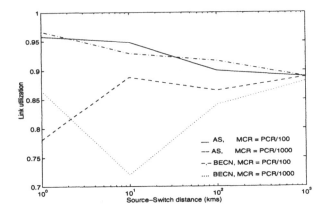

Fig. 8. Server / output link utilization

5 Summary

BECN and proposed AS congestion control schemes for ABR service in ATM networks are compared in the presence of two traffic classes - ABR and VBR, under heavy load conditions exceeding 0.95. The discussion relates to the traffic management at the segment of an ATM network between terminals generating traffic and the switch. By ensuring much shorter queue in the ATM switch output buffer, AS scheme provided for delay sensitive VBR traffic class, while retaining approximately the same utilization, sharply reduced mean queuing delay and queuing delay variance. This disproportions between AS and BECN schemes grew huge on long, i.e. WAN links. At the same time, delay insensitive ABR traffic class experienced either in considerably smaller proportion increased queue size and mean queuing delay or even shortening of queue and mean queuing delay.

References

1. The ATM Forum Technical Committee: Traffic Management Specification Version 4.0, April 1996.
2. M. Hassan, H. Sirisena, J. Breen: Design and   Analysis of a Congestion Control Architecture using a Proportional Feedback Controller, ATNAC, December 1996.
3. K. Kawahara, Y. Oie, M Murata, H. Miyahara: Performance Analysis of Reactive Congestion Control for ATM Networks, IEEE JSAC, vol. 13, May 1995.
4. W. Matragi, K. Sohraby: Combined   Reactive/ Preventive Approach for Congestion Control in ATM Networks, IEEE ICC, May 1993.
5. C. Ikeda, H Suzuki: Adaptive Congestion Control Schemes for ATM LANs, IEEE INFOCOM, June 1994.
6. G. Pecelli, B. Kim: Dynamic Behavior of Feedback Congestion Control Schemes, IEEE INFOCOM, vol. 1, 1995.

7. A. Kolarov, G. Ramamurthy: End-to-End Adaptive Rate Based Congestion Control Scheme for ABR Service in Wide Area ATM Networks, IEEE ICC, June 1995.
8. J. Ren, J. Mark: Design and Analysis of a Credit Based Controller for Congestion Control in BISDN/ ATM Networks", IEEE INFOCOM, vol 1, 1995.
9. A. Arulambalam, X. Chen, N. Ansari: Allocating Fair Rates for Available Bit Rate Service in ATM Networks, IEEE Communication Magazine, November 1996.
10. D. Gaiti, N. Boukhatem: Cooperative Congestion Control Schemes in ATM Networks, IEEE Communications Magazine, November 1996.
11. S. Kalyanaraman, R. Jain, S.Fahmy, R Goyal, B.Vandalore: The ERICA Switch Algorithm for ABR Traffic Management in ATM Networks, IEEE/ACM Transactions on Networking, November 1997.

An Admission Control Framework for Applications with Variable Consumption Rates in Client-Pull Architectures*

Silvia Hollfelder, Karl Aberer

GMD - Integrated Publication and Information Systems Institute (IPSI)
Address: Dolivostraße 15, D- 64293 Darmstadt, Germany
E-Mail: {hollfeld | aberer}@darmstadt.gmd.de

Abstract. Highly interactive multimedia applications require variable data rates during their presentation. Current admission control mechanisms do not address the variable data rate requirements appropriately for the following reasons: (1) classical admission control mechanisms are based on the server-push approach, where the required data rate has to be estimated in advance, and (2) worst-case resource reservation is not economic. Client-pull models are more appropriate to serve these kinds of applications. At the current state, there are no suitable mechanisms that support admission control in client-pull architectures at the server. In this paper, a session-oriented framework for admission control is introduced that is based on two steps: (1) the admission of new clients and (2) the scheduling of the single requests of admitted clients to balance the load. The goal of this approach is to improve the server utilization and the Quality of Service. Evaluation studies demonstrate the benefit of the framework.

1 Introduction

Enhanced multimedia applications like computer-based training (CBT), product documentation, or digital libraries enable a flexible user behavior since the user has various options to realize its preferences interactively. Examples of interaction types that occur in such applications are the usage of VCR-functionality for the playback of continuous media, browsing in media archives [10] and the interactive control of preorchestrated composite multimedia presentations [1]. These different interaction types cause highly varying data consumption rates of the application and makes it difficult to specify resource demands in advance. Thus, the media storage components have to provide mechanisms that are able to deal with these characteristics of highly, interactive multimedia applications. These mechanisms differ from those required by

---

* This work has partly been funded by the European Union within the framework of the ESPRIT Long Term Research Project HERMES, No. 9141.

S. Jajodia, M.T. Özsu, and A. Dogac (Eds.): MIS'98, LNCS 1508, pp. 82–97, 1998.

multimedia applications with more uniform access characteristics, like video-on-demand.

For illustration purposes, we discuss the characteristics of browsing applications in digital libraries as one typical example. In a digital library, the users have to deal with a huge amount of data, including video data. Therefore, they want to scan quickly through data that has been roughly specified by a query in order to inspect and compare it. In contrast to a video-on-demand application where the users generally want to view complete, single videos, in this scenario, the user makes full use of VCR-functionalities, like fast forward, rewind and pause, and might require to view several videos in parallel. Thus, within this application the data requests arrive aperiodically at the server, and the data rates vary within a wide spectrum. Another example for applications with variable data consumption are composite multimedia presentations where the user gets presented various media, like text, image, audio and video, simultaneously and the course of the presentation is controlled interactively by the user. The task of the multimedia data management system in such scenarios is to support the qualitatively adequate presentation of the required media data. Especially in distributed environments, this is a challenge.

Distributed multimedia applications require the support of continuous data flows from the server to the client satisfying Quality of Service (QoS) parameters. In order to achieve the required presentation quality, the clients compete for limited resources on the server. The basic strategies to deal with limited resources can be distinguished into optimistic and pessimistic ones.

With optimistic strategies all requests are served as well as possible (best effort). These strategies are typically used in client-pull architectures, where the client subsequently requests small chunks of media data during presentation. The server triggers the delivery of data only after a single, "small" request has arrived. The data requests arrive aperiodically at the server [15]. In case of user interactions the client changes its request behavior, e.g., it will request larger blocks of a media or send more frequent requests. The client-pull architecture is suitable for interactive applications with varying resource requirements since it is not assumed that the required data rate will be constant for the duration of a presentation. Bottlenecks are dealt with either by the server or clients with various strategies, e.g., by means of quality adaptation mechanisms at the client [9] or at the server [18].

With pessimistic strategies resource reservations are made at the server, in advance. An admission control mechanism usually checks at the server, if enough resources for the adequate delivery of data to a new client are available. If there are enough resources available, the client is admitted and the resources are reserved for this client until the end of the presentation. Most approaches for admission control mechanisms consider the request of single media streams within a server-push architecture. Since the whole presentation is pre-specified by the request the server manages the delivery of the whole media stream and pushes the data continuously to the client. Admission control mechanisms for "pure" server-push architectures assume that during a presentation the data rate consumed by the client will be nearly constant [15]. The available system resources are calculated by stochastic [11,19] or deterministic approaches [20,12]. Based on the knowledge about the already reserved and freely available resources it is possible to reject requests in case of server overloads. Admission control mechanisms are harder to use for interactive applications since it is difficult to estimate server resources consumed by the applications. We discuss some of the strategies that can be considered.

A priori reservation. To guarantee a given Quality of Service worst case assumptions about the data rate required can be made. Obviously, the reservation of the worst case data rate wastes server resources and decreases the number of clients that can be served in parallel. Dey-Sircar et al. [5] reserve separate server bandwidth for VCR-interactions, using statistical methods. The drawback of their work is that they assume that interactions occur rarely.

Re-admission at interaction points. A straightforward way to use standard admission control policies with interactive applications is to perform admission control for each single media object request, that can occur as the result of an interaction as described in Gollapudi and Zhang [7]. One drawback of their approach is that each client request is subject to the admission control. For example, when the first scene of a video is admitted there is no guarantee for the admission of the subsequent scenes of the same presentation. This may lead to unacceptable delay in presentation when too many clients send requests. The main problem of their approach is that the admission is not performed for a client session. Thus, the admission of one continuous media stream of a multimedia presentation does not necessarily guarantee the admission of another continuous media stream that has to be synchronized with the already admitted streams. But, especially in composite, interactive presentations, temporal requirements between multiple media, like start_with, or finish_with, have to be considered.

Smooth the application data rates. Some approaches to admission control for interactive applications propose to 'smooth' the data rate deviations to achieve a relatively constant workload. Shenoy and Vin [16] reduce the high data rate for fast forward and fast rewind of MPEG-videos by encoding the stream in base and enhanced layers. The encoding of the base layer is done by reducing the temporal and spatial resolution. For fast forward only the base layer is used. Chen, Kandlur, and Yu [3] suggest segment skipping where a segment can be a set of Group of Pictures (GoP) of an MPEG-video. For fast forward or fast rewind some segments are skipped. Chen, Krishnamurthy, Little, and Venkatesch [2] change the order of MPEG-frames to a priority sequence. For fast forward and fast rewind only the most important frames (I- and P-Frames) are pushed to the client. The higher data rate is reduced by quality adaptation on the temporal dimension of other requests by a dynamic resource reservation. Reddy [14] reduces the latency of 'urgent' requests, but neglects varying bandwidth requirements. The smoothing approach is, however, restricted to relatively simple interactive scenarios where interactions take place within the presentation of one single media stream.

Reviewing the different approaches, up to date, no admission control mechanism has been developed which is applicable for varying resource requirements of highly interactive applications requiring a client-pull architecture. We presented first ideas on admission control for client-pull architectures in [8]. In this paper, we propose an admission control framework to support interactive multimedia applications, assuming that no user profile is available that gives any information about the resources required by a pending client. It consists of (1) the admission of new clients, in the following called pending clients, when server resources are available and (2) the scheduling and adaptation of requests of admitted clients. We evaluate different strategies, both for admission and scheduling. With the approach we benefit from the relative safety provided by admission control, but still provide fallback strategies in the case of overloads. The admission control mechanism we propose is session-oriented such that requests related to the same presentation or session do not require separate admissions. This gives adequate support for composite multimedia presentations. The main problem to be adressed is the criterion upon which the admission decision can be performed. The inital request of a session does not provide the necessary information to predict future requests. Here, we use statistical features of the running sessions for determining the admission criterion. For a large number of parallel session the average client consumption is a good estimate for prediction. Data rate variations are accounted for by introducing a safety margin. Thus, an admitted client is supposed to obtain sufficient resources. If in spite of the admission control resource bottlenecks occur, strategies for rescheduling of requests are used to achieve high QoS by means of load balancing. In the worst case quality adaptations are required to enable guaranteed continuous delivery.

We first introduce the underlying system model in Section 2.1. Then we introduce the admission and scheduling strategies in Sections 2.2 to 2.4. In Section 3 we present the results of evaluation studies and conclude the paper with some remarks on future research directions.

2   Admission Control Framework

We describe a framework that is under implementation for a Multimedia Database Management System at GMD-IPSI. It is designed to support highly interactive applications with variable data consumption. The goal is to provide better QoS than best effort delivery and to achieve better server utilization than worst-case-based reservation.

2.1   System Model

The system model is based on a client-pull architecture. Clients request multiple chunks of data from the server within a single multimedia session. A multimedia session contains the presentation of at least one time-dependent media, like a video or an audio. Single media as well as composite media presentations are possible.

One task of the server is to limit the number of active clients by means of an admission control mechanism. At the beginning of a session, a client requests the server for admission (see Figure 1). Then the server informs the client about its admission. After a client has been admitted, it can send data requests to the server. When a client terminates its multimedia session it informs the server. The server handles data requests from admitted clients within service periods of fixed length, which are indexed by $k \in \mathcal{Z}$. Data requests specify which part of which media object is requested by the client and at which time it has to be delivered. Thus, a data request has the form <b, t>, with t ∈ $\mathcal{Q}$.

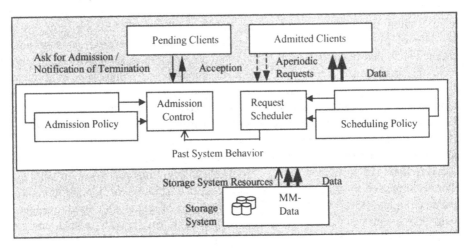

Fig. 1. The System Model

The specifications used for a block b can be of different types. In the simplest case, they indicate the beginning and the end of a block within a media stream. For example, for a video stream this can be the first and the last frame of a scene requested by the client. More complex cases are, for example, requests of data required for fast forward, which may require only every second frame of a video, and requests of parts of different media like an audio with the corresponding video. The server is responsible for mapping the specification of the data requests to the corresponding data accesses to the media data.

The deadline t specifies the time in number of service periods that a client is willing to wait until its request is scheduled. These deadlines may vary between the single requests of a client. The clients are able to specify deadlines since they have more information on the presentation state. For example, the buffer state of a client may be used as an indicator for the urgency of a request. By sending requests in advance the client can also account for delays of the request that can occur, for example, due to network transmission time, or can plan ahead for future presentation. This means that it has to send the data request in time to the server to avoid that data will be delivered too late. It overcomes deviations in delivery by using a local buffer [4]. The client assumes that requested data will be delivered within the given deadline, e.g., at the earliest within the next service period.

In each period k, the server collects the incoming requests, schedules the requests for the next service period, and when the system resources are not sufficient it delays the remaining requests for later periods. Since the delay of requests depends on the scheduling policy and not on the arrival time of the request, the arrival order does not necessarily determine the scheduling of requests, even for the same client. Still the arrival time can be used as one priorization criterion.

In addition to scheduling single requests, the server has to be able to fragment single requests $<b,t>$ into several disjoint requests $<b_1, t>, ..., <b_n, t>$, such that $b_1, ..., b_n$ specify the same data as b, for two reasons. First, though we assume that single requests are small, it may happen that data requests are too large to be served within one service period. Second, for optimization it can be advantageous to split a request, such that part of the request is served with the remaining resources of a current service period and utilization is increased.

The storage system is responsible for the execution of the schedule. It maps the schedule to accesses to the storage system. This opens the opportunity to increase the throughput by optimizing the reading order for all requests scheduled for one service period. It is assumed that the request scheduler has a model for the storage system throughput and uses this for determining the scheduling.

The approach described in this paper abstracts from the properties of the storage system like disk scheduling policies, data placement strategies, and buffer size but it assumes that the throughput of the underlying storage system is given as a bandwidth value [5]. This assumption is realistic because todays' storage systems that consist of disk arrays do not offer access to single disks. The storage system reads the requested data from the disk, buffers it in the server cache, and sends it to the client over the network. It is also assumed that the network will be able to send the data appropriately to the client.

2.2   Admission of Pending Clients

In the following, several strategies for admission control are introduced. They are based on an admission criterion that automatically adapts to the system load. It has to adapt to different client consumption types, both for uniform and for bursty ones. The goal of the strategies is to achieve a high system utilization and to avoid overload situations since they degrade the temporal QoS by delayed requests.

Before a client session is allowed to issue data requests it requests admission from the server. This request is called admission request.

Let Res_{max} be the maximal amount of resources provided by the storage system. For each period k we introduce the following parameters: the set of currently admitted clients C_k, the set R_k of open requests that need to be handled by the server in the next period, and the set S_k of requests that are scheduled for the next period. Assume that for a given period k we have $R_k=\{r_1, ..., r_n\}$ and $S_k=\{s_1, ..., s_m\}$. The number of admitted clients is given by $|C_k|$. Then we define the server load l_k by

$$l_k = \frac{1}{Res_{max}} \sum_{i=1}^{n} res(r_i)$$

where $res(r_i)$ are the resources required to serve request r_i. Note that the server load can be larger than 1.0 thus not all requests can be handled within the next period.

Next, we define the server utilization u_k by

$$u_k = \frac{1}{Res_{max}} \sum_{i=1}^{m} res(s_i)$$

where $res(s_i)$ are the resources required to serve the scheduled request s_i. Note that the server utilization always is smaller or equal to 1.

In the simplest case the admission control can admit new clients as long as storage system resources are available, i.e., $u_k \leq 1$, which basically amounts to a best effort strategy. However, the current server utilization in service period k is only a good prediction on the future server utilization, as long as the resource demands of single sessions vary only little. Thus, in approaches that smooth the resource demands for each session, as discussed in Section 1, the current server utilization is a viable measure for the admission, while for highly interactive applications, that we consider, it is not. Similarly, the current server load can be considered as an admission criterion, with $l_k \leq 1$.

In order to adapt to the long term system behavior, we introduce a 'lookback' value λ that determines the number of service periods we look back to observe the past system behavior. The choice of this value determines how fast the admission control can adapt to new load patterns, or how strongly it compensates for short term deviations in server load. Based on the quantities u_k and l_k we can now define two quantities that will be considered for an admission criterion.

The *average server load* $l_{k,\lambda}$ of the past λ periods is given by

$$l_{k,\lambda} = \frac{1}{\lambda} \sum_{i=1}^{\lambda} l_{k-i}$$

The *average server utilization* $u_{k,\lambda}$ of the past λ periods is given by

$$u_{k,\lambda} = \frac{1}{\lambda} \sum_{i=1}^{\lambda} u_{k-i}$$

In the following, we introduce two approaches for defining an admission criterion that considers the past system behavior. For these criteria we introduce a quantity $\tau \in [0,1]$ that is used as safety margin. This quantity determines how close the average utilization and load values may approach the maximum value of 1, and thus how much tolerance is available to compensate for short term deviations. High values of τ represent an aggressive admission policy, while low values of τ represent a defensive admission policy. In the first case, overload situations may happen more frequently, while in the latter case the utilization will be lower and less clients are admitted.

Strategy 1: Lookback to server behavior. This strategy considers the past server resource values as admission criteria. For the admission, both average server load and the average utilization can be used. Pending clients are admitted if the average server load or the average utilization are under the safety margin, i.e.,

$$u_{k,\lambda} < \tau \quad \text{or} \quad l_{k,\lambda} < \tau.$$

This strategy does not consider the information on the number of admitted clients.

Strategy 2: Lookback to client behavior. The idea is to estimate the client consumption by considering the average request or average consumption rate of the admitted clients, in the past. The advantage of this approach is that the number of admitted clients is considered for the admission criteria.

The average client request rate $r_{k,\lambda}$ of the past λ periods is given by

$$r_{k,\lambda} = \frac{1}{\lambda} \sum_{i=1}^{\lambda} \frac{l_{k-i}}{|C_{k-i}|}$$

The average client consumption rate $c_{k,\lambda}$ of the past λ periods is given by

$$c_{k,\lambda} = \frac{1}{\lambda} \sum_{i=1}^{\lambda} \frac{u_{k-i}}{|C_{k-i}|}$$

A pending client is admitted in service period k, if

$$c_{k,\lambda} * (|C_k|+1) < \tau \qquad or \qquad r_{k,\lambda} * (|C_k|+1) < \tau$$

With this admission criterion a pending client is admitted when in addition to the sum of the average consumption or average request rate of the admitted clients C_k resources for at least one new client are available. This means that resources required for a pending client are estimated to be equal to the average resources required by the admitted clients. Furthermore, it is expected that the average past behavior of admitted clients will be an indicator for the future. Note that we neglect their individual behavior since it is not necessarily representative for future resource demands.

2.3   Scheduling Policies for Data Requests

After pending clients have been admitted the server has to deliver the clients' requests in the forthcoming periods until their sessions are terminated. In each period k, the server collects the incoming requests I_k together with the requesting client and the time of arrival. Thus I_k consists of tuples $<c, t_{in}, b, t>$, $c \in C_k$, $t_{in} \in \mathcal{H}$, where C_k is the set of admitted clients and t_{in} the arrival time of a request at the server. By means of a scheduling policy the server generates a schedule S_k that determines which requests are scheduled for the next period, where $S_0 = \emptyset$. The set of open requests R_k in each period k is then determined by the incoming requests I_k and requests from previous periods that are not scheduled yet by $R_k = I_k \cup (R_{k-1} \setminus S_{k-1})$, where $R_0 = \emptyset$. During scheduling it may happen that the available system resources are not sufficient to handle all open requests. Then, the scheduling policy as a first option can move a request $<c, t_{in}, b, t>$ to period k+1 without harm as long as t > k.

As soon as the open requests cannot be satisfied within the forthcoming service period the scheduling algorithm has to priorize the open requests. In the following, we discuss different scheduling policies with two goals in mind: (1) serve open requests within their time constraints (see Section 2.1), and (2) balance the system load between different service periods. Load balancing is important since the system load varies in between consecuting periods. In contrast to the admission control mechanism, which targets at avoiding long term bottlenecks, short-term deviations in system load can be smoothed through request scheduling. The following scheduling policies can be considered [8].

- First Come First Serve (FCFS): The simplest policy is to serve the requests by their arrival order. This policy has only small potential for load balancing since it does not consider the request urgency for scheduling.
- Resource-driven Scheduling: *LORF* (Low Resource Requests First Serve) reduces the negative effects of overload by first scheduling the requests with lowest resource requirements. This increases the number of requests that can be served. This strategy is useful in applications where the benefit of the system is related to the number of requests served within the time constraints.
- Earliest Deadline First Serve (EDF): *EDF* gives those requests priority that have the closest deadline. The further the deadlines of requests reach into the future, the higher is the potential of this policy. The goal of the policy is to achieve a high percentage of requests that have to be served within their deadlines, i.e., increase QoS in terms of jitter.
- Quality of Service-driven Scheduling: This policy requires a QoS-metric representing the relevant QoS parameters that determine acceptable quality ranges. High Quality First Serve (*QUF*) prefers requests that require high QoS parameters, assuming that applications with high quality requirements are most interested in good service.

When the advanced scheduling policy is not able to schedule open requests within their time constraints their service will be delayed. If the admission and load balancing techniques can no longer guarantee the full service quality, additional mechanisms for quality adaptation can be used to overcome bottleneck situations. The goal of quality adaptation is to balance quality degradation, of which lost or delayed requests is one type. With adaptation the required data volume is reduced by modifying the quality of the delivered data in the temporal and/or spatial dimension. For example, it is possible to modify the resolution of a video or audio, or drop frames of a video [9]. When the server decides to adapt it has the responsibility to reduce the data rate and deliver the data with reduced quality in a way such that the client is able to interpret the returned data, which then deviates from its original request. This might be a non-trivial problem for compressed stream data like MPEG with interframe dependencies. The quality adaptations are in the simplest case distributed over all clients equally, or can be based on individual QoS profiles of the clients. Related work on quality adaptation can be found, e.g., in [17].

Thus, the combination of an admission control mechanism, a scheduling mechanism with load balancing, and a quality adaptation mechanism is the way to enable the server to optimally adapt to the requirements of highly, interactive multimedia applications and at the same time achieve high resource utilization. The admission control and scheduling mechanism cannot guarantee that system overload does not occur but, by an appropriate choice of parameters, allow to reduce the number of overload situations.

2.4   Service Algorithm

We now give the detailed algorithm for admission control and request scheduling. The algorithm is given in pseudo code. In the algorithm, the average client consumption is used as admission criterion. The algorithm for the other admission criteria is analogous. For periods with $k < \lambda$ the value $c_{k,k}$ is used for the admission criterion, instead of $c_{k,\lambda}$.

```
S₀:= ∅;  R₀:= ∅;  C₀:= ∅;  k:=1;
While(true)
Begin
P_k := requests for admission;
While(P_k ≠ ∅ and c_{k,λ} (|C_k| +1) < τ)
        Begin
        C_k := C_k ∪ {first(P_k)};
        P_k := P_k \ {first(P_k)}; End;
I_k := requests from admitted clients;
R_k := I_k ∪ (R_{k-1} \ S_{k-1});
Sort R_k according to priority criterion;
Free_res = Res_max; S_k:= ∅;
While(free_res > res(first(R_k)))
        Begin
        S_k := S_k ∪ {first(R_k)};
        R_k := R_k \ {first(R_k)};
        free_res := free_res - res(first(R_k)); End;
Execute scheduled requests in S_k;
Update c_{k,λ};
Remove terminated clients from C_k;
k++; End;
```

Fig. 2. Pseudo Code of Admission Control and Scheduling Algorithm.

After performing admission control the algorithm schedules open requests until all resources of the next service period $k+1$ are reserved. After that, the schedule is sent to the storage system. In addition, the average client consumption is updated for the admission control mechanism in each service period.

3   Evaluations

In this section, we present experimental results that were obtained in a simulation environment implemented in the Mathematica [21] system. We compare two quantities for determining the quality of an admission and scheduling strategy, namely the average server utilization versus the number of delayed requests, which we use as a QoS criterion. In the course of this investigation a particular focus was on the stability of the admission control mechanism we propose. Stability means in this context that the system is able to control itself in phases with low and high load. For example, in underloaded periods the danger exists that too many clients get admitted, and in overloaded periods too many pending clients get rejected which leads to system underload in the future. In the worst case, oscillating behavior of the system load occurs. This is a critical point for any feedback system.

We describe the configuration that was used for simulating client behavior. The client switches between periods, where it requests data, and idle periods, in which it does not request data (e.g., the user is inspecting discrete data). During the request periods the client requests a varying load of media data (a media stream). All duration parameters are generated using the exponential probability distribution, while the request sizes are generated using the normal distribution. The server is assumed to have 30000 units of resource within a service period. The duration parameters are chosen under the assumption that a service period has a length of one second. In the chosen configuration, there exist two types of clients. The first has an average request period duration of 10 service periods with an average request size of 1400 units of resource per service period, an average idle period duration of 10 service periods, and average total session duration of 100 periods. The second client has an average request period duration of 30 periods with an average request size of 4200 units of resources, an average idle period duration of 3 service periods, and an average total session duration of 200 service periods. While the first client is intended to simulate average quality presentations for a browsing application, the second client simulates a VCR access to a high quality video. Low quality clients are created five times as often than high quality clients. Furthermore, clients are created such that the server periodically has to deal with phases of low load and high load. One such phase has 100 periods. In this way, the server has to continuously deal with the stability problem. Our configuration allows only around 10 parallel clients. This low number of clients generates still a rather bursty distribution of requests and thus imposes a more difficult challenge to the admission control than a larger number of clients.

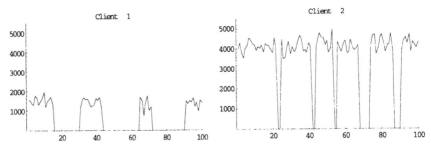

Fig. 3. Client Request Behavior of Type 1 and Type 2.

Figure 3 illustrates the typical behavior of both types of clients over their lifetimes. The x-axis represents the service periods and the y-axis gives the requested resource units. The graphs represent the request behavior of a client during its request and idle times. The request behavior varies around 1400 resource units in the left figure and around 4200 units in the right figure during a multimedia presentation. The clients request no data during their idle periods.

First we evaluate the different strategies that we have proposed. As a first experiment we take strategy 2 and run a prescreening for (λ, τ)-values for both, average client consumption rate $c_{k,\lambda}$ and average client request rate $r_{k,\lambda}$, as admission criterion. As scheduling policy we use EDF. The results are summarized in Table 1.

λ	τ	average utilization $c_{k,\lambda}$	variance of utilization $c_{k,\lambda}$	fraction of requests served in time $(c_{k,\lambda})$	average utilization $r_{k,\lambda}$	variance of utilization $r_{k,\lambda}$	fraction of requests served in time $(r_{k,\lambda})$
1	0.8	0.827701	0.132783	**0.774411**	0.856366	0.160017	**0.649223**
10	0.8	0.801515	0.168636	0.968677	0.818404	0.258037	**0.410026**
100	0.8	0.744060	0.164218	0.976362	0.705767	0.164979	0.977320
1	0.9	0.882038	0.152534	**0.246973**	0.924667	0.089782	**0.324022**
10	0.9	0.840137	0.141908	**0.890563**	0.793205	0.179114	**0.711840**
100	0.9	0.790747	0.140999	0.979186	0.719280	0.145321	0.976081
1	0.95	0.904935	0.122163	**0.438073**	0.883451	0.101035	**0.818325**
10	0.95	0.890717	0.119438	**0.521545**	0.814924	0.173354	**0.767916**
100	0.95	0.825157	0.157906	**0.712329**	0.732246	0.173858	0.900999

Table 1. Results of Strategy ´Lookback to Client Behavior´ (Strategy 2).

The left side of the table displays the results with $c_{k,\lambda}$ and the right one the results with $r_{k,\lambda}$ as decision criterion. This experiment shows that low values of λ (e.g., 1, 10) and high values of τ (e.g., $\tau = 0.95$) can immediately lead to unstable behavior (see bold values). This means that short lookback phases are not sufficient for the admission control because the system load varies in this experiment in larger time-windows. Further, in our configuration, a safety margin of $\tau = 0.95$ and higher is not sufficient to compensate short-term load deviations.

For better illustration we give one typical example of a stable system behavior for the values $\tau = 0.9$, and $\lambda = 100$, using $r_{k,\lambda}$ as a criterion for the admission which served more than 97% of the requests in time and achieved average utilization of almost 72% (see Figure 4). The best system utilization would be achieved by an average server load of value 1. The left figure shows that short term peaks in the server load can be dealt with. In the right figure, the dotted line gives the number of requests served within their deadline, and the solid line gives the number of delayed requests over the service periods. For example, it is shown how EDF balances the highest server load, occurred some periods just before service period 50. The request scheduler is able to avoid delayed requests at this period. This high server load leads to single delayed requests just after period 50.

Next, we evaluate alternative admission and scheduling strategies. The following experiment shows that average server utilization $l_{k,\lambda}$ and similarly average server load $u_{k,\lambda}$, used for strategy 1, are no adequate admission criteria. One reason for this worse behavior is that for a long lookback the values $l_{k,\lambda}$ and $u_{k,\lambda}$ increase and decrease very slowly when new clients get admitted or rejected since these values represent average values over the past. In this case, it may happen that with a long lookback, phases of low past server load lead to uncontrolled admission of new clients, and vice versa. This leads in the extreme case to a strongly oscillating behavior and extreme server overload. On the other hand, short lookbacks do not sufficiently reflect the varying resource requirements. This worse behavior does not occur with strategy 2 since this admission criteria does account for the current number of admitted clients.

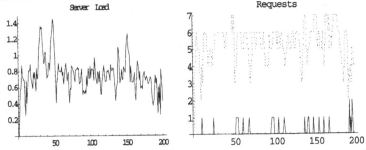

Fig. 4. Example of a stable System Behavior using 'Lookback to Client Behavior' (Strategy 2).

We performed an experiment with (λ, τ)-values of $(20, 0.9)$, as displayed in Figure 5. The left side of Figure 5 demonstrates the extremely high server load with multiple peaks (server load > 10). The right side shows that the number of delayed requests (solid lines) is extremely high, and only a few requests are served within their deadlines (dotted lines). With larger values of λ the behavior becomes even worse.

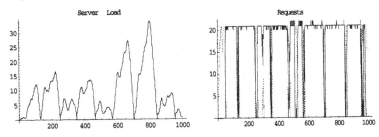

Fig. 5. Example Using 'Lookback to Server Behavior' (Strategy 1).

The next experiment (Figure 6) illustrates the benefit of using the EDF scheduling strategy. We performed the experiment with (λ, τ) -values $(100, 0.9)$ with the average client request rate as admission criterion, which behaved well when using EDF.

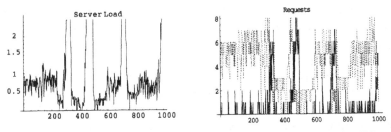

Fig. 6. Example Using 'Lookback to Client Behavior' (Strategy 2) and FCFS.

For the same experimental parameters the FCFS scheduling strategy performs substantially high variations in server load (left figure). The temporal QoS, measured in percentage of requests served in time, degraded to a rate of 0.85 in this experiment (right figure).

With regard to the question, whether average client consumption or average client request rate is the preferable admission criterion the results are not fully conclusive, yet. However, the Table 2 reports results of an experiment with $\lambda = 200$ that is one of several experiments, which indicate that the average request rate appears to be the admission criterion leading to more stable behavior. This experiment was run over 1000 periods.

decision criterion	λ	τ	average utilization	variance of utilization	fraction of requests served in time
ck,λ	200	0.8	0.753404	0.209823	0.802239
	200	0.9	0.797481	0.164365	0.85
rk,λ	200	0.8	0.703255	0.166676	0.972553
	200	0.9	0.73551	0.17511	0.958729

Table 2. Comparison of Client Consumption and Client Request Rate.

In order to verify our results for using the average client request rate as a criterion, we performed a long term run over 30.000 service periods with parameters ($\lambda = 200$, $\tau = 0.8$). In this experiment, too, the system behavior remained stable, with an average utilization of 0.75 and average Quality of Service of 0.97.

A question that requires further investigation is the dependency between the optimal safety margin τ and the variance of the average request rate and the average consumption rate. This quantities obviously depend on each other and a quantitative approximation of this relationship would be very useful. First experiments on relating the threshold value with the variance of the average request rate and the average consumption rate showed the following behavior: Using the variance of the average consumption rate as a safety margin for the admission criterion the system turned immediately unstable. Using the variance of the average request rate as a safety margin for the admission criterion showed acceptable, but still less stable behavior than in using predetermined values of τ. An alternative possibility would be to dynamically adapt the safety margin, i.e., to increase it when the quality decreases and, to decrease it when the server utilization decreases.

We also compared our admission control framework with a worst case based admission control. For that purpose we used a client that generates only few, but data intensive requests, and then remains idle for longer periods. In the configuration for this experiment the average request size is 4200, the average idle period 30, the average request period 3, and average total duration 200. Our admission control mechanism based on the average request rate achieved a utilization value of 0.67 and a QoS value of 0.92. A pessimistic admission strategy that admits only that many clients that can be served if all of them issue simultaneously requests, admits at most 7 clients at a time, since 7 * 4200 = 29400 (29400 < 30000). This strategy achieved a utilization value of 0.09 (!) and QoS value of 0.93. Note that, due to random variations in the request size, overloads are still possible with the pessimistic approach. Our strategy achieved a more than seven times higher utilization with the same QoS.

4   Conclusions

In this paper, a framework for an admission control mechanism for applications with variable data rates is introduced that is based on two steps: the admission of pending clients and the scheduling of the single requests of admitted clients. The admission of pending clients is based on the past client behavior. Various policies for the scheduling of single requests are used to balance the server load. Simulations show the benefit of the admission control framework for applications with variable data consumption with respect to QoS and server utilization. The experimental results can be summarized as follows:

- Using average server utilization and average server load are no adequate criteria.
- EDF achieves a substantial performance gain as compared to FCFS.
- Very short lookbacks do not work reliably.
- In general, the average client request rate behaves more stable in the long run and achieves comparably better performance than average client consumption.
- For uneven load patterns in the number of requesting clients the lookback should be at least over a whole period of load variation.

Currently, we are developing a distributed implementation of the admission control framework in Java that will be used both for evaluation purposes and for the implementation of the admission control module in a multimedia server.

Future work will include the evaluation of our approach within a multimedia database system. We also expect to obtain data on consumption rates of real world applications which we can use to further evaluate and to refine the admission control framework. However, we do not expect qualitative changes in its behavior since, in the experiments we performed, the admission control mechanism adapted very well to quite different types of load patterns. For the admission and scheduling method we see two important questions that need to be addressed. First, the dynamic adaptation of the safety margin values and, second, the use of dynamic QoS adaptations in the scheduling strategy.

References

1. Susanne Boll, Wolfgang Klas, and Michael Löhr: Integrated Database Services for Multimedia Presentations. In: S. M. Chung (Ed), Multimedia Information Storage and Management, Kluwer Academic Publishers, 1996.
2. Huang-Jen Chen, Anand Krishnamurthy, Thomas D. C. Little, and Dinesh Venkatesch: A Scalable Video-on-Demand Service for the Provision of VCR-Like Functions. In: Proc. 2nd Int. Conf. on Multimedia Computing and Systems, 1995.
3. Ming-Syan Chen, Dilip D. Kandlur, and Philip S. Yu: Support for fully interactive Playout in a disk-array-based Video Server. In: ACM Multimedia 10/1994.
4. Asit Dan, Daniel M. Dias, Rajat Mukherjee, Dinkar Sitaram, and Renu Tewari: Buffering and Caching in Large-Scale Video Servers. In COMPCON' 95: Technologies for the Information Superhighway, 1995.
5. Jayanta K. Dey-Sircar, James D. Salehi, James F. Kurose, and Don Towsley: Providing VCR Capabilities in Large-Scale Video Servers. In: Proc. of ACM Multimedia, 1994.

6. Craig S. Freedman and David J. DeWitt: The SPIFFI Scalable Video-on-Demand System. In: M. Carey and D. Schneider (Eds.): In: Proc. of Int. Conference on Management of Data (ACM SIGMOD), 1995.

7. Sreenivas Gollapudi and Aidong Zhang: NetMedia: A Client-Server Distributed Multimedia Environment. In: Proc. of 3rd Int. Workshop on Multimedia Database Management Systems, 1996.

8. Silvia Hollfelder: Admission Control for Multimedia Applications in Client-Pull Architectures. In Proc. of 3rd Int. Workshop on Multimedia Systems (MIS), 1997.

9. Silvia Hollfelder, Achim Kraiss, and Thomas C. Rakow: A Client-Controlled Adaptation Framework for Multimedia Database Systems. In Proc. of Europ. Workshop on Interactive Distributed Multimedia Systems and Telecommunication Services (IDMS), 1997.

10. Rune Hjelsvold, Roger Midtstraum, and Olav Sandstå: Searching and Browsing a Shared Video Database. In: Kingsley C. Nwosu, Bhavani Thuraisingham, and P. Bruce Berra (Eds), Multimedia Database Systems, Kluwer Academic Publishers, 1996.

11. Guido Nerjes, Peter Muth, and Gerhard Weikum: Stochastic Performance Guarantees for Mixed Workloads in a Multimedia Information System. In: Proc. of the IEEE Int. Workshop on Research Issues in Data Engineering (RIDE), 1997.

12. Banu Özden, Rajeev Rastogi, Avi Silberschatz, and P. S. Narayanan: The Fellini Multimedia Storage Server. In: S. M. Chung (Ed): Multimedia Information Storage and Management, Kluwer Academic Publishers, 1996.

13. Seungyup Paek and Shih-Fu Chang: Video Server Retrieval Scheduling for Variable Bit Rate Scalable Video. In: Proc. of the IEEE Int. Conference on Multimedia Computing and Systems, 1996.

14. Narasimha Reddy: Improving Latency in Interactive Video Server. In: Proc. of SPIE Multimedia Computing and Networking Conference, 1997.

15. Siram S. Roa, Harrick M. Vin, and Asis Tarafdar: Comparative Evaluation of Server-push and Client-pull Architectures for Multimedia Servers. In: Nossdav 96, 1996.

16. Prashant J. Shenoy and Harrick M. Vin: Efficient support for Scan Operations in Video Servers. In: Proc. of the Third ACM Conference on Multimedia, 1995.

17. Heiko Thimm and Wolfgang Klas: Delta-Sets for Optimized Reactive Adaptive Playout Management. In Proc. 12th Int. Conference On Data Engineering (ICDE), 1996.

18. Heiko Thimm, Wolfgang Klas, Crispin Cowan, Jonathan Walpole, and Calton Pu: Optimization of Adaptive Data-Flows for Competing Multimedia Presentational Database Sessions. In Proc. of IEEE Int. Conference on Multimedia Computing and Systems, 1997.

19. Harrick M. Vin, Pawan Goyal, Alok Goyal, and Anshuman Goyal: A Statistical Admission Control Algorithm for Multimedia Servers. In: Proc. of the ACM Multimedia, 1994.

20. Harrick M. Vin, Alok Goyal, and Pawan Goyal: Algorithms for Designing Large-Scale Multimedia Servers. In: Computer Communications, 1995.

21. Stephen Wolfram: The Mathematica book, 3rd ed., Wolfram Media/Cambridge University Press, 1996.

Accurate Modelling of VBR Coded Video Sources in ATM Networks

Gajendra Sisodia[1], Mark Hedley[2], Subrata De[3], and Ling Guan[1]

[1] Department of Electrical Engineering, University of Sydney,
Sydney 2006, Australia
{Sisodia, Ling}@ee.usyd.edu.au
[2] CSIRO Australia, Marsfield NSW 2122, Australia
mark.hedley@tips.csiro.au
[3] Vodafone Pty Limited, Chatswood NSW 2006, Australia
de@vodafone.com.au

Abstract. In this paper, we summarise the previous work in the area of modelling variable bit rate (VBR) coded video sources in asynchronous transfer mode (ATM) networks. We verify these models, especially in the area of measuring the quality of their predictions for network performance and the grade of service experienced by a user. In addition to verifying these models, we suggest a new modelling approach of VBR coded video sources. In previous cases, the number of cells generated by the coder for a sequence of video frames are modelled. In the new modelling approach, the number of cells in each type of macroblocks of a frame are modelled. This model is tested by comparing the cell loss rate in simulation of an ATM switch to cell loss rate produced when traces generated by the model were used as source.

1 Introduction

The modeling of variable bit rate (VBR) coded video sources becomes an important issue in ATM networks since it provides the starting point, in both theoretical analysis and engineering design, for network traffic management, delay-buffer trade offs, cell loss probability and related issues. The statistical source models of different types of video traffic are needed to design and study the performance of the network. The variable bit rate (VBR) video is considered to be a major source of traffic for the cell-relayed asynchronous transfer mode (ATM) network. Typically, the number of bits generated by the video coder for each video frame is modelled. Since video will be one of the major high data rate sources in future service requirements, there are considerable research activities aimed at designing VBR codecs and examining their feasibility in ATM networks [1].

The VBR video transmission allows consistent picture quality in contrast to the constant bit rate (CBR) where quality varies to match the constant nature of the channel. In CBR, it is easy for network provider, since it allows a fix amount of

S. Jajodia, M.T. Özsu, and A. Dogac (Eds.): MIS'98, LNCS 1508, pp. 98–109, 1998.

network resources to be allocated to the service. The efficient use of the network resource is left to the user and the demand is limited. In the cell-relayed ATM network, many services share the same link and each service places information in cells of length 5 byte header and 48 byte information. The cell header contains the information like the destination to which cell is to be directed. The cell loss in real time services is always a problem. For example in real time audio or video transmission, if cells are lost they can not be retransmitted and this affects the quality of the transmitted audio or video. This is because in real time, new video frame (in video service) arrives after a every fraction of second (if frame rate is 30 frames per second, it arrives after every 1/30th second) and by the time lost cells are retransmitted it is too late to use them. If the network load increases there is a high probability of loosing more number of cells and this results in decrease of the quality of service. In the design of video service the peak cell loss rate is a very important measurement.

Several different models based on the actual data measurement have been proposed for VBR video traffic (e.g. [2], [3], [7]). The statistical performance for full motion and videoconferencing VBR video is studied by using those models.

In this paper, we implement some of those models and study the statistical performance and the cell loss probability of H.263+ coded [4] VBR video traffic. We also proposed a new modelling approach to model VBR traffic model. Some tests are performed to verify this modelling approach, using video data derived from H.263+ coder. It is found that this modelling approach outperforms DAR(1) model in predicting network performance.

The video coding scheme used, and VBR statistics, are discussed in section 2. The previous source models which we use for our statistical analysis and simulation are discuss in section 3. In this section we also discussed the advantage, disadvantages and limitations of those models and how we fit our real data. In the section 4, we presented our new modelling approach of H.263+ coded data. In section 5, we discuss verification of models a using statistics of the real data, and data generated by using different models. The simulation study of cell loss rate is done in section 6 for real data, and each model data using an ATM multiplexer switch.

2 Source Data

We acquired two long real video sequences for analysis with QCIF (176 × 144 pixels) resolution. They were:

A. A typical videoconference sequence showing head and shoulders of a speaker. This consists of 10,000 frames at 10 frames per second.

B. This is from a football game which has full camera movement. This consists of 10,000 frames at 15 frames per second.

These sequences were coded using a H.263+ coder (public domain software from the University of British Columbia [5], which in turn is based on the ITU TMN7

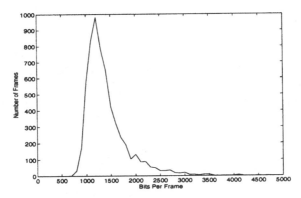

Fig. 1. The frequency distribution for the number of bits per frame for sequence 'A', with QP=10.

software [6]). There are a number of optional modes available, all of which were turned off. The quantisation parameter was set to 10, which provides a high degree of compression. The cells required per frame for the first five hundred frames of each sequence are shown in Fig. 3 and Fig. 6. Each frame is divided into a number of ATM packets (48 data bytes each), and the statistical properties of the number of cells per frame are shown in Table 1. The frequency distributions of the sequences are shown in Fig. 1 and Fig. 2 respectively. As can be seen in both the sequences, the negative binomial distribution provides a good approximation to the distribution of the number of bits or cells per frame.

Table 1. Summary statistics of coded data sequences

Parameter	Sequence 'A'	Sequence 'B'
Mean [cells]	4.04	28.38
Variance [cells]	1.41	272.13
Max [cells]	13	193
Min [cells]	2	10
ρ	0.98	0.91

3 Previous Modelling Work

Since the negative binomial is discrete analog of a gamma distribution, a discretized version of the latter can be used when it is more convenient to do so. The different source models can exploit this statistical behaviour of the sequences. We implemented three different models which exploit this property.

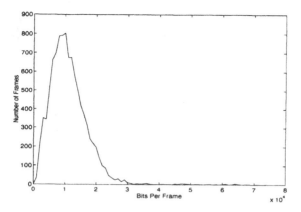

Fig. 2. The frequency distribution for the number of bits per frame for sequence 'B', with QP=10.

3.1 DAR(1) Model

The source of the video using VBR encoding is modelled as a multistate Markov chain. The Markov chain gives the number of cells in each frame, and determined by three parameters; the mean and variance of the number of cells per frame and the correlation between the number of cells in successive frames. These parameters can be easily estimated from the mean and variance of the real data sequences. Although the DAR model [7] is effective as a source model when several sources are multiplexed, it is not effective as a source model for a single source in isolation because its sample paths have flat spots. This means that the model data trace is constant for long interval, and do not look like the real data trace. This difference between model data and real data is mitigated when several sources are multiplexed. The DAR model was used successfully to compute effective bandwidth by Elwalid [14].

The basic idea of the DAR(1) model is to generate a sequence of cells per frame using a first order finite state Markov chain, determined using three parameters: mean, variance and correlation (shown in Table 1). The transition matrix P = (p_{ij}) of Markov chain is given by

$$P = \rho I + (1 - \rho)Q \tag{1}$$

where ρ = autocorrelation factor (for first lag), I is the identity matrix and each row of Q consists of the negative binomial probabilities.

3.2 GBAR Model

The GBAR(1) [8] process was introduced by McKenzie [9], which has inherent feature that the marginal distribution is gamma and the autocorrelation is geometric. The GBAR(1) model is based on two well known results: a) the sum of independent Ga(α,λ) and Ga(β,λ) random variables is a Ga($\alpha+\beta,\lambda$) random variable, and b) product of independent $Be(\alpha,\beta-\alpha)$ and $Ga(\beta,\lambda)$ random variables is a $Ga(\alpha,\lambda)$ random variable. Thus if X_{n-1} is $Ga(\beta,\lambda)$, A_n is $Be(\alpha,\beta-\alpha)$, and B_n is $Ga(\beta-\alpha,\lambda)$, and these three are mutually independent, then

$$X_n = A_n X_{n-1} + B_n \tag{2}$$

defines a stationary stochastic process $\{X_n\}$ with a marginal $Ga(\alpha,\lambda)$ distribution. The process defined by (2) is called a GBAR(1) processes. This process is used as a source model by generating noninteger values from (2) and rounding to the nearest integer, which can be interpreted as the number of cells per frame. Table 2 shows the values obtained for the different parameters when the model is fitted to the real data.

Table 2. GBAR model parameters

Parameter	Sequence 'A'
ρ	0.98
α	1.20
β	1.23
λ	0.305

The GBAR model is a more accurate representation of an individual VBR video source and easy to simulate but it is not useful for modelling full motion video sources.

3.3 SCENIC Model

The SCENIC model [3], which is a generalised form of the DAR(1) model, is used to generate data for full motion type video sequences. In this model the scene is considered as a combination of frames. The scene boundary is defined to be the frames where the bit rate changes sharply. The PDF of the scene length is defined as

$$p(x) = \frac{a}{x^n + b^2} \tag{3}$$

The mean and variance of this sequence can be calculated, and with this mean and variance, parameter r and p of the negative binomial distribution can be obtained. The parameter n and b were obtained by the application of a curve fitting technique to the histogram of the scene length. Table 3 shows the values obtained for the different parameters when the model is fitted to the real data.

The SCENIC model has been shown to provide more accurate approximation to the cell per frame of VBR full motion video source, but it is not able to model videoconferencing video traffic.

Table 3. SCENIC model parameters

Parameter	Sequence 'B'
ρ	0.91
r	3.29
p	0.104
b	52
n	2.8

4 New Modelling Approach

In previous modelling work, typically the number of cells generated by the video coder for each video frame is modelled. Among models DAR(1) model has the advantage of being very general and can be used with any distribution for the number of cells per frame. This model can be used to model VBR videoconference and full motion video traffic. The disadvantage of this model is that it generates same number of cells for long sequences and its sample paths have flat spots (Fig. 4 and Fig. 7), which is not a real case. This (flat spots) affects the accuracy to predict the network performance by using this model. The accuracy of this model can be improved if the model do not have flat spots in its sample paths (cells per frame) and generate different number of cells per frame.

We suggested a new modelling approach to model the coded sequences at macroblock (MB) level using DAR(1) model. As discussed before we used H.263+ coder to code our two long video sequences of QCIF format. While coding each frame is divided into fix number of macroblocks (For example in QCIF format (in our case) each frame is divided into 99 macroblocks) and each MB in every frame is either intra coded (I-coded) or predictive coded (P-coded) or not coded (N-coded) at all. Therefore each frame has three types of coded macroblocks and the sum of these macroblocks is equal to the total number of Macroblocks in one frame (99 in our case).

When real video sequences were coded, we separated the total number of coded bits for each type of MB in each frame. It was observed that the negative binomial distribution provided a good approximation to the distribution of the number of bits for each type of macroblocks (I-coded, P-coded and N-coded). We used DAR(1) model to model each type of MB which uses the negative binomial marginal distribution. This new model is named as DAR(M) model. This model generated total number of bits for each type of MB (for both sequences) and all MB bits were added to get total number of bits in each frame. The generated number of cells per frame for the first five hundred frames of each sequence are shown in Fig. 5 and Fig. 8. As it can be seen that this model generates different number of cells per frame and do not have flat spots in its sample path as compared to Fig. 4 and Fig. 7 (DAR model).

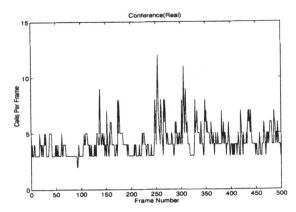

Fig. 3. Output traffic rate in terms of the number of cells per frame for sequence 'A', from frame 1 to 500.

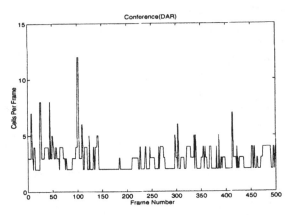

Fig. 4. Output traffic rate in terms of the number of cells per frame using DAR model for sequence 'A', from frame 1 to 500.

5 Model Verification

In this section, we use two tests to verify the models. The first is to see if the autocorrelation function matches well, the second to determine if the cell loss rate predicted (section 6) by a model lies within the range of the real data.

The autocorrelation function of the generated sequences should be very close to the real data. Ideally, it should be the same as to the model data including the tail behaviour. As shown in the Fig. 9 and Fig. 10, this is not the case for the source models. The autocovarince is computed for the real data sequences and, DAR(1), GBAR, SCENIC and DAR(M) model data sequences as a function of the lag measured in number of frames. Fig. 9 and Fig. 10 shows the autocovariance for sequence 'A' and 'B', and for the different models fitting to this sequence. For sequence 'A', the autocovariance for the DAR(1), GBAR and DAR(M) models decaying exponentially at large lags(video frame). Since GBAR model has only short range dependence [8], the autocovariance is not matching well for small lags(approximately 15 lags), but it matches well for large lags. It could be seen that autocovariance for the DAR(M) model is matching well for large leg as compared to other models. For the sequence 'B', the autocovariance for the DAR(1) and SCENIC is very close to the real data. It can be seen in the figure that DAR(M) model is matching well at the tail end of the real data. So the H.263+ coded real data sequences fits well to the sequences generated by the DAR(M) source models.

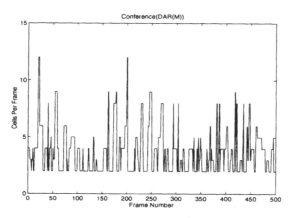

Fig. 5. Output traffic rate in terms of the number of cells per frame using DAR(M) model for sequence 'A', from frame 1 to 500.

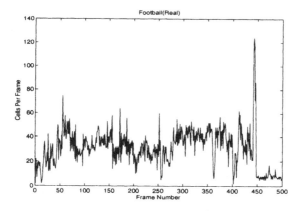

Fig. 6. Output traffic rate in terms of the number of cells per frame for sequence 'B', from frame 1 to 500.

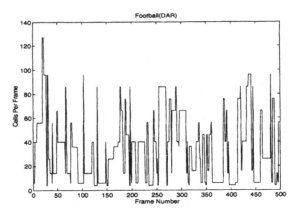

Fig. 7. Output traffic rate in terms of the number of cells per frame using DAR model for sequence 'B', from frame 1 to 500.

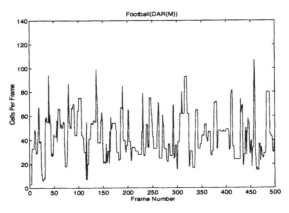

Fig. 8. Output traffic rate in terms of the number of cells per frame using DAR(M) model for sequence 'B', from frame 1 to 500.

6 ATM Network Simulation

6.1 Cell Loss Prediction

The usefulness of models for predicting cell loss rate for a number of different buffer sizes was verified by simulation. The ATM multiplexer shown in the Fig. 11, was used for simulation. The buffer was a part of the ATM switch. The departure process of the buffer was deterministic with first in first out (FIFO) discipline. Each video source was generating cells per frame at the rate of 10 frames per second (for sequence 'A') and 15 frames per second (for sequence 'B') giving different fixed number of cells for each frame. In order that the input sequences for each source be approximately independent, each source was started at a different frame in the sequence. In addition, video frames from different sources began at different times. Each ATM cell was made of 5 byte header, along with 48 bytes of data. Each video source generated and sent fixed number of cells to the ATM switch buffer. This size of cells represented the frame size. When all the cells of a frame transmitted to the switch buffer, video source input generated another value of frame size for the next frame.

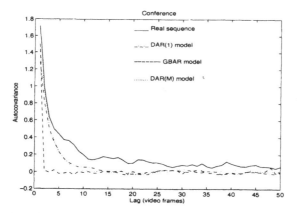

Fig. 9. Autocovariance function for sequence 'A' data and different models fitted to it.

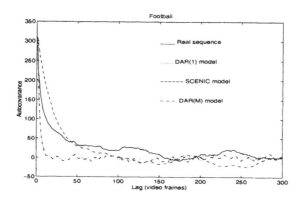

Fig. 10. Autocovariance function for sequence 'B' data and different models fitted to it.

For the sequence 'A', an output link speed of 150 Mbits per second was used. Fig. 12 shows the cell loss rate observed using each of the models at different buffer sizes, along with that of real data sequence. It could be seen that DAR(M) model provides good fits for the real data as compared to DAR(1) model. For these models no cell loss was observed for large buffer sizes. Since SCENIC model is used to model full motion video sequences, it was not used for sequence 'A'.

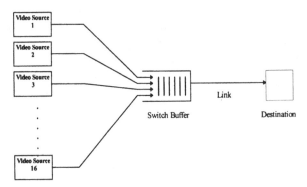

Fig. 11. The ATM multiplexer model.

For the sequence 'B', the output link speed 320 Mbits per second was used. Fig. 13 shows the cell loss rate observed using each of the models at different buffer sizes, along with that of real data sequence. The DAR(1) and SCENIC model provides good fits for the real data. As compared to DAR(1), the DAR(M) model provides much better fits for real data because in DAR(1) model, cells per frame are constant for fix number of frames which is not a reality in full motion video sequences. The SCENIC models predicts CLR much better than other models but it is restricted only for full motion video sequences.

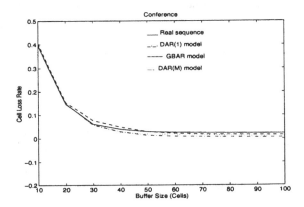

Fig. 12. Cell Loss Rate vs. Buffer size for the sequence 'A', using real data and data generated by various models with link speed of 150 Mbits per second.

7 Conclusion

In this paper, we have proposed a new modelling approach for data generated by variable bit rate video coder and can be used to model conference and full motion video sequences. In this model, data was modelled at macroblock level instead of at frame level. This model generates data for each type of macroblock in every frame and all generated macroblock bits are added to get bits per frame. This new model has been shown to provide a more accurate approximations to the cell loss rate and autocorrelation function than previous DAR(1) model on data from H.263+ video coder. We used this model and verified for multiplexed video traffic but this model could also be used as single source model and the performance of this model could be verified.

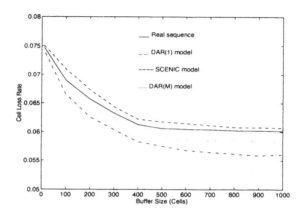

Fig. 13. Cell Loss Rate vs. Buffer size for the sequence 'B', using real data and data generated by various models with link speed of 320 Mbits per second.

References

1. Verbiest, L. Pinnoo, and B. Voeten.: The impact of the ATM concept on video coding, IEEE J. Selected Areas in Communications, vol. 6, pp. 1623-1632, Dec. 1988.
2. Maglaris, D. Anastassiou, P. Sen, G. Karlsson and J. D. Robbins.: Performance models of statistical multiplexing in packet video communications, IEEE Tans. on Communications, vol. 36, No. 7, July 1988.
3. Frater, J. F. Arnold, P. Tan.: A new statistical model for traffic generated by VBR coders for television on the broadband ISDN, IEEE Trans. Circuits and Syst. for Video Technol., vol. 4, pp. 521-526, Dec. 1994.
4. ITU-T Recommendation. H263+.: Video coding for low bitrate communication, 1997.
5. TMN encoder, University of British Columbia, Canada, http://www.ee.ubc.ca/Image, 1997.
6. ITU-T , H.263+ Ad Hoc group.: Video Codec Test Near_Term, Version 7 (TMN7), 1997.
7. Jacobs and P. A. W. Lewis.: Time series generated by mixtures, J. Time Series Analysis, vol. 4, No. 1, pp. 19-36, 1983.
8. Heyman, D.: The GBAR source model for VBR videoconferences, IEEE/ACM Trans. Networking, vol. 5, No. 4, pp. 554-560, August 1997.
9. McKenzie.: Autoregressive moving-average processes with negative-binomial and geometric marginal distributions. Adv. Appl. Prob., vol. 18, pp. 679-705, 1986.

Retrieving Images by Content: The Surfimage System

Chahab Nastar[1], Matthias Mitschke[1]*, Nozha Boujemaa[1],
Christophe Meilhac[1], Hélène Bernard[2], Marc Mautref[2]

[1] INRIA Rocquencourt, BP 105, F-78153 Le Chesnay, France
[2] Alcatel Corporate Research Center, Route de Nozay, 91460 Marcoussis, France

Abstract. Surfimage is a versatile content-based image retrieval system allowing both efficiency and flexibility, depending on the application. Surfimage uses the query-by-example approach for retrieving images and integrates advanced features such as image signature combination, multiple queries, query refinement, and partial queries. The classic and advanced features of Surfimage are detailed hereafter. Surfimage has been extensively tested on dozens of databases, demonstrating performance and robustness. Several experimental results are presented in the paper.

1 Introduction

The ideal content-based image retrieval system should be versatile:

- for image databases with *ground truth*, the system should be as *efficient* as possible on the specific application. Examples include face recognition or pathological image retrieval. A quantitative evaluation of the system can then be reported in terms of recognition rate, precision/recall graph, etc.
- for image databases where *no ground truth* is available, the system should be *flexible*, since the notion of perceptual similarity is subjective and context-dependent. Smart browsing, query refinement, multiple queries, and partial search on user-defined regions are among the desirable features of the system. Applications include stock photography and the World Wide Web.

Unlike most of the earlier systems (e.g. [3]), Surfimage can deal with both categories of image databases. For a specialized database, the ground truth is well-defined and a dedicated image signature will lead to optimal performance. This has been experimented on the MIT face database of 7,652 images where we report a recognition rate of 97%, the best reported recognition rate on this dataset [10].

In order to deal with generic databases, Surfimage includes advanced features such as signature combination (i.e. how to combine color and shape within the same query), query refinement through relevance feedback (i.e. learning from user interaction), multiple queries, and partial search on image sub-regions.

These features are detailed hereafter.

---

* The author is now with: Siemens AG, Med GT 5, Henkestr. 127, D-91052 Erlangen, Germany

S. Jajodia, M.T. Özsu, and A. Dogac (Eds.): MIS'98, LNCS 1508, pp. 110–120, 1998.

2 Surfimage: Classic Features

For the algorithm designer, the hardest step is image indexing, i.e. the computation of image signatures. This is typically an off-line processing. For doing this, genericity or specificity of the signature and conservation (or non-conservation) of the spatial arrangement of the image are key issues. The corresponding images signature categories with examples are summarized in table 1.

arrangement	generic sig.	specific sig.
encoded	*Fourier spectrum*	*eigenfaces*
lost	*color histogram*	*distance ratios*

Table 1. Image signature categories & examples

Surfimage offers a large selection of signatures in all the different categories mentioned in table 1. Among the signatures we can mention:

- Low-level signatures capturing color, shape and texture. Examples include color, orientation and texture histograms, Cooccurrence, Fourier and Wavelet transforms.
- High-level signatures which are derivated from a complex modeling of image content and sometimes a statistical analysis of the database. Examples include eigenimages [15,6], flexible images [10] or image shape spectrum [7].

The similarity metric is usually defined via a distance measure which will be used for nearest neighbor match in feature space. Various similarity metrics are implemented in **Surfimage**: the Minkowski L_p distances, the Cosine metric, the Hellinger metric, and M-estimators for outlier rejection. In our experience, the city-block distance L_1 is convenient since it is fast to compute and well-suited to signatures which are histograms.

Surfimage uses the query-by-example approach for querying. In the classic querying scheme, the user (i) loads a database, (ii) selects a signature, (iii) chooses a similarity metric, and clicks on a query image from the database to find more similar images with respect to the chosen signature and metric. Experiments are shown in section 4.

3 Surfimage: Advanced Features

The specificity of **Surfimage** is its advanced features which makes it uniquely flexible among image retrieval systems. Advanced features include signature combination, relevance feedback, and partial queries. They are presented hereafter.

3.1 Signature Combination

Combination of different features has been a recent focus of image retrieval [12,4,2,5]. But how do we combine "apples and oranges", i.e. features that have different number of components, different scales etc.?

Simple rescaling of the features is not suitable since it would alter the discrimination properties of each feature. A weighted linear combination of feature vectors is another possible method, and the weights have to be estimated (learned) after various experimentations with the database [4,2].

We have experimented with two combination methods. Under Gaussian assumption, *the normalized linear combination* method uses the estimated mean μ_i and standard deviation σ_i of the distance measure d for each feature i, providing the normalized distance:

$$d'(\mathbf{x}^{(i)}, \mathbf{y}^{(i)}) = \frac{d(\mathbf{x}^{(i)}, \mathbf{y}^{(i)}) - (\mu_i - 3\sigma_i)}{6\,\sigma_i}. \tag{1}$$

where $\mathbf{x}^{(i)}$ and $\mathbf{y}^{(i)}$ are the vector signatures of images X and Y within feature i (see also [11]). The new distance measure d' will essentially have its values in $[0...1]$. Let $\alpha_i = \frac{\mu_i - 3\sigma_i}{6\sigma_i}$. The combined distance between X and Y is then:

$$D(X, Y) = \sum_i \rho(d'(\mathbf{x}^{(i)}, \mathbf{y}^{(i)})) - \sum_i \rho(-\alpha_i) \tag{2}$$

where ρ is an increasing function (e.g. $\rho(x) = x$, $\rho(x) = x^3$ etc.).

The voting procedure operates as follows: in response to a query, each feature retrieves images and grades them by increasing order of distance. The ranks of the retrieved images within each feature can then be combined by a weighted sum (e.g. averaging) to output the retrieved images according to the combination of features. Alternative methods include the use of the median rank and the gymnastics-rule (i.e. ignoring the worst and the best ranks of an image) for robustness.

For evaluating the combinations, we experiment on benchmark databases with ground truth, and draw the precision-recall graphs, with:

$$\text{Precision} = \frac{|\text{retrieved relevant images}|}{|\text{retrieved images}|} \tag{3}$$

$$\text{Recall} = \frac{|\text{retrieved relevant images}|}{|\text{relevant images}|} \tag{4}$$

where $|D|$ denotes the number of elements in D.

For most applications, it is impossible to maximize precision and recall simultaneously, but these values should ideally be as large as possible. Figure 1 shows the precision-recall graphs for a database with ground-truth adapted from the MIT *Vistex* database, consisting of 384 homogeneously textured images as used in [14]. From this figure, it is obvious that *any version of feature combination is more performant than a single feature*, as noted elsewhere [13]. We have quantitatively verified the better performance of the combination on a number of other

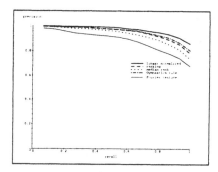

Fig. 1. Precision-recall graph for the MIT *Vistex* database. Note that the Fourier texture, the most performant single feature that we have computed, is not as good as any of the combined features.

benchmark public-domain databases with ground truth (Columbia database of 3D objects, ORL face database etc.).

3.2 Relevance Feedback

We now can combine several features for a single query. Our objective in this section is to enable query refinement by user interaction. Before describing our method, consider the following example that will clarify our motivations. Suppose the user is a customer willing to purchase a shirt. In most cases they have some ideas about the features connected with shirts, like color, texture, size, quality, price. Their idea about these features can either be very precise ("I want a cotton shirt"), other features can vary in a range ("I am ready to spend 30 to 40 dollars on it"), other features might be unimportant ("I don't care about the color"). The salesman's job is to *guess* these different distributions to come up with the ideal shirt.

What we want to do is similar to the above example. In practice, we wish to integrate both the positive (relevant) and the negative (non-relevant) examples of the user. Our idea is to estimate the distribution of relevant images for each feature component from the examples provided by the user and to simultaneously minimize the probability of retrieving non-relevant images. Note that the distribution of the non-relevant images cannot be easily estimated for various reasons: (i) for a given query, the number of non-relevant images is usually much higher than the number of relevant images (ii) non-relevant images tend to be multimodal (iii) since the system tends to retrieve relevant images, the sample of non-relevant retrieved images is not representative of the non-relevant images in the database. Nevertheless, we take the user-provided non-relevant examples into account (see [8,9] for details). A key issue is that our estimation of the distribution is based on a few data points (e.g. less than a dozen) and therefore it is not reliably representative of the true distribution of all the images in the database relevant to the query. Therefore we draw random variables according to the estimated distributions, retrieving more "varied" images than the classic maximum likelihood estimator.

One of the nice properties of our relevance feedback algorithm is that, in cases where relevant and non-relevant images are all mixed up within a feature component, the estimated distribution will tend to be flat (large standard deviation). This means that the corresponding feature component is not discriminant for the query.

3.3 Partial Queries

The user is often interested in a particular object or region rather than the whole image. This observation motivates recent research on spatially-localized features and sub-region matching (e.g. [1]).

There are several problems with sub-region (or partial) matching. The first one is segmentation: accurate segmentation of an image into regions in the general case is very difficult. Another problem is invariance: is the user interested in finding other occurrences the object (or region) with the same position, orientation, and scale, or do they require invariance against these transformations?

In order to deal with partial queries, we use a multiresolution quadtree representation (similar to [16]) that localizes image features in structured subregions (figure 2). This approach avoids image segmentation and allows for matching accross scales, if necessary.

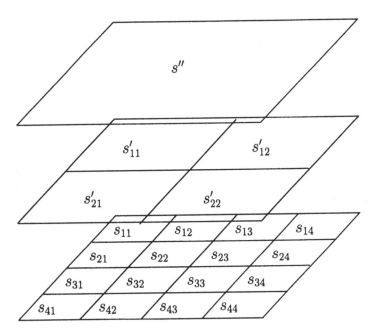

Fig. 2. Computation of image signatures on the multiresolution quadtree representation of the original image

4   Retrieval Results

Figure 3 shows an example of querying with Surfimage on the MIT face database (7,652 images). We have developed a specific, arrangement-preserving signature for this database called *flexible images* [10]. With the MIT face database, Surfimage produced a recognition accuracy of 97% based on a nearest neighbor rule. This corresponds to only six mistakes in matching views of 200 people randomly chosen in the database of 7,562 images. This is significantly better than had previously been reported for this dataset [12].

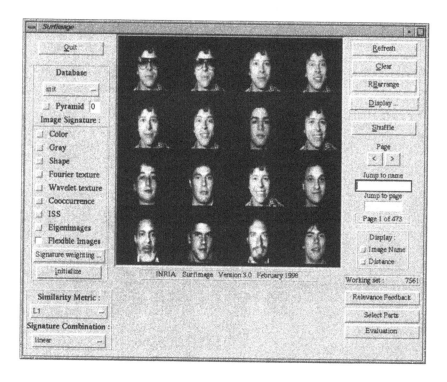

Fig. 3. Single specific features: retrieval of the top left face using flexible images [10]. Retrieved images are from top left to bottom right in order of best match. Note that the second and third best matches are faces of the query person without sunglasses.

Combining image features (up to a dozen image signatures) increases the discrimination power of the index. We illustrate this property by presenting the results on our homebrew *bigdatabase*, which was built by merging the MIT *Vistex* database of textures, the *BTphoto* database of city and country scenes, a homebrew *paintings* database, and the *homeface* database of people in the lab. The total number of images in *bigdatabase* is 3670. Figure 4 shows the ability of finding more city scenes from a query, thus essentially performing a classification task. A combination of features was used for increased performance.

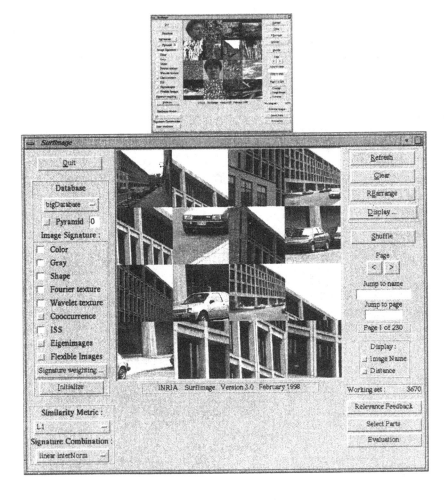

Fig. 4. Classification: Up: a sample of the heterogeneous *bigdatabase* of 3670 images. Bottom: classifying city scenes.

Figures 5 present the results of a multiple query on the Columbia database. The user is shuffling through the database and decides to retrieve more ANACIN and TYLENOL packs by selecting a couple of images. The technique used is the relevance feedback technique detailed above, but in this case no nonrelevant image was specified.

We illustrate query refinement on the *bigdatabase* described above. The user refines their query to obtain more portraits (figure 6). Note that many of the retrieved images can be classified as portraits, although the total number of portraits in the database is small (about 2% of the images in the database are portraits).

Partial querying with **Surfimage** are currently being investigated. The first results using the multiresolution method are promising (figure 7).

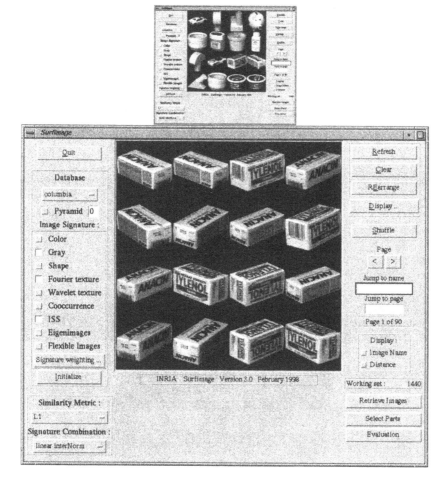

Fig. 5. Multiple queries: specifying a couple of images (up) for finding more ANACIN and TYLENOL packs (bottom).

5   Conclusion

We introduce Surfimage, a versatile content-based image retrieval system, that has been extensively tested on dozens of databases, proving efficiency on databases with ground truth and flexibility on databases without ground truth. More precisely, the flexibility of Surfimage comes from its advanced features such as signature combination, relevance feedback and partial queries. This last feature is currently being improved.

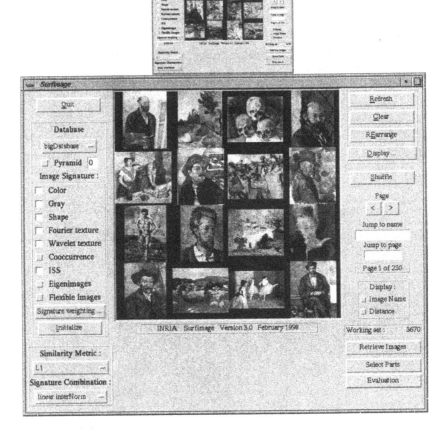

Fig. 6. Relevance feedback: Using user's feedback (up) to find more portraits (bottom).

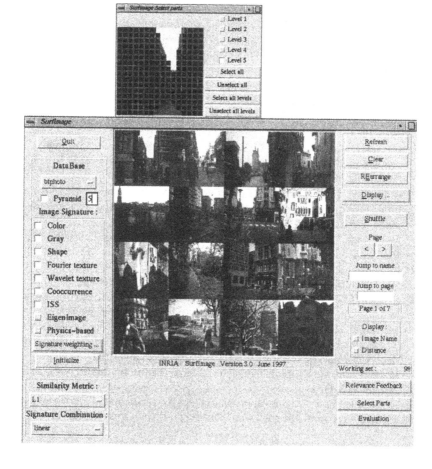

Fig. 7. Illustration of a partial query on two subregions

References

1. S. Belongie, C. Carson, H. Greenspan, and J. Malik. Color- and texture-based image segmentation using em and its application to content-based image retrieval. In *Proceedings of the Sixth International Conference on Computer Vision (ICCV '98)*, Bombay, January 1998.
2. I. Cox et al. PicHunter: Bayesian relevance feedback for image retrieval. In *Proceedings of 13th International Conference on Pattern Recognition*, Vienna, Austria, 1996.
3. M. Flickner et al. Query by image and video content: the qbic system. *IEEE Computer*, 28(9), 1995.
4. A. Jain and A. Vailaya. Image retrieval using color and shape. *Pattern Recognition*, 29(8), 1996.

5. T. Minka and R. Picard. Interactive learning using a society of models. *Pattern Recognition*, 30(4), 1997.
6. H. Murase and S. K. Nayar. Visual learning and recognition of 3D objects from appearance. *International Journal of Computer Vision*, 14(5), 1995.
7. C. Nastar and M. Mitschke. Real-time face recognition using feature combination. In *3rd IEEE International Conference on Automatic Face- and Gesture-Recognition (FG'98)*, Nara, Japan, April 1998.
8. C. Nastar, M. Mitschke, and C. Meilhac. Efficient query refinement for image retrieval. In *Computer Vision and Pattern Recognition (CVPR '98)*, Santa Barbara, June 1998.
9. C. Nastar, M. Mitschke, C. Meilhac, and N. Boujemaa. Surfimage: a flexible content-based image retrieval system. In *ACM-Multimedia 1998*, Bristol, England, September 1998.
10. C. Nastar, B. Moghaddam, and A. Pentland. Flexible images: Matching and recognition using learned deformations. *Computer Vision and Image Understanding*, 35(2), February 1997.
11. M. Ortega, Y. Rui, K. Chakrabarti, S. Mehrotra, and T. Huang. Supporting similarity queries in MARS. In *ACM Multimedia*, Seattle, November 1997.
12. A. Pentland, R. Picard, and S. Sclaroff. Photobook: Tools for content-based manipulation of image databases. *Int. Journal of Comp. Vision*, 18(3), 1996.
13. R. Picard, T. Minka, and M. Szummer. Modeling subjectivity in image libraries. In *IEEE Int. Conf. on Image Proc.*, Lausanne, September 1996.
14. Y. Rui, T. Huang, S. Mehrotra, and M. Ortega. A relevance feedback architecture for content-based multimedia information systems. In *Workshop on Content Based Access of Image and Video Libraries*, Porto Rico, June 1997.
15. M. Turk and A. Pentland. Eigenfaces for recognition. *Journal of Cognitive Neuroscience*, 3(1), 1991.
16. A. Vellaikal and C. Kuo. Joint spatial-spectral indexing of jpeg compressed data for image retrieval. In *Int'l Conf. on Image Proc.*, Lausanne, 1996.

Weakly Constraining Multimedia Types Based on a Type Embedding Ordering

Christian Altenschmidt, Joachim Biskup, Jürgen Freitag, and Barbara Sprick

Fachbereich Informatik, Universität Dortmund, Germany
{altensch|biskup|jf|sprick}@ls6.informatik.uni-dortmund.de

Abstract. We present a concept of weakly constraining types which balances heterogeneity and fixity of data structures. This concept is designed for a multimedia mediator that uses fixed type declarations on schema level but allows variations of actual structures on instance level. The concept is based on a notion of embedding a fixed type declaration into a variation structure such that essential aspects of the fixed declaration are preserved. Finally we show how multimedia types gain from our type system.

1 Introduction

1.1 Balancing Heterogeneity and Fixity of Structure

In the evolving information society users increasingly expect informational services that can deal with various kinds of heterogeneity. At the same time traditional database schemas fix the structure of stored data by declaring its types. When designing advanced information systems we are faced with the challenge of integrating the benefits of heterogeneity and the advantages of fixing the structure of data. In this paper we report on the fundamentals of a specific solution to this challenge. This solution is part of our overall design of a *multimedia mediator* (MMM), that is currently implemented in a prototype fashion [5,6].

From the perspective of a user, the MMM provides a well-structured gateway to some application dependent part of a federated multimedia system. Seen from inside, the MMM employs proxy objects for external multimedia items, hides all details of external communication, and its query optimization takes advantage, among other things, of materializing previous query answers in the proxy state. We intend the MMM to be set up in a top-down approach. Based on the analysis of an application, an administrator first declares a schema tailored for potential users. Then conditions for the access to external sources are specified, partly automatically and partly on a case by case basis. Later on, whenever the users refer to proxy objects, the system transparently supplies all translations that are necessary to access the actual sources.

S. Jajodia, M.T. Özsu, and A. Dogac (Eds.): MIS'98, LNCS 1508, pp. 121–129, 1998.

1.2   Design of a Type System

The services of the MMM are based, among others, on a new concept of weakly constraining types that constitute our specific solution to allow restricted heterogeneity while partially fixing the structure of data. Our new concept is part of the intended type system of the MMM. The mediator should automatically supply certain standard translations between fixed type expressions in the schema and various actual structures on the instance level. More special kinds or specific aspects of translations have to be individually supplied by appropriate wrappers on a case by case basis.

In this paper we define a suitable notion of *embedding* one type into another. Strictly speaking, we should always clearly distingish the syntactic and semantic aspects of a type, i.e. the (syntactic) type expression, as occuring in a schema, and its (semantic) extension which is defined as the set of complying instances. Furthermore, even if a particular data item is not statically considered to be a member of the type extension, it nevertheless can explicitly or implicitly have a structure which might comply with the type expression. In that case we can reasonably speak about the data item having that type as a dynamic type. Though being important for our considerations [8], in the following these distinctions are often blurred by abuse of language, as usual in computer science.

Our notion of an embedding is expressed by a function that maps nodes of (the syntax tree of) a first type (expression) onto nodes of (the syntax tree of) a second type (expression). Roughly speaking, this function indicates how each edge of the first type is translated into a path of the second type. Based on this definition of type embedding, we introduce a new type constructor **self_describe** that can be used for partial structural descriptions on schema level. This constructor associates a type on schema level with a set of structures on instance level such that the schema level type expression can be embedded in each of the instance level structures.

1.3   Achievements and Comparison

Recently a lot of research on semi-structured data has been done (cf. [1,8,12]). Many approaches adopt the Object Exchange Model (OEM) to describe heterogeneous objects, and corresponding schemas [9,11] essentially describe all possible paths to (components of) objects.

Two recent implementations of dbs with semi-structured objects, Lore [11] and the OQL-doc project [2], can be seen as extensions of the ODMG proposal. Lore meets the problem of object heterogeneity by avoiding typing, while OQL-doc explicitly enriches the type system with a union type. To overcome the differences in data structure resulting from heterogeneity many approaches, like [10,2,3], employ regular path expressions. Lorel [3] uses coercion for comparing objects of different types. In UnQL coercion is avoided by exploiting pattern matching [10].

The main difference between the approaches mentioned above and our concept is our top down approach to mediation. We design a uniform schema, describing all essentials by a type definition that ignores heterogeneity. Queries are well-typed and related to this uniform view, thus they can be answered transparently without the need of regular path expressions. We define when values can be translated into our uniform view. We argue, that this is possible in an algorithmically generic way, if we can apply some kind of natural coercion [7], namely a mapping of "finer" values onto "coarser" values. This way a type union is not explicitly needed and we are open to add new structures without the need of changing the schema.

2   A New Type System and Its Requirements

We are looking for a specific approach to maximize the allowed heterogeneity of data while sufficiently fixing its structure. We propose to introduce a new kind of types that allow variations in the structure of data instances (for the sake of heterogeneity), but also insist to specify *essential constraints* on them (for the sake of semantic clarity and computational efficiency).

2.1   A New Type System

We design a new type system with the following goals in mind: The type system should potentially *integrate a broad spectrum* of types. It should *deal with semi-structured data* and it should support the intended *top-down usage* of the MMM. For meeting well-typedness, a *path expression* should correctly and efficiently be interpreted on the instance level which may be spread across various sources.

With these overall goals in mind, our concept of *weakly constraining types* is devised to supply certain standard translations for reasonably manageable situations. On schema level, we will interpret certain *types* as time-independent partial structural descriptions of the anticipated data instances. On instance level, any single data item has a particular, possibly time-dependent structure that must *conform* to the schema type. Then, for any data item the raw data is supplemented with some kind of self-description consisting of its particular structure and the relationship between this actual structure and the schema type.

2.2   Objects as Abstractions of Reality

Our MMM is based on maintaining proxy objects for external multimedia items. A first set of requirements is derived from the following interpretation of values of proxy objects as *abstractions* of the external multimedia items.

First we emphasize that a multimedia item and its representing proxy object refer to the same "entity of the real world". A multimedia item is a database object identified by a unique object identifier and containing a description of the entity as its value. Thus the multimedia item is designed as an abstraction with respect to the essential aspects of the world. The corresponding proxy object further abstracts from the multimedia item.

How can we produce abstractions? Basically, we abstract by *removing actual information* from the original object, for instance by neglecting certain aspects, making data coarser or aggregating data. We argue that to some extent removing information can be accomplished in an algorithmically generic way. However, if we want to *add conceptual information* we cannot do so in an algorithmically generic way but have to employ case specific wrappers.

We argue that we could remove arbitrary information, but intuitively the removal should preserve a certain property of object relationship, namely, whenever the values of two objects are indistinguishable before the removal they should still be indistinguishable afterwards.

2.3   Essential Constraints

As mentioned above the mediator administrator specifies essential constraints to be placed on the source objects by declaring a type on schema level, i.e. he defines a *tree* with inner nodes describing the desired hierarchical structure and leaves describing the desired content data.

Now we look for a mechanism to actually place these essential constraints on source objects. We know that a source object is primarily restricted by its particular (dynamic) type, no matter whether this type is defined explicitly in the source level schema or generated adhoc by a wrapper. So it suffices to place the essential constraints on this type. We do this by demanding that an *embedding function* i from the nodes of the schema level type tree t_1 into the nodes of the instance level type tree t_2 exists. This function should have two additional properties described in the following.

We want to guarantee that all atomic components of the first type (identified with) t_1 are also present as *independent* components in the second type (identified with) t_2. Then, the flat information contained in a data unit of type t_1 can also be expressed by a data unit of type t_2. More formally, function i *discriminates leaves*, i.e. i is *injective* on the set of leaves of t_1 in such a way that for any two leaves n and m of t_1 the nodes $i(n)$ and $i(m)$ are *not connected* in t_2. Note that by this definition it is possible to map leaves onto inner nodes, which allows atomic values on schema level to be structurally more differentiated on instance level.

We want to ensure that the internal structure of the first type t_1 is also somehow represented in the second type t_2. Then, the structural information contained in a data unit of type t_1 can also be somehow expressed by a data unit of type t_2. More formally, function i *strictly preserves connections*, i.e. for each edge (n, m) in t_1 there exists a corresponding *nonempty* path in t_2 connecting the nodes $i(n)$ and $i(m)$. As an immediate consequence, also for each path in t_1 from node n to node m there exists a corresponding path in t_2 connecting the nodes $i(n)$ and $i(m)$.

2.4 Requirements for Path Expressions

Having discussed the type system from a conceptual point of view we will now specify some more pragmatic requirements. For query evaluation we would like to query source objects as if they were of a type defined in the schema. This means it is necessary to correctly and efficiently interprete path expressions being well-defined with respect to the essential constraints specified in the schema. More precisely, a path in a constraint type should be *faithfully* translated into a path in a variation type, i.e. if a path p_1 in the constraint type is a strict initial part of a path p_2 then the translation of p_1 is a strict initial part of the translation of p_2. Summarizing, the embedding should maintain the structural data of a constraint type also in the variation types, and it should allow conversion of content data in a variation instance into content data for the constraint instance.

3 An Embedding Ordering and Its Algebraic Properties

We build our type system from some atomic types, e.g. **boolean, integer** and **string**, by applying some type constructors, e.g. **n_tuple_of**, for cardinals n, **set_of**, and **reference_to**. For all scalar values, we will omit an explicit constructor **scalar**. Any type σ is described by its syntax tree, where the leaf nodes denote the involved atomic types and the nonleaf nodes denote the use of type constructors. Thus a type σ can be considered as a pair $\langle temp, label \rangle$, where *temp* describes the pure graph theoretical structure of the syntax tree, and *label* describes the annotations at the nodes of the syntax tree. Figure 3 shows a

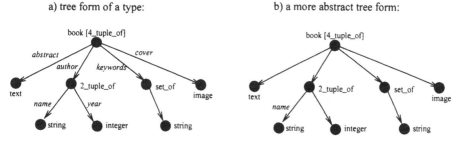

Fig. 1. Different kinds of type presentation

simple example of a type in different forms. Part a) depicts a type in tree form. Attribute names appear as labels on the edges. Part b) is derived from part a) by omitting the attribute names. Later on, for the convenience of presentation, we will mostly use this kind of presentation.

In this context, we assume that for any nonleaf node of any tree the descending edges are marked with (locally unique) identifiers. Thus for any node with k successors we can distinguish the corresponding k subtrees by these marks even if they are isomorphic. We will, however, omit the identifiers for the sake of succintness.

If we understand values as abstractions, a value of type σ is seen as an equivalence class of values of type τ, namely of those τ-abstractions that are coarsened to the σ-abstraction. For atomic types this means in terms of a type system that an atomic type σ is contained in τ, $\sigma \leq \tau$, iff the domain of σ is considered as a subdomain of τ. For example, we specify that **boolean** $\leq$ **integer** $\leq$ **string**. If τ is a complex (= structured) value, we still demand at least $|\sigma| \leq |\tau|$.

Abstractions of constructors are coarsened by deleting components. In terms of a type system this means, a constructor c_2 is a refinement of a constructor c_1, $c_1 \leq c_2$, iff all components of c_1 are also components of c_2. For instance, considering tuple constructors, we can specify that for $n \leq m$, **n_tuple_of** $\leq$ **m_tuple_of**. Note, that the constructor **m_tuple_of** can also be simulated by a cascade of tuple constructors each of which may have an arity less than m.

Essential constraints as mentioned in section 2.3 are placed on the type trees as a whole. Their effects on our embedding will be more formally investigated in the next subsections.

3.1   Types Involving Only One Atomic Type and Tuple Constructors

We first treat the special case that we have only one atomic type *atom* and only the tuple constructors **n_tuple_of**, for all cardinals n.

Definition 31 (embedding of (type) trees) *A tree $temp_1$ is* embeddable *into a tree $temp_2$, $temp_1 \leq temp_2$, iff there is a mapping i of the nodes of tree $temp_1$ on the nodes of tree $temp_2$ such that the following two properties hold:*

1) Mapping i discriminates leaves (see section 2.3).

2) Mapping i strictly preserves connections (see section 2.3).

Lemma 31 *The embedding $\leq$ is closed for subtrees: Suppose $temp_1 \leq temp_2$ via some mapping i, and consider the subtree $temp_{1,n}$ determined by a node n of type $temp_1$ and the subtree $temp_{1,i(n)}$ determined by the corresponding node $i(n)$. Then also $temp_{1,n} \leq temp_{1,i(n)}$ via the same mapping i.*

Lemma 32 *The embedding $\leq$ is reflexive and transitive.*

To proof transitivity, we argue that if an embedding maps a leaf of $temp_1$ onto an inner node of $temp_2$ we can find an equivalent embedding which maps the leaf of $temp_1$ onto a leaf of $temp_2$, such that we gain injectivity on leaves.

So our definition of embedding $\leq$ turns out to result in the useful algebraic structure of a partial ordering. Here we define two trees to be in the same equivalence class iff they are identical except of a systematic (bijective) renaming of their nodes and edges. We always take a tree as a representative member of its equivalence class. With this convention in mind we can state the following theorem.

Theorem 31 *The embedding $\leq$ is antisymmetric, and thus the embedding $\leq$ is a partial ordering on types.*

Proof (sketched) We first show that we can choose the mappings i and j as inverse functions on the leaves. Then it is a fact that a rooted tree is completely characterized by the set of its leaves and the ancestor function. With this we can proof (by induction on the distance from leaves) that the ancestor function of tree $temp_1$ is equal (up to renaming) to the ancestor function of tree $temp_2$. $\square$

In section 2.2 we have treated values as abstractions and discussed their property of being indistinguishable. Let us now define that two abstractions are *indistinguishable* if their trees can be mutually embedded such that contents of corresponding leaves are equal. Then theorem 31 can also be interpreted as follows.

Theorem 32 *The embedding $\leq$ preserves indistinguishability of abstractions as stated in section 2.2.*

3.2   Impact of Additional Atomic Types and Type Constructors

We now relax the assumed restrictions, namely that we have only one atomic type *atom* and only the tuple constructors **n_tuple_of**, for all cardinals n. The first restriction can be dropped as follows. Remember that, by the construction principle of types, atomic types only appear as leaves and that, by the property of discriminating leaves, leaves are injectively mapped on independent subtrees. We first discuss the special case where these subtrees are leaves again. If we now assume that we have several different atomic types, then, in all cases, we only have to take care that any leaf type t_1 is mapped on a leaf type t_2 such that, considered as atomic types, $t_1 \leq t_2$, i.e. t_1 is contained in t_2. When we deal with "semantic domains", i.e. syntactic types with specialized operations, or the general case that a leaf is mapped on a nontrivial subtree, the notion of containment might be quite subtle and is subject to semantically motivated decisions to be taken by the mediator administrator.

Unfortunately, when differentiating atomic types our embedding loses transitivity. This results from the possibility of mapping leaves onto inner nodes combined with our demand for containment of the atomic type of the leaf in the complex value of the inner node. For instance, in 2 we can neither map both v_1 and v_2 on w since this mapping would not discriminate leaves, nor can we guarantee that both v_1 and v_2 are contained in one of the leaves in σ_3. For now we have to leave

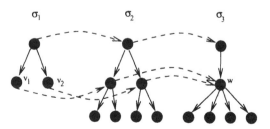

Fig. 2. An example for loss of transitivity

this problem open. For relaxing the second restriction we have to deal with the specific properties of any additional constructor. For the sake of space we just mention that we can appropriately treat two powerful constructors that appear in object-oriented databases, namely the set constructor **set_of** and the reference constructor **reference_to**. Further constructors still need to be investigated, see also section 5.

Summarizing, we can formally define a generalized notion of type embedding. For an example, see [6]. This notion is based on two more fundamental definitions:

- any given definition of containment $\leq$ of atomic types
- the specific definition of refinement $\leq$ of the type constructors **n_tuple_of**, **set_of**, and **reference_to** that comprises only the trivial containments **set_of** $\leq$ **set_of** and **reference_to** $\leq$ **reference_to** as well as, for $n \leq m$, **n_tuple_of** $\leq$ **m_tuple_of** as already stated in the introduction of this section.

Definition 32 (embedding ordering on types) $\langle temp_1, label_1 \rangle \leq \langle temp_2, label_2 \rangle$: *iff $temp_1 \leq temp_2$ via a mapping i (satisfying the conditions given in definition 31), and $label_1(n) \leq label_2(i(n))$, for all nodes n of $temp_1$ such that $label_1(n)$ is not a tuple constructor.*

4   A Concept of Weakly Constraining Types

We are now ready to introduce our new concept of weakly constraining types. For this goal we propose a new type constructor **self_describe** with two parameters. The first parameter must be a usual type specifying the time-independent essential constraints on the structure of allowed instances. Any processing of data has to be well-typed with respect to this type, possibly by using an embedding.

The second parameter, a *meta-type* the values of which are types, is used to restrict the allowed instances more concretely. Both parameters must be *compatible* in the sense that the first parameter can be embedded in all types given by the second parameter. Some data unit is allowed as an instance iff the particular structure of the data unit (i.e. its dynamic type) is an element of the second parameter.

For any type σ occuring as a first parameter, we can use the corresponding meta-type Σ, consisting of all types τ such that σ can be embedded into τ, as a default for the second parameter. Again, the reader is referred to [5,6] for an example.

5   Embedding Multimedia Types

Starting with traditional types as described in section 3 we can sketch some multimedia types and discuss reasonable embeddings by some simple examples. A first characteristic type for multimedia systems is *text*, which differs from plane strings by including structural information. Following our argumentation for traditional types we would like to embed a less structured text in a more structured one, and viewing a string as a text without any structure we define *string* $\leq$ *text*.

Images stored in a database are usually enriched by visual features to allow a content-based retrieval. Thus we may view an image as a tuple consisting of the image itself and additional attributes covering information like colour and texture, or even a set of identifiable objects together with their spatial interrelationships. We again can take over definition 32 leading to common-sense emdeddings of different image types, where the coarser image type lacks some attributes and therefore some kind of information. Seeing colour as meaningful information, we may define *greyscale image* $\leq$ *colour image*. Finally, in the presence of a process which detects text within an image, we can argue *string* $\leq$ *image*.

The most significant features of multimedia data result from its representation and demand the incorporation of time-related concepts. The main ingredients are composition principles like sequential composition and parallel composition. When talking about embedding we would expect information of time to be removed in the coarser type, which is introduced by two simple examples: a sequential constructor may arrange images to be shown one after one with a certain delay, and the set of images is embedded in the sequential arrangement. Likewise a parallel constructor synchronizes the presentation of different objects to be shown in parallel, and the tuple of objects is embedded in its parallel arrangement.

References

1. S. Abiteboul. Querying semi-structured data. In Afrati and Kolaitis [4], pages 1–18.
2. S. Abiteboul, S. Cluet, V. Christophides, T. Milo, G. Moerkotte, and J. Simon. Querying documents in object databases. *Journal of Digital Libraries*, 1(1):5–19, 1997.
3. S. Abiteboul, D. Quass, J. McHugh, J. Widom, and J. L. Wiener. The lorel query language for semistructured data. *Journal of Digital Libraries*, 1(1):68–88, 1997.
4. F. Afrati and P. Kolaitis, editors. *6th Int. Conf. on Database Theory*, Delphi, Greece, Jan. 1997. Springer-Verlag.
5. J. Biskup, J. Freitag, Y. Karabulut, and B. Sprick. A mediator for multimedia systems. In *Proc. 3rd Int. Workshop on Multimedia Information Systems*, pages 145–153, Como, Italy, Sept. 1997.
6. J. Biskup, J. Freitag, Y. Karabulut, and B. Sprick. Query evaluation in an object-oriented multimedia mediator. In *Proc. 4th Int. Conf. on Object-Oriented Information Systems*, pages 31–43, Brisbane, Australia, Nov. 1997.
7. K. B. Bruce and G. Longo. *A modest model of records, inheritance, and bounded quantification*, pages 151 –195. MIT Press, Cambridge, London, 1994.
8. P. Buneman. Semistructured data. In *Proc. 16th ACM SIGACT-SIGMOD-SIGART Symp. on Principles of Database Systems*, pages 117–121, Tucson, AZ, May 1997.
9. P. Buneman, S. Davidson, M. Fernandez, and D. Suciu. Adding structure to unstructured data. In Afrati and Kolaitis [4], pages 336–350.
10. G. Fernandez, L. Popa, and D. Suciu. A structure-based approach to querying semi-structured data. In *Proc. Workshop on Database Programming Languages*, 1997.
11. J. McHugh, S. Abiteboul, R. Goldman, D. Quass, and J. Widom. Lore: A database management system for semistructured data. *SIGMOD Record*, 26(3):54–66, 1997.
12. D. Suciu. Management of semistructured data. *SIGMOD Record*, 26(4):4–7, 1997.

Balancing Workload and Communication Cost for a Distributed Virtual Environment

John C.S. Lui, M.F. Chan, Oldfield K.Y. So, and T.S. Tam

Department of Computer Science & Engineering
The Chinese University of Hong Kong

Abstract. Recent advancement in computer graphics and networking technologies enable researchers to experiment and build the distributed virtual environment (DVE) system. In general, a DVE system allows many clients to simultaneously explore a virtual world and at the same time, users in this virtual environment can interact with each other and can manipulate the objects in the virtual world. To implement such a system, there are many challenges that researchers have to face so as to build an efficient DVE system that can represent a large virtual world and at the same time, support large number of concurrent users. In this work, we present some of these important issues, such as the necessity to balance the workload among different servers as well as minimizing the inter-server communication. We show that the problem, in general, is NP-complete and we proposed several algorithms so as to find the partitioning policy efficiently.

1 Introduction

With the advances in multimedia systems, parallel/distributed database systems and high speed networking technologies, it is now possible to build a distributed system which allows many users to virtually explore and interact under the same 3D virtual world. This 3D virtual world is composed of many high-resolution 3D graphics sceneries that represent a real-life world. This type of shared, computer-resident worlds are called the *distributed virtual environments* (DVEs)[8] and like other ground-breaking computer technologies, DVEs can change the way we learn, work, and interact with other people. It is a challenging task to design and implement a cost-effective and high performance DVE system. Some of the challenges include 1) how to maintain various object consistency in the virtual world, 2) how to maintain different user's view consistency and, 3) balancing workload and reducing communication cost in the DVE system. Some of the previous work on DVE system can be found in [1,2,4,5,6,7]

2 System Architecture, Models, and Avatars

In general, there are two possible architectures for implementing a DVE system. These two types of architectures are 1) the single server distributed virtual environment architecture (SSDVE) and 2) the multiple servers distributed virtual

S. Jajodia, M.T. Özsu, and A. Dogac (Eds.): MIS'98, LNCS 1508, pp. 130–135, 1998.
© Springer-Verlag Berlin Heidelberg 1998

environment architecture (MSDVE). In the SSDVE architecture, all the clients are connected to the dedicated server. In order to make sure that all clients have the same consistent view of the virtual world, any action or activity generated by a client has to be transmitted to other clients. The initiating client will send a message to the DVE server, the DVE server will first transform the message to the corresponding database operations and then the server will broadcast (or multicast) the new information to other clients in the system so that each client can update the local view of the virtual world. Since the SSDVE architecture can only handle a small number of concurrent clients, to support a large number of concurrent clients, one can adopt the MSDVE architecture. In the MSDVE architecture, multiple servers will be used and each server is responsible to handle a subset of the virtual world database operations, the communication of its attached clients as well as the communication between servers. In general, the communication cost between servers is more *expensive* than the communication cost between the server and its attached clients because the server and its attached clients may reside in the same local area network while different servers may reside at two extremes edges in the Internet.

A virtual world is a 3D model which represents a real world environment. Depending on the type of application and the environment we want to model, a virtual world can represent a small environment (e.g., a small classroom) or a large real world setting (e.g., the city of Los Angeles). For a small DVE world, all the DVE clients can simply attach to the dedicated server, which is responsible for database updates and broadcasting (or multicasting) messages to each DVE clients within the virtual world. On the other hand, if the virtual world that we want to represent is large or if there is a large number of concurrent DVE clients in the same virtual world, then a single server may not have enough computational power to handle the aggregate workload. To overcome this, we divide up the virtual world into different *disjoint cells*. Clients can still explore the entire virtual world concurrently and they can move from one cell to another cell. If we adopt the MSDVE architecture, we can assign different cells to different servers. In this case, the total workload of the virtual world can be shared by multiple servers. It is important to note that because a DVE client has the capability to move from cell to cell in the virtual world, therefore, the workload of each server is time-varying. Another important point to note is that some form of communication between servers is needed to maintain the consistency of the view to the virtual world. Therefore, we need to balance the server's workload as well as the inter-server communication.

In the DVE system, we usually use an avatar, which is a 3D active object, to represent a DVE client in the virtual world. The avatar can move or travel in the virtual world. The client can also use his/her avatar to communicate with other avatars (or other users in the virtual world), or use his/her avatar to access any 3D objects in the virtual environment. One simple way to maintain the consistency of the avatars in the virtual world is to broadcast any action taken by any avatar to all other avatars in the system. However, this will incur a significant communication overhead. In general, each avatar only needs to know the activity that happened near his/her vicinity. Therefore, one way to greatly reduce the total communication overhead is to allow every avatar to define his/her own *area of interest* (AOI). In this case, the avatar only needs to know the activity within his AOI and update it's own state and to make his/her view consistent. In [3], we present the mathematical model of predicting the cell location of each avatar in the virtual world.

3 Problem Formulation and Partitioning Algorithms

3.1 Problem Formulation

First, let us define the following terms that we use in this paper.

N = Number of cells that compose the whole virtual world.
P = Number of partitions or servers in the DVE system.
n = Number of avatars in the DVE system.
A_i = Avatar i where $i = 1, 2, \ldots, n$.
W_i = Workload in cell c_i, $i = 1, \ldots, N$.
L_{ij} = Communication cost for the link between cell c_i and c_j, $1 \leq i, j \leq N$.
w_1 = A non-negative relative weight to represent the computational workload cost on a server.
w_2 = A non-negative relative weight to represent the importance of the server-to-server communication cost. Note that $w_1 + w_2 = 1.0$.
C_P^W = Workload cost for a given partition configuration $\mathcal{P}$.
C_P^L = Communication cost for a given partition configuration $\mathcal{P}$.
$C_{\mathcal{P}}$ = Total cost for a given partition configuration $\mathcal{P}$.

Given the state of the DVE system and the number of servers P, we first perform the *graph transformation* so as to represent the workload in each cells as well as the communication cost. The graph transformation can be performed as follow:

Graph Transformation: (*input*: State of DVE system, number of partition P; *output*: a weighted graph $G = (V, E)$)

For each cell c_i, create a node v_i in G.
Compute W_i which is the workload in cell c_i and it is equal to the number of avatars in c_i or the expected number of avatars in c_i, depending on the DVE state representation.
If cell c_i and c_j are adjacent to each other, then there is an edge $E_{ij} \in E$ such that E_{ij} is between node v_i and v_j in V.
Compute L_{ij} which is the communication link cost for E_{ij}. Since we assume that the AOI of each avatar covers only the adjacent cells, therefore, we let $L_{ij} = W_i + W_j$ if v_i and v_j are in different partitions and $L_{ij} = 0$ otherwise.

We are now in the position to formally define our workload partitioning problem. Given a graph $G = (V, E)$ with $|V| = N$, $\mathcal{P}$ is the partition that divides V into P (where P is the number of servers) disjoint subsets $V_1, V_2, \ldots, V_P$ such that $V_i \cap V_j = \emptyset$ for $i \neq j$ and $\cup_{i=1}^{P} V_i = V$. Given a partition $\mathcal{P}$, we can define the workload cost $C_{\mathcal{P}}^{W}$ on this partition such that:

$$C_{\mathcal{P}}^{W} = \sum_{j=1}^{P} \left(\sum_{v_i \in V_j} \left| W_i - \frac{n}{P} \right| \right) \qquad (1)$$

Let us define the following function between a cell u and a partition V_l:

$$ADJ(u, V_l) = \begin{cases} 1 \text{ if } \exists v \in V_l \text{ such that } u \text{ and } v \text{ in } G \text{ are connected (or } E_{uv} \in E); \\ 0 \text{ otherwise.} \end{cases}$$

Then, given a partition $\mathcal{P}$, let C_{ij} be the communication cost between partition V_i and V_j and C_{ij} can be expressed as:

$$C_{ij} = \sum_{u \in V_i} W_u \cdot ADJ(u, V_i) + \sum_{u \in V_j} W_u \cdot ADJ(u, V_j) \qquad (2)$$

Let $C_{\mathcal{P}}^{L}$ be the communication cost for partition $\mathcal{P}$ and it is $C_{\mathcal{P}}^{L} = \sum_{i=1}^{P} \sum_{j>i}^{P} C_{ij}$. Therefore, $C_{\mathcal{P}}^{L}$ represents the total server-to-server communication cost given the partition $\mathcal{P}$. The overall cost for the partition $\mathcal{P}$, denotes by $C_{\mathcal{P}}$, is:

$$C_{\mathcal{P}} = w_1 C_{\mathcal{P}}^{W} + w_2 C_{\mathcal{P}}^{L} \qquad (3)$$

where w_1 and w_2 represent the relative importance of the workload cost and the communication cost respectively. Lastly, the cells-servers assignment problem is to find an optimal partition $\mathcal{P}^{*}$ such that

$$C_{\mathcal{P}}^{*} = \min_{\mathcal{P}} \{C_{\mathcal{P}}\} \qquad (4)$$

Before we discuss the workload partitioning algorithms, we show that:

Theorem 1. *The workload partitioning problem of Equation (4) is NP-complete.*

Proof: please refer to [3]   ∎

3.2   Partitioning Algorithms

Exhaustive Partitioning (EP) Algorithm: One simple way to partition the cells among different servers is by the exhaustive approach, that is, given N cells in the DVE system and P servers, then each cell can have at most P choices, therefore, the total number of partition policies are

$$|\mathcal{P}| = (P)(P) \cdots (P) = P^N \qquad (5)$$

Baseline Partitioning (BP) Algorithm: Given the NP-completeness nature of the workload partitioning problem, let us propose a heuristic algorithm which we called the *baseline partitioning (BP) algorithm*. The BP algorithm assumes that if the positions of the avatars are uniformly distributed over the whole virtual world, then the workload of a partition, which is proportional to the number of avatars inside it, should be proportional to the area of that partition. To evenly distribute the workload among different partitions, the algorithm tries to assign equal area to all partitions. The BP algorithm is to divide the virtual world with a grid of squares such that the number of squares is equal to the number of available servers P. In the case that the number of servers P is not a square number, the largest square number which is less than P is used while the rest of the cells in the virtual world will be assigned evenly among the remaining servers.

Bisection Partitioning (Bi-P) Algorithm: The previous discussed BP algorithm assumes that avatars are uniformly distributed across the virtual world. To handle different location distributions, we propose the the *bisection partitioning* (Bi-P) algorithm, which is based on the concept of bisection. Without the loss of generality, let us first present the Bi-P algorithm for N cells system and $P = 2$. Let P_k^n be the partition for the kth server with n cells, we have:

$$P_1^N = V = \{v_1, v_2, \ldots, v_N\} \quad ; \quad P_2^0 = \emptyset \tag{6}$$

Let $\mathcal{P}_i$ be the ith partition configuration and let $C_{\mathcal{P}_i}$, the cost based on Equation (3), be the cost of partition configuration $\mathcal{P}_i$. Based on the initial partition, we have $\mathcal{P}_0 = (P_1^N, P_2^0)$ and the corresponding $C_{\mathcal{P}_0}$. We can then find $\mathcal{P}_1$ by moving one cell from P_1^N to P_2^0 and compute the cost $C_{\mathcal{P}_1}$. Note that the cell can be chosen in such a way that the total cost of $C_{\mathcal{P}_1}$ is minimized, which can be achieved by considering each cell in P_1^N and this process takes a linear time with respect to the total number of cells in the system. Formally, we have:

$$\mathcal{P}_i = (P_1^{N-i}, P_2^i) \qquad i = 0, 1, \ldots, N \tag{7}$$

where $\mathcal{P}_{(i+1)}$ can be derived by:

$$\mathcal{P}_{(i+1)} = (P_1^{(N-(i+1))}, P_2^{i+1}) = (P_1^{(N-i)} - \{v_j\}, P_2^i \cup \{v_j\})$$
$$\text{for } v_j \in P_1^{(N-i)} \text{ and } C_{\mathcal{P}_{(i+1)}} \text{ is minimized} \tag{8}$$

Note that $C_{\mathcal{P}_0}$ and $C_{\mathcal{P}_N}$ represent the two extremes of the highest load imbalanced cost (i.e., all cells are assigned to one server and there is no server-to-server communication). Therefore, the Bi-P algorithm is to choose a configuration that:

$$\mathcal{P}_{i*} = \{\mathcal{P}_i \mid C_{\mathcal{P}_i} = \min_{0 \le j \le N} \{C_{\mathcal{P}_j}\}\} \tag{9}$$

The above algorithm applies for $P = 2$. For a larger number of P, we can first use the Bi-P algorithm mentioned above, then choose a partition that has the largest workload and then apply the Bi-P algorithm again.

Cell Shifting Operation: Since only the EP algorithm can generate an optimal partition while the BP and the Bi-P algorithm can only general a sub-optimal partition (of course, the advantage of these two algorithms is that they require a much lower computational cost of finding a partition). One way we can further reduce the cost $C_\mathcal{P}$ from the resulting partition $\mathcal{P}$ that was generated by either BP or the Bi-P algorithm is to perform some form of *post-processing*. In general, cell shifting operation is a process of assigning a cell from one partition to its neighboring partition such that the resulting partition $\mathcal{P}'$ has a lower total cost $C_{\mathcal{P}'}$ than $C_\mathcal{P}$. The cell-shifting operation terminates when there is no more cell shifting operation that can be performed so as to reduce the total cost $C_{\mathcal{P}'}$. Therefore, it is intuitively clear that the resulting partition $\mathcal{P}'$ after the cell-shifting operation should be as least as good as the original partition $\mathcal{P}$, which was generated by the BP or the Bi-P algorithm. Please refer to [3] for the performance study of various partitioning algorithms.

4 Conclusion

Distributed virtual environment allows different people to interact with each other without leaving their homes and offices. This form of communication or collaboration, will surely change the way we interact. In this paper, we present some of the research issues in designing and building a distributed virtual environment. In particular, we consider how to assign workload to different servers and at the same time, reducing the overall workload and communication cost. We show that in general, the partitioning problem is NP-complete and therefore, we proposed several heuristics, the BP, Bi-P and cell-shifting operations. We show that the bisection partitioning algorithm, together with the cell-shifting operation, can efficiently assign the workload and at the same time, reduce the communication cost.

References

1. W. Broll. *Distributed Virtual Reality for Everyone: a Framework for Networked VR on the Internet.* Proceedings of the IEEE Virtual Reality Annual International Symposium, March 1997.
2. John C.S. Lui, M.F. Chan, T.F. Chan, W.S. Cheung, W.W. Kwong. *Virtual Exploration and Information Retrieval System: Design and Implementation.* The third International Workshop on Multimedia Information Systems (MIS'97), 1997.
3. John C.S. Lui, M.F. Chan, K.Y. So, T.S. Tam, *Balancing Workload and Communication Cost for a Distributed Virtual Environment.* Technical Report, The Chinese University of Hong Kong, May, 1998.
4. R. Muntz, J.R. Santos, and S. Berson. *RIO: A Real-time Multimedia Object Server,* ACM Performance Evaluation Review, ACM Press, vol. 25(2), p.29-35, Sept, 1997.
5. R.R. Muntz, J. Renato Santos, S. Berson. *A Parallel Disk Storage System for Real-time Multimedia Applications,* accepted for publication in the Journal of Intelligent Systems.
6. M. R. Macedonia, D.P. Brutzman, M.J. Zyda, D. R. Pratt, P.T. Barham, J. Falby and J. Locke. *NPSNET: A Multi-player 3D Virtual Environment over the Internet,* Proceedings of ACM Symposium on Interactive 3D graphics, April 1995.
7. O. Stahl and M. Anderson. *DIVE: A Toolkit for Distributed VR Applications.* Swedish Institute of Computer Science, SICS.
8. R. C. Waters, J. W. Barrus. *The rise of shared virtual environments.* IEEE Spectrum, pp. 20-25, March, 1997.

Network Visualization of Heterogeneous US Army War Reserve Readiness Data

Joseph H. Schafer [1], Timothy J. Rogers [2], and John A. Marin [3]

[1] Office of Artificial Intelligence, United States Military Academy, West Point, New York 10996 , Telephone: (914) 938-2407; Facsimile: (914) 938-3807, Email: Joseph-Schafer@usma.edu, WWW: http://www.ai.usma.edu/

[2] Institute for Systems Research, University of Maryland, College Park, MD 20742, Telephone: (301) 405-6741; Facsimile: (301) 405-6707, Email: rogers@cs.umd.edu, WWW: http://www.cs.umd.edu/~rogers

[3] Office of Artificial Intelligence, United States Military Academy, West Point, New York 10996, Telephone: (914) 938-4628; Facsimile: (914) 938-3807, Email: Jack-Marin@usma.edu, WWW: http://www.ai.usma.edu/

Abstract. We have prototyped a multimedia tool to visualize the readiness of US Army War Reserve equipment. In contrast to previous efforts, our system allows the readiness to be visualized across several dimensions and to mediate existing heterogeneous data sources. Our front end Java applet enables multimedia and multidimensional visualization and allows a small client to access the mediation server from any networked location. The mediation server employed in this application is the Heterogeneous Reasoning and Mediator System (HERMES) which works with *existing* data and knowledge paradigms to resolve conflicts and generate sophisticated conclusions.

1 Background and Motivation

Logistical planning for an Army of the 21st Century will require the quick and efficient visualization and manipulation of databases with quantitative data, symbolic entries, and diverse forms of data structures. For example, consider the problem where a logistical planner must devise a plan to supply a land-based contingency force with items located on pre-positioned supply ships. The creation of such a plan would require access to the following sources of data:

1. The demand database containing the requisitions of the land-based forces.
2. The supply databases reflecting the current inventory of the ships.
3. A Geographic Information System (GIS) to locate ports for ship docking.
4. A planning tool to devise a supply strategy according to some objective function.

Since the above databases are in different locations, on different platforms, and stored in different database or file formats, this becomes an extremely difficult database problem. Currently, in a labor and time intensive effort, Army War Reserve (AWR) analysts manually combine sources such as those described above into a

S. Jajodia, M.T. Özsu, and A. Dogac (Eds.): MIS'98, LNCS 1508, pp. 136–147, 1998.

common format on a common platform. The AWR Community, spearheaded by the Logistics Integration Agency1 (LIA), is developing a planning and analysis information system that will manipulate multimedia objects, such as GIS data, automatically and seamlessly combine data from disparate sources, and covert this data into useable information. Given the immense size of the Army War Reserve databases, the logistical planning and analysis information system will also summarize, visualize, and navigate through appropriate databases and infer sophisticated conclusions from the distributed data sources.

The approach we applied to the AWR planning process is to create a prototypical planning and analysis information system using a tool called HERMES - Heterogeneous Reasoning and Mediator System [1]. HERMES was developed by the University of Maryland under contract to the Army Research Office (ARO) and Army Research Laboratory (ARL) and provides a good approach for mediating between diverse data sources and reasoning systems. Thus, the objective of this research is twofold: first, we wish to demonstrate the capability to maintain up-to-date and on-demand data access for AWR planning and analysis. The second objective is to assess the potential of HERMES to provide a secure, remote, collaborative multimedia presentation of summarized, distributed data.

The remainder of this paper will describe this prototypical system, to include the multimedia visual presentation of the summarized information such that "drilling down" to more detailed information is evident. Additionally, we will present some observations concerning the implementation of HERMES and some initial results regarding the operation of this prototypical system.

2 Applying the HERMES System and Related Work

In order to integrate disparate data sources, there exist two obvious alternatives: (1) Integrating the data into a single source such as a data warehouse; (2) Allow the databases to remain with the originator, and create a system to go out and get the data as needed. Combining the data into a single source has the advantage of centralizing the data and providing users with a common interface. However, disadvantages of importing data into central warehouses include failures due to single-source centralization and keeping the imported data current and consistent. Also, one data structure may not efficiently support all required functions, for example, storing GIS map data in a relational database is very inefficient [2].

Our challenges with respect to visualizing [3, 4] networked [5] heterogeneous data, relationships, and structure are similar to those related to other very large data sources whether in data ware houses or mediated from raw legacy files [6].

Combining the necessary AWR data into a single warehouse is a difficult task currently being researched and worked-on by the Army Strategic and Advanced Computing Center (ASACC) [7]. The data warehouse allows logistics analysts to locate data files centrally and ensure data integrity and synchronization. However, the centralization approach does not satisfy all the AWR logistic planner needs since

1 This research was supported in part by the US Army Logistics Integration Agency, Alexandria, VA and New Cumberland, PA, USA.

currency of the data is critical. Thus, we developed an improved hybrid method that encompasses the data warehouse employing HERMES.

HERMES defines a platform for building mediators, or programs that semantically integrate different and possibly heterogeneous information sources and reasoning systems. Mediators (see the pioneering work by G. Wiederhold, [8]) typically express methods to resolve conflicts, unify mismatches in measurement units (e.g. convert centimeters to inches) and generate sophisticated conclusions based on information contained in a wide variety of data structures [9]. HERMES mediators employ annotated logic-based rule sets that define precise domain function execution over target data sources. HERMES domain modules encode the actual conduit through which the system accesses native data files.

3 Visualizing Army War Reserve Data with HERMES

The AWR project requires secure, collaborative network access to heterogeneous, distributed data sources. Using HERMES as the glue necessary to implement the back-end data server, we employed the following four basic steps to build an initial prototypical system.

1. Identify, locate and collect the target data sources.
2. Encode new HERMES domain modules (software interfaces) as necessary and leverage the existing *Oracle* domain for the imported warehouse data.
3. Design and implement the mediator (rules to map queries to data sources).
4. Design the client graphical user interface (GUI) and encode the remote client front-end.

3.1 Identifying and Collecting the Data

We identified and accessed over a dozen unclassified samples of representative databases from those used in current Army War Reserve analysis and obtained unclassified portions of actual data. Additionally, we developed appropriate synthetic databases for the demonstration in lieu of actual, classified data. The data and schema descriptions were obtained from both LIA and the Army Strategic and Advanced Computing Center Data Warehouse.

The prototypical system currently mediates among four representative data sources. We will continue to develop techniques to update and interface new data sources with applicable standards, data dictionaries, and ontologies [10]. While our initial priority was to visually summarize and enable drill down through the heterogeneous data, we envision a unified framework that will also encompass multimedia and GIS data sources provided later.

3.2 Required HERMES Domains -- LOGTAADS and *Oracle*.

Once we amassed the project data the next step was to forge the necessary data interface. This required implementing the LOGTAADS (Logistics - The Army Authorization Document System) domain, and warehousing the remaining files on an *Oracle 8* server. The LOGTAADS data set exists in "flat-file" form but envelopes four distinct record types, typical of many legacy COBOL data files. It is basically a single-file multi-table relational database that lacks an application-programming interface (API). Access to this legacy data required writing the LOGTAADS domain (a HERMES software interface) which defined basic relational database operations over the native LOGTAADS tables.

The data exists on three separate servers, connected via 10 Megabit Ethernet LAN. Clients connect through the Internet via any Java 1.1.5 compatible browser. The Web, remote HERMES server, and the LOGTAADS servers all run on Sun Sparc Ultra 1's, a 167 MHz 64 bit machine running Solaris 2.5. Our *Oracle 8* server runs on a 233 MHz P5 MMX Gateway PC running Windows NT Server 4.0. The databases, servers, and network communication processes for this prototypical system are depicted below in Figure 1.

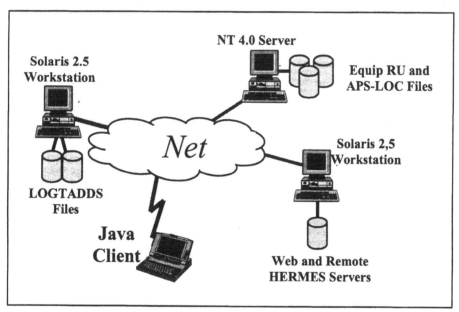

Fig. 1. Overall view of HERMES process and databases accessed in this AWR prototypical system

3.3 Designing the AWR Mediator

HERMES mediator files list declarations and rules for accessing and combining diverse software and data. Basically, the mediators map query requests onto data sources through domain function calls. Mediators generally correspond to applications. For example, HERMES mediators have been constructed for applications such as inventory management, travel planning, and networked banking systems.

The mediators for the AWR planning system defines the query predicates, data sources, rule bodies, and security conditions necessary to instantiate the appearance of a unified homogeneous database. Again, it is important to emphasize the mediator must integrate disparate U.S. Army data sources by invoking required sequences of LOGTAADS and *Oracle* domain function calls. At this point in time, the most complex query exists in the loc_force_DUIC_totals (location force totals) predicate which is a query stub. The mediator rules for this query, depicted below in Figure 2 and subsequently explained, describes a distinct sequence of steps necessary for answer resolution.

3.4   The Client Interface

Conceptually, the client graphical user interface (GUI) implements a forest of multi-branch HERMES query trees which enable logistic planners to drill-down all necessary (predefined) data paths while shielding users from the underlying HERMES syntax. The multi-tree, multi-branch aspect allows the user to visualize the data from many different perspectives. For example, several attributes may characterize a particular data set uniquely. The client interface allows the operator to select a set of data visually by one set of attributes and then examine the data by another view [11].

Architecturally, the client interface exists as an HTML embedded Java (version 1.1.5) applet which communicates with the remote HERMES server via standard TCP/IP socket protocols. This allows logistic planners at multiple locations, working often from diverse operating systems and platforms, to visualize the required army readiness data using standard Java enabled web browsers.

The LIADBook Java class encodes the query tree. Each query can map to zero, one, or more sub-queries. As users select to drill-down, the client interface maps data from the parent query answer to its child sub-query masks. For example, suppose a user wishes to see what equipment is located on the fictitious supply ship *Alexandria*. To drill into the *Alexandria* data the client interface maps data (the location selection) from the *loc_totals* query answer: loc_totals(3, *Alexandria*, 9510, 8471, 89.0747):1 onto its child query nodes. In this case it generates two sub-queries:

```
loc_ERC_totals (D_Status, Alexandria, SzERC, D_AuthQty, D_OnHand,
                    D_Percent):1.0
loc_force_totals (D_Status, Alexandria, SzFrc, D_AuthQty, D_Onhand,
                    D_Percent):1.0.
```

that ultimately render the six answers appearing indented beneath the *Alexandria* location data.

```
loc_force_DUIC_totals (D_Status, SzLOC, SzFrc, SzDUIC, D_AuthQty, D_OnHand, D_Percent,
SzDesc):1 <-

   constant( SzLOC)&
   constant( SzFrc)&

   loc_force_DUICs (SzDUIC, SzLOC, SzFrc):1 &
   is( 'Qtys.hrm', oracle:project_select('equipru:2b', "lia98apr@bester/******",
                                     "Auth_qty, Net_short",
                                     "DUIC", "=", SzDUIC))&

   =( D_AuthQty, hermes:sum_double( 'Qtys.hrm', "Auth_qty"))&
   =( D_Short,   hermes:sum_double( 'Qtys.hrm', "Net_short"))&
   =( D_OnHand,  math:subtract( D_AuthQty, D_Short))&
   percentage( D_Percent, D_OnHand, D_AuthQty):1&
   readiness (D_Status, D_AuthQty, D_OnHand, D_Percent):1&
   taads_UICs( SzDUIC, SzDesc):1.

loc_force_DUICs (SzDUIC, SzLOC, SzForce):1 <-

   variable( SzDUIC)&
   constant( SzLOC) &
   constant( SzForce)&
   is( 'TgtDUICs.hrm', oracle:project_selectN ('aps_loc:2e', "lia98apr@bester/******",
                                     "Duic", 2,
                                     "LOC", "=", SzLOC, "frc_type", "=",
SzForce))&

   in( DUIC_Recd, hermes:unique( 'TgtDUICs.hrm'))&
   =( SzDUIC, DUIC_Recd.Duic).
```

Fig. 2. Partial depiction of a HERMES mediator used to collect and integrate data from an *Oracle* database and nested flat file containing LOGTAADS data. The `loc_force_DUIC_totals` predicate, listed in Figure 2, calls the `loc_force_DUICs` predicate to obtain unit identifiers for the target location (**SzLOC**). The `loc_force_DUICs` predicate, in-turn, instructs the remote HERMES server to select *Oracle* Aps_Loc table tuples which match the target SzLOC location input data, and then project the Duic table fields to TgtDUICs.hrm, a temporary working-file, for all selected tuples.   For each unique TgtDUICs.hrm tuple, the system then assigns the corresponding Duic field entries to the resulting answer SzDUIC variable. Such instantiated SzDUIC variables ultimately return to the calling `loc_force_DUIC_Totals` predicate which then applies them as selection constraints for the *Oracle* EquipRU table. EquipRU tuples which match the target SzLOC and SzDUIC values are then projected (Auth_qty and Net_short fields only) to the Qtys.hrm temporary file for all selected tuples. The system then adds the Qtys.hrm column data and stores the results to the D_AuthQty and D_OnHand answer variables. Finally the HERMES server calculates the percentage and readiness value, and instantiates the SzDesc answer variable (descriptive text) with data extracted from the LOGTAADS database (via the taads_UICs predicate).

3.5   Remote Client Front End and Multimedia Presentation

As of this writing, the interactive client interface adheres to a data pull mode of operation; as the user graphically specifies a desired query the system responds with the requested data, (presented as a drill-down table). Figures 3 through 5 below show the screens generated as a user drilled first into the *Alexandria* readiness data, and then specified *Alexandria* Battalion Task force (BNTF) readiness data.[2]

Note the plus (+) and minus (-) drill control button color coding currently represents a simplistic percentage based readiness level indicator implemented for this demonstration (Green >= 90% > Yellow => 80% > Red < 80%); the final implementation would render the coloring based on a much more complex user specified data function call. [12, 13]

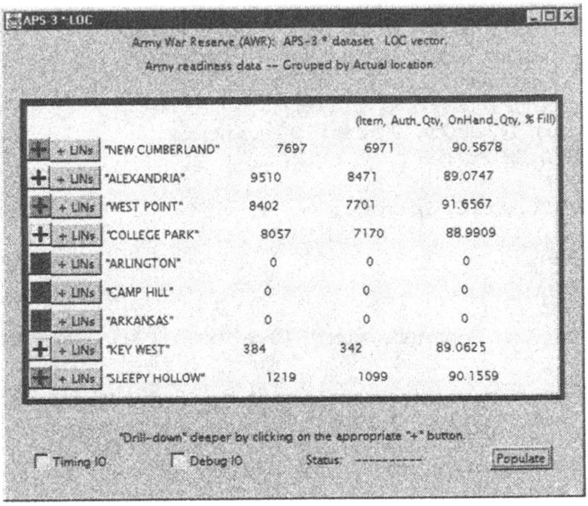

Fig. 3. Screen capture generated for equipment readiness on fictitious supply ships

Clicking on a table entry plus ("+") button causes the system to drill a level deeper into the data. The next levels data then appears indented in the table beneath its parent entry, and the plus button changes mode to minus ("-"); subsequently, clicking on a minus button for any level causes that drill path to collapse.

In the next few months, we will improve the somewhat immature user interface to provide a unified framework for navigating additional AWR multimedia and GIS data via indirect manipulation [14]. We will also add a data "Cut & Paste" and Object Linking and Embedding (OLE) support which will enable users to export client generated data directly into other common documentation editors such as graphical word-processors, spreadsheets, and charting packages.

---

[2] The *actual location* is the same as the *ship name* for Army Prepositioned Stocks-3 (APS-3) afloat stocks. Figure 4 also illustrates two dimensions of the *Alexandria* readiness (1) by Equipment Requirement Code (ERC): P, A, B/C and (2) by next lower unit: BNTF, Brigade (BDE) and Echelons Above Division (EAD) Combat Support and Combat Service Support (CS/CSS).

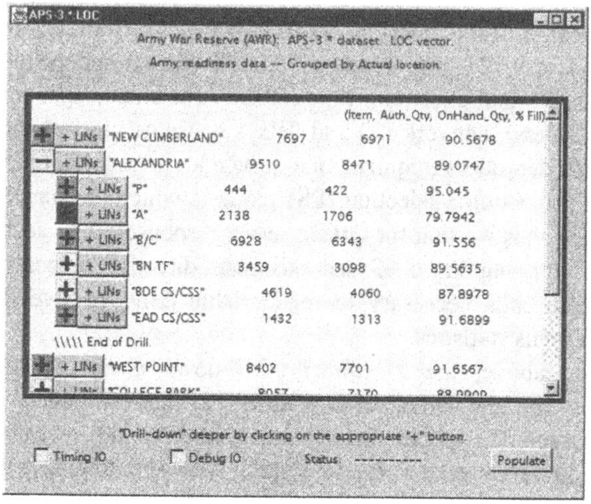

Fig. 4. Screen capture generated for a drill down of the fictitious supply ship *Alexandria*

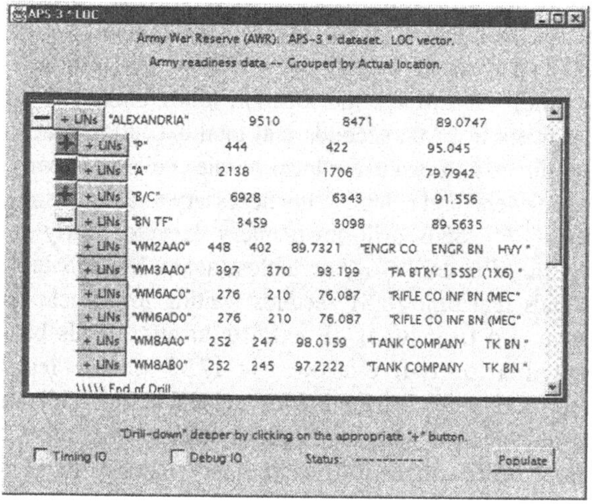

Fig. 5. Screen capture generated for a drill down to the unit level

3.6   Preliminary Execution Timings on Four Queries.

As stated earlier, the data servers exist on three separate machines, connected via 10 Megabit Ethernet LAN.   Clients connect through the Internet via any Java 1.1.x compatible browser (we use HotJava for our demonstrations).   Both Jilad (the Web and remote HERMES server), and Oryx (the LOGTAADS server) are Sparc Ultra 1's, a 167 MHz 64 Bit architecture running Solaris 2.5.   We serve Oracle 8 from Bester, a 233 MHz P5 MMX Gateway PC, running NT Server 4.0.

The initial location status query accesses two Oracle database files (*Aps_Loc* and *EquipRU*, a 155 x 4,721 join renders 731,755 tuples) independently across the network. While the total execution time (at the Java client) appears extreme (14.52 seconds for 9 answers), network I/O and delays consume most of the time. A closer look reveals that this query requires one server login request (expensive) and ten separate Oracle projection / selection (PS) requests which consumed 11.87 Seconds real time (9.74 seconds waiting for Oracle server responses, 2.13 seconds System and User time). The remaining 2.65 seconds map directly to local hermes domain function and math calls necessary to render table joins, resolve the answers, and calculate simple totals statistics.

As mentioned above, the *Alexandria* drill-down query actually invokes two separate queries into the Oracle *EquipRU* (4,721 tuples) table. The first query executes three Oracle PS operations consuming 3.08 seconds real time (2.55 seconds waiting for Oracle server responses, 0.53 seconds System and User time). It returns the *Alexandria* location totals broken down by equipment readiness codes (ERC), three answers in 3.92 seconds real total execution time. The remaining 0.83 seconds map directly to local hermes calls necessary to render table joins, resolve answers, and calculate simple totals statistics.

The second *Alexandria* drill-down query requires thirty-six Oracle PS requests on the *EquipRU* and *Aps_Loc* tables (again 731,755 tuples total) which consume 9.18 seconds real time (8.46 seconds waiting for Oracle server responses, 0.73 seconds System and User time). It extracts the location totals broken down by task force identifiers, three answers in 22.06 seconds real total execution time. The remaining 12.88 seconds map directly to extensive local hermes calls necessary to regroup and join tables, resolve answers, and calculate the necessary totals statistics.

The "*Alexandria – P*" totals drill-down query executes thirty seven Oracle PS operations on the *EquipRU* and *Aps_Loc* tables (again 731,755 tuples total) which consume 9.13 seconds real time (8.81 seconds waiting for Oracle server responses, 0.31 seconds System and User time). It extracts location totals broken by the "P" level readiness identifier, thirty-five answers in 17.95 seconds real total execution time. The remaining 8.82 seconds map directly to local hermes calls necessary to join tables, resolve answers, and calculate the necessary totals statistics.

The "*Alexandria – BNTF*" totals drill-down query accesses two Oracle tables and LOGTAADS data (*Aps-Loc*, *EquipRU* and *WM_MOC* tables), a 155 x 4,721 x 68,146 join which renders 49,866,176,230 potential tuples. This required fourteen Oracle PS requests, consuming 9.13 seconds total real time (8.81 seconds waiting for Oracle server responses, 0.32 seconds System and User time), and sixteen LOGTAADS PS operations, consuming 34.60 seconds total real time (24.50 seconds waiting for the remote hermes server, 10.10 seconds System and User time). It extracts location totals broken down by the "BNTF" force identifier, six answers in 95.74 seconds real total execution time. The remaining 52.01 seconds map directly to local hermes calls necessary to join tables, resolve answers, and calculate the necessary totals statistics.

Please note that this system is currently a proof-of-concept prototype; planned mediator and domain code optimizations should greatly reduce the system execution times [15, 16].

The LOGTAADS data domain, in particular, does not yet support a select function; Pending implementation of such will simultaneously decrease both the required LOGTAADS domain call network traffic and the required search engine answer resolution work. This alone should reduce the "*Alexandria – BNTF*" totals drill-down query by roughly factor of ten. Additionally, the LOGTAADS WM_MOC.txt data file is six months older than the Oracle EquipRU table; several key identifiers cited in the EquipRU table do not exist in our WM_MOC table. As such the seven of thirteen potential "*Alexandria – BNTF*" answers fail in the final join (cited execution time basically applies to rendering thirteen vice six answers).

4 Future Research

A future component of this research may address the computer-assisted extraction of meaningful information and knowledge from large quantities of remote data, text documents, and other media. We envision an experimentally derived [17] heuristic visual tool to allow humans to generate queries against the data to answer questions that would be very hard for unassisted humans to formulate [18]. Other research may include extending the project with an advanced scheduling package that creates delivery schedules for requested items. This may require the development or extension of a temporal database calculus and algebra for queries [19].

We are carefully considering the software engineering and interface [4] characteristics of the presentation tools to ensure it may easily adapt to new sources of data, analysis algorithms, and hardware platforms. Specifically we envision a Java byte-code enabled interface that will allow platform independent access from all major client workstations. [20]

We will also investigate and recommend solutions to various security implications of the mediated data gathering and collaborative planning environment. We will report on the current state of Security Infrastructure Assurance and Information Protection as it relates to our project [21].

Finally, the next stage of this project may utilize the University of Maryland's Collaborative Heterogeneous Interactive Multimedia Platform (CHIMP) technologies [22]. Drawing information directly from distributed networked resources, via Internet or direct data server connections, CHIMP effectively allows us to create dynamic multimedia (data, images, sound, video, and more) packed readiness briefings based on the most current information available. CHIMP technologies allow such briefings to be both interactive, and tailored on-the-fly for specific audiences (according to authenticated privileges).

5 Conclusion

We have built a prototypical system and demonstrated the capability to maintain up-to-date and on-demand data access for AWR planning and analysis. Additionally, we have shown that HERMES can provide a secure, remote, collaborative multimedia presentation of summarized, distributed data.

The type of problem we discuss in this paper is not unique to Army logistics planners. A group of prominent database researchers met, discussed, and published their collective opinion on future prospects concerning database research in February 1990 and again in May 1995 [23]. These researchers stated that significant database research problems included support for multimedia objects, distribution of information, and ease of database management and use [24].

Since the problems we attacked for AWR databases is not unique, we feel the application of HERMES to the networked visualization of heterogeneous AWR data is a significant advancement in database technology and remote multimedia visualization of networked data.

References

1. Subrahmanian, V.S., *et al.*, *HERMES: A Heterogeneous Reasoning and Mediator System.* 1997.
2. Adali, S. and V.S. Subrahmanian, *Amalgamating Knowledge Bases, III - Algorithms, Data Structures, and Query Processing.* Journal of Logic Programming, .
3. Nielson, G.M., *Visualization Takes its Place in the Scientific Community.* IEEE Transactions on Visualization and Computer Graphics, June 1995. 1(2): p. 97-98.
4. Sears, A. and A.M. Lund, *Creating Effective User Interfaces.* IEEE Software, July/August 1997. 14(4): p. 21-24.
5. Horowitz, E., *Migrating Software to the World Wide Web.* IEEE Software, 1998. 15(3): p. 18-21.
6. Antis, J.M., S.G. Eick, and J.D. Pyrce, *Visualizing the Structure of Large Relational Databases.* IEEE Software, January 1996. 13(1): p. 72-79.
7. ASACC, *Information Briefing on Army Data Warehousing.* 1998, Army Strategic and Advanced Computing Center: Washington, DC.
8. Wiederhold, G., *Mediators in the Architecture of Future Information Systems.* IEEE Computer, March 1992. 25(3): p. 38-49.
9. Lu, J.J., A. Nerode, and V.S. Subrahmanian., *Hybrid Knowledge Bases.* IEEE Transactions on Knowledge and Data Engineering, 1996. 8(5 October): p. 773-785.
10. Luke, S., *et al.*, *Ontology-based Web Agents.* Proceedings of First International Conference on Autonomous Agents 1997, AA-97.
11. Stoffel, K., *et al. Semantic Indexing For Complex Patient Grouping.* in *American Medical Informatics Association Annual Fall Symposium (AMIA-97).* 1997.
12. *Army Regulation 220-1, Unit Status Reporting for Field Organizations*, Washington DC: Headquarters, Department of the Army.
13. Smith, T.L. and J.H. Schafer. *Using Machine Learning to Determine United States Army Readiness.* in *Tenth Annual Software Technology Conference (STC '98).* 1998. Salt Lake City, UT.
14. Shneiderman, B. and P. Maes, *Direct Manipulation vs Interface Agents: Excerpts from debates at IUI 97 and CHI 97.* ACM Interactions, 1997. IV(6): p. 42-61.
15. Adali, S., *et al. Query Processing in Distributed Mediated Systems.* in *1996 ACM SIGMOD Conference on Management of Data.* 1996. Montreal, Canada.
16. Chaudhuri, S. and K. Shim. *Query Optimization in the Presence of Foreign Functions.* in *19th VLDB Conference.* 1993.
17. Tichy, W.F., *Should Computer Scientists Experiment More?* IEEE Computer, May 1998. 31(5): p. 32-40.

18. Ullman, J.D., *The database approach to knowledge representation*. Proceedings of the 13th National Conference of the American Association for Artificial Intelligence. AAAI Press, MIT Press, 1996.

19. Voss, D., *Timestamps to Support Valid-Time Indeterminacy in Temporal Databases*, in *Computer Science Doctoral Dissertation*. 1997, Vanderbilt University: Nashville, TN. p. 94.

20. Taft, S.T. *Programming the Internet in Ada 95*. in *Ada Europe*. 1996.

21. Sternal, P. *Information Protection for the 21st Century*. in *Research and Development for Infrastructure Assurance / Information Warfare - Defend*. 1997. Alexandria, VA.

22. Candan, K.S., B. Prabhakaran, and V.S. Subrahmanian. *CHIMP: A Framework for Supporting Multimedia Document Authoring and Presentation*. in *1996 ACM Multimedia Conference*. 1996. Boston, MA.

23. Siberschatz, A., *et al.*, *Database Systems: Achievements and Opportunities*. SIGMOD Record, 1990. **19**(4): p. 6-22.

24. Silberschatz, A., M. Stonebraker, and J. Ullman. *Database Research: Achievements and Opportunities Into the 21st Century*. in *Report of an NSF Workshop on the Future of Database Systems Research, May 26-27 1995*.

A Museum-Oriented Authoring Tool [1]

Alessandro Grimaldi and Tiziana Catarci

Dipartimento di Informatica e Sistemistica
Università degli Studi di Roma "La Sapienza", Via Salaria, 113 - 00198 Roma, Italy
E-mail: [grimaldi | catarci]@infokit.dis.uniroma1.it

Abstract. The multimedial capacities of the last generation computers meet the needs of the recent, new impulse to catalogue, restore and preserve the archaeological patrimony. In this paper we propose an easy-to-use authoring tool suitable to a) help the user in setting up an exhibition or a museum in such a way to match different criteria and satisfy user-defined or structure constraints; and b) prepare several kinds of visits to such exhibitions/museums, each visit being tailored to a certain type of visitor and/or giving particular emphasis to different aspects of the exhibition/museum. In order to lay the foundations of our work a precise definition of the terms *museum* and *visit* is also given.

1   Introduction

In the last few years a lot of work has been done to catalogue and coherently organize the huge artistic and cultural Italian patrimony (see, for instance, Progetto Finalizzato CNR Beni Culturali, 1996). One of the main aspects in this context is the possibility to *virtualize* museums, so to allow anyone to access their exterminate historical-cultural resources without even leaving their homes. However, not much has been done to allow computer unfamiliar people to take active part to this process: most of the existing software is conceived (often unintentionally) for computer experts, and it is hard to use by those who do not possess a computer-oriented culture and mentality. The result is that those programs are often misused by those who would have the possibilities to exploit them at their best, that is the experts of cultural areas (archaeologists, museologists, students of art and so on), yielding a waste of energy and resources. It becomes therefore necessary a further effort in software designing, in the sense that software should be "intelligent" enough to do most of the job, yet simple enough to be used even by those who still see the computer as a *hostile being*. This is one of the goals of our job.

An *authoring system* (e.g. [6],[7],[8]) is one of the possible approaches to the problem of integrating audio, video and graphical resources into one composite

---

[1] Work funded by Programmi MURST, Settore Multimediale, Programma Rete Multimediale nell'evoluzione verso UMTS, linea di ricerca "Applicazione ai Beni Culturali"

S. Jajodia, M.T. Özsu, and A. Dogac (Eds.): MIS'98, LNCS 1508, pp. 148–160, 1998.

document. An authoring system provides visual tools to help the author composing the multimedia application, and the system automatically generates the necessary code. Our work fits in this particular approach. Its main goal is to realize an authoring tool simple enough to allow a non-expert user to set up an exhibition, or a museum, equipped with a certain number of multimedial guided tours. The main features of our proposal are:

a)   *Setting up and visiting real exhibitions/museums*: the author has a "physical" structure (rooms) at her/his disposal, and a number of objects s/he wants to accommodate, according to some subdivision criteria. The structure plan, the physical characteristics of the objects as well as the sorting and the subdivision criteria are input to the system, which produces as output a reasonable disposition, that the author is free to modify in a subsequent step;

b)   *Virtualization of a real exhibition/museum*: the museum is already set up, and the author just wants to "reproduce" it on the computer: in this case the only needed inputs are the room plan and the coordinates of each object;

c)   *Setting up and visiting a virtual exhibition/museum*: as in a), with the relevant difference that there is no constraining physical structure. Objects are arranged in virtual rooms, built by the system itself.

This paper is organized as follows. In Section 2 we briefly present the basic concepts on which the tool builds, namely *exhibition, museum* and *visit*, while in Section 3 we describe the basic features of the proposed authoring tool. Finally, in Section 4 we show how *Matthew* supports the main user's task, namely building an exhibition, by giving a simple example of how it works.

2   Basic Definitions

2.1. *Exhibition* and *Museum*

As a first approximation, an exhibition can be seen as a display of objects related to a single, "enough limited" subject, while a museum collects a number of objects related one another by broader scopes. However, defining precisely what a *single subject* is may be a hard task, also because it is often difficult to establish "who is a minor subject of who": as an example, "*The silex*" can be seen as a minor subject of "*The Mid-Paleolithic*", but the viceversa is also true. It is all up to what the authors have in their minds when preparing an exhibition (or a museum). The solution to this problem is in defining *subject* with the most "open" definition we can find: that is, assuming that a *subject* is simply *any argument we can use for an exhibition* (or a museum). According to this choice, we can formulate the difference between the two terms as follows:

DEFINITION 1. An *exhibition* is a showing of objects related to one subject, and a *museum* is a set of exhibitions.   ♦

Thus, if we find a reasonable model for an exhibition, we automatically get a reasonable model for a museum.

The exhibition of a set of objects is characterized by three elements: a *subject*, a *period of time*, and some *constraints*.

Subject and period of time

Sometimes the period of time is strictly determined by the subject, sometimes the relation is not that obvious; in some cases it can even collapse in a single year, or day. Thus, in general, we can say that for an exhibition to be completely defined we need both of these elements to be specified. We can derive a graphic formalization of these concepts.

Consider a bidimensional space (Figs. 1 and 2); let the x axis be the time axis. We can imagine to enumerate on the y axis all the possible subjects, or at least all the interesting ones. Then, a horizontal segment (or a half line) will represent what we call the *temporal development* of that particular subject. By following this formalism, the terms *exhibition* and *museum* are associated with windows in this space, as shown in figures 1 and 2. Of course, the main difference between them is the height of the window, which in the exhibition case will be such to enclose only one subject, while in the other case it will enclose more than one.

Constraints

There exist different kinds of constraints that either the author wants to impose upon the exhibition, or derive from external circumstances. We classify them as being *objective* or *subjective*. Objective constraints are determined by existing external

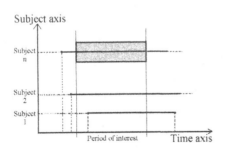

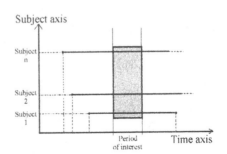

Fig. 1. Representation of an exhibition.   **Fig. 2.** Representation of a museum.

conditions (for example, number and dimensions of the available rooms), while subjective constraints are due to author's choices. We singled out five subclasses of subjective constraints:

- Type of multimedia supports (*audio*, *video*, *sound*, *image* and *text*);
- Final user (*child*, *generic*, *expert*);
- Sorting rules;

- Grouping rules;
- Placement rules (e.g.: space between objects)

Summarizing, we can give the following, more precise, definition of *exhibition*:

DEFINITION 2. If O is the set of objects relevant to an exhibition M, we will say that M *is an exhibition over* O. Given a set of objects O, an exhibition over O is characterized by a triple *{Subject, Period of time, Constraints}*, where

- all objects in O are related to *Subject*
- *Period of time* is a temporal development of *Subject* itself
- *Constraints* is a couple *{Objective constraints, Subjective constraints}* determining a particular arrangement of the objects in O

A *museum* is a set of exhibitions.   ♦

2.2.   Visit

It is reasonable to say that a *visit* refers to a certain subject, developed along a certain period of time. Therefore, from this point of view a visit coincides with what we have just called *exhibition*. However, not all available objects have always to be exposed, for technical, bureaucratic or safety reasons. Indeed, there are limitations that must be imposed upon the visit one wants to build. Among them we can include those constraints specified by the author for teaching or aestethical reasons (object order, disposition, relevance). So, we can define a visit as follows:

DEFINITION 3. A *visit* is a couple *{Exhibition, Temporary Constraints}*, where *Exhibition* is over a set O of objects, and *Temporary Constraints* is a set of rules that both determines a subset of O and forces a new placement of this subset.   ♦

3   *Matthew*

The above definitions have been used as basis for the creation of an authoring tool called *Matthew* (*Museum-oriented Authoring Tool - THEsis Work* [2]). This tool gives an author the possibility to define a structure (that is, a set of rooms), select a set of objects from the available database, and possibly impose sorting, grouping and placement rules. Then, the system generates the exhibition, trying to satisfy all constraints, both deriving from the structure (objective constraints) and specified by the author (subjective constraints). The result is shown to the author, who can make any change s/he desires. *Matthew* can also perform a *self check*, pointing out any problem occurred while satisfying the constraints, together with suggestions and solutions to improve the exhibition quality.

---

[2] This name derives from the fact that the tool was the subject of the Master Thesis of the first author.

It must be pointed out that, though managing multimedia objects, *Matthew* does not actually deal with the typical problems of multimedia authoring (such as media synchronization), since it is meant to be put "on top" of a traditional authoring tool. Indeed, *Matthew*'s output is a high level description of the museum, which will be equipped with visit paths in a near future. This description and the visit paths will be given as input to the lower stratum of the system (i.e., the authoring tool) which will take care of the media related aspects.

Matthew deals with three classes of objects:

- *Pictures*, which includes all objects that can be hung to a wall (i.e., not only paintings but also drawings, carpets, tapestries, etc.).
- *Islands*, comprising those objects which can be placed upon a pedestal (e.g. statues and vases) or placed "horizontal", such as carpets, plastics, and so on.
- *Showcase objects*, comprising all those objects which can be placed inside a *showcase*. Showcases are built by *Matthew* in a pre-processing step of the automatic disposition routine. The author may define size and number of the showcases to be used.

A particular attention has been reserved to the interface. As a basic hypothesis, the author is not an expert computer user, so s/he is supposed to have some difficulties even in using a graphical interface. Trials we made with a set of potential users (e.g.: archaeologists and museum directors) highlighted the features that a "simple enough" interface should offer, namely:

- No menus. Surprisingly enough, such users see a menu as a way to hide information, rather than a tool to organize it.
- Few icons. The iconic language is powerful, but using too many icons may give rise to confused and puzzled users.
- Large use of buttons. A button has an advantage upon an icon: a caption may evidentiate its function, sometimes much better than an image can do.
- Feedback. A change in the appearance of the interface is necessary to inform the author that her/his action has been recognized, and yielded some results.
- *Don't set the user up for a fall* (see [3]). The program must not give the author the chance to accomplish wrong or useless actions. This means that at any step only the minimum set of useful objects must be enabled, and that a strict control must be performed upon any action performed by the author, to trap any dangerous operation and alert her/him before proceeding.

3.1. *Matthew*'s Architecture

Matthew is formed by six modules:

- *Master*, which is the main module. Here the author can select a structure, a set of objects to be shown, sorting, grouping and placement rules, and can start the automatic placement process. The problem of placing different kinds of objects (including showcases) in a predefined set of rooms may be seen as a more general and much complex version of the well-known knapsack problem, as long as each room can be considered as a knapsack. Thus, we propose a heuristic-based solution (see below for more details, or [4] for a complete discussion). The experiments we performed gave good results with respect to both effectiveness of the placement and computation time. This module also lets the author modify the resulting disposition, and (if requested) performs the self check.

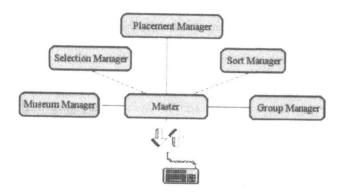

- *Museum Manager*, by which the author defines the rooms to be used in the exhibition. At the present stage of implementation this is a simple editor, allowing one to draw only rectangular rooms with windows and doors.
- *Selection Manager*, which helps the author in selecting, editing and saving sets of objects. A selection is made by specifying the subject of the visit (identified through a suitable set of keywords), the type of final user the exhibition is addressed to, and the multimedia supports to be used. Then the Manager allows the author to browse the resulting selection and discard one or more objects, or some or all of the multimedia components of each single object.
- *Group Manager*, to be used for defining grouping rules. Objects may be grouped in order to highlight particular features of each group, or just to create subsets to be displayed in different rooms. For the moment, a sort rule corresponds to a logic condition created by using the *And/Or* logical connectors.
- *Sort Manager*, a powerful module to create sorting rules.
- *Placement Manager*, which allows the author to specify several parameters, such as the minimum distance between two adjacent objects, the position of the pedestals (along the walls or grouped in the middle of the rooms), and many more.

3.2. Algorithms

As we already stated, disposing some objects in a set of rooms may be a time consuming task given its similarity with a more complex version of the knapsack problem. In fact, roughly speaking, a knapsack problem can be regarded as being a 3-dimensional problem: the involved variables are *size* for the knapsack, and *size* and *weight* for each object. In our problem we not only have many "knapsacks" (rooms), each one with 3 dimensions (width, depth and height, that may differ from one room to another), but also 3 dimensions for each object (again, width, depth and height). Furthermore, we have one more complication: as we said before, the objects we deal with belong to one of three different classes (*pictures*, *islands* and *showcase objects*), each one with its own properties, namely:

- a picture has only two relevant dimensions, and can not be placed in the middle of a room;
- an island has three relevant dimensions, and can be placed in the middle of a room as well as along its walls;
- a showcase object has three relevant dimensions, and has to be put inside a showcase together with other similar objects. Showcases then behave like islands.

Intuitively, it is easy to see how our problem is harder than a simple knapsack, *which is itself an NP-complete problem!* [3]. As a consequence, the placement algorithms we implemented do not try to compute an optimal solution; on the contrary, they search a reasonable object disposition (note that they might have to manage many hundreds of objects). Apart form computational reasons, there is more behind this choice. We must never forget that the solution a computer can provide is (and *must be*) only a starting point, which the author can use to make changes according to her/his own mental model of the exhibition, model that a computer is of course unable to reiterate. There would not be much sense in trying to generate an optimal placement, since the author will modify it anyway. [4]

3.2.1   First Step: Sorting and Grouping

First of all, objects are divided in three sets (of course *pictures*, *islands* and *showcase objects*). Each set is then sorted according to the author's directives (see Section 4). *Matthew* gives the author the possibility to sort objects on any of their features (in ascending and descending order, but even on a custom order), using all or part (enumerated list) of the values that feature takes in the database. If the author doesn't specify a grouping rule, objects are considered as forming one single group; otherwise, they are grouped following that rule.

---

[3] - It is straightforward to prove both that the knapsack problem may be expressed in terms of our problem, and that our problem is in NP.

[4] - This conclusion comes from a wide analyses of the final users' requirements and expectations.

3.2.2   Second Step: Showcase Generation

Showcase objects are then placed in the available showcases. The idea behind the algorithm[5] is to take in consideration one object at a time, to compare its dimensions with the current showcase dimensions and eventually discard it, if it doesn't fit. Showcases are filled one shelf at a time. All the objects remaining after the last showcase has been filled are discarded.

3.2.3   Third Step: Object Placement

Once the necessary showcases have been built, *Matthew* accomodates the objects in the selected rooms. The algorithm used to place the objects is similar to the algorithm used to generate showcases: this sounds obvious, if we think of a showcase as a room, and regard its shelves as room walls. The main difference, of course, is that showcases contain only one class of objects (namely, *showcase objects*), while rooms hold three different classes (the above mentioned *pictures*, *islands* and *showcases*).[6] Let us discuss it with some more details.

The system conceives a museum as a list of *segments*, that is *portions of wall*. Some of these segments are free and available for placing objects, while others cannot be used at this purpose, since they represent doors and windows (or other architectural elements such as columns, niches, curtains, possibly signs, and so on).

The algorithm considers each object in turn and assigns it to one of the free segments by means of a greedy strategy, trying to minimize the number of discarded objects. The main problem that may arise is a *conflict*, i.e. the current object overlaps a previously placed object (see figure 3, where object A conflicts with object B). If this event occurs, the algorithm first tries to shift the conflicting object (A) on the segment until the conflict is resolved. If this is not possible, it looks for an object which can be swapped with A. If such an object can not be found, the algorithm starts moving objects to other segments, until either a) there are no more objects to move (so that A is discarded) or b) enough space has been freed to set A in place. Notice that no swapping or moving violating author's sorting rules is performed.

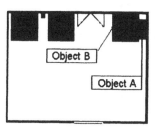

Fig. 3. Conflicting objects.

---

[5] The following holds when the author explicitly mentions the dimensions of the available showcases. Actually, *Matthew* can manage "automatic" showcases, but in such a case the algorithm is extremely simple, and we will not discuss it here. See [4] for details.

[6] In the following we will cover the most general case, leaving particular cases (e.g.. virtual structures) out of consideration.

4   Building an Exhibition

The best way to understand how *Matthew* works is providing an example. So, let us suppose we are building an exhibition about "The Celts". This main task can be divided in six sub-tasks, each one corresponding to a module:

- Definition of a structure (set of rooms) (*Museum Manager*)
- Selection of the objects to be exposed (*Selection Manager*)
- Definition of a sorting rule (*Sort Manager*)
- Definition of a grouping rule (*Group Manager*)
- Definition of a placement rule (*Placement Manager*)
- Object disposition and self check (*Master*)

4.1   Definition of a Structure

Clicking on the "Museum Manager..." button on the *Master* module (see Fig. 11) we enter the building editor, by which we can define a two room building, as in Fig.

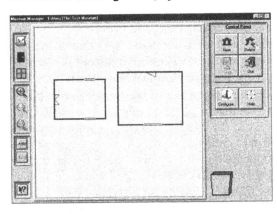

4, by just dragging and dropping the upper left corner icons: these will be the rooms in which our exhibition will be realized. We decide to save them (using the "Save" icon) under the name "The Test Museum", and then the "Quit" icon takes us back to the *Master*.

Fig. 4. The *Museum Manager*.

4.2 Selection of the Objects

The a set of objects to be shown has now to be selected, so click on the "Selection Manager... " button. The window shown in Fig. 5 opens, and in the first combo box we can input the subject of our exhibition: "The Celts", along with some keywords defining this subject. Let us assume we want to set up an exhibition for *generic* and *expert* users, using all available multimedia components. Now, pressing the "Start..." button causes the

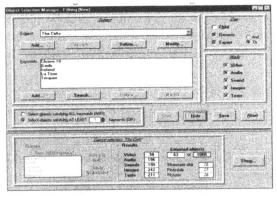

Fig. 5. The *Selection Manager*.

selection process to start, and the results to be shown in the lower frames. In this example we have 83 objects satisfying the query. Clicking on the "Show..." button a new window opens, where we can discard some objects or any of their multimedia components. At the end of this phase we save this set of objects for later use (say we choose the name "Exhibition for Generic and Expert Users"), finally quitting back to the *Master*.

4.3   Definition of a Sorting Rule

Third step. Suppose we need a sorting rule, so open the *Sort Manager* and enter the window shown in Fig. 6. We build a rule with "*Place of construction*" as the main key

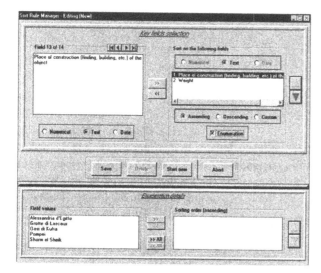

and "*Weight*" as a secondary key. Note that a key may be enumerated: using the lower lists we can choose which field values are to be considered in the sorting process. We decide to save this rule with the name "*Place (Enum) + Weight (Asc)*", and get back to the *Master* once again.

Fig. 6. The *Sort Manager*.

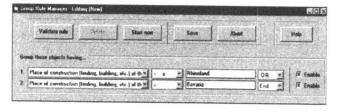

Fig. 7. The *Group Manager*.

4.4   Definition of a Grouping Rule

Now, imagine that we want to group the objects, since we need to highlight all those objects found or built in Germany. The "Group Manager..." button opens the window in Fig. 7, where we compose the condition "Place = 'Rhineland' OR Place = 'Bavaria'", which will act as a

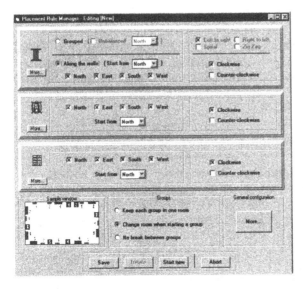

Fig. 8. The *Placement Manager*.

filter during the placement routine, grouping together all objects which satisfy it. Let us save the condition as "German sites".

4.5   Definition   of   a   Placement Rule

Finally, we decide to change the default placement rule, which puts pedestals in the middle of the rooms, as we want to put all pedestals along the walls. So, we enter the *Placement Manager* (Fig. 8) and set up this parameter (see the upper frame). In this simple example we decide not to change any of the remaining parameters (space between objects, screen colors, size, number and dimensions of showcases, group emphasizing, and so on). We save this rule with the name "Default + Pedestals along the walls".

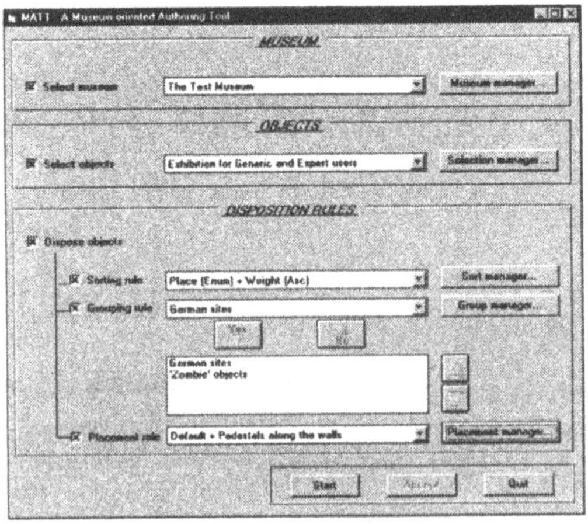

4.6 Object Disposition and Self Check

Exiting the *Placement Manager* takes us back to the *Master* form (Fig. 9) where all fields have been automatically updated. The button "Start" starts the automatic disposition process. After few seconds (10 seconds on a PC 486/100 with 8 Mb of RAM) the result is shown (Fig. 10), and we have the possibility to move objects around, by simply dragging them with the mouse, to build the

Fig. 9. The *Master* module.

exhibition exactly the way we mean it. Additional information may be obtained acting on the leftmost icons in the frame.

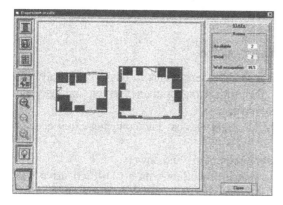

Fig. 10. The resulting disposition.

For example, the bulb icon activates the self check (Fig. 11). The system analyzes the results and gives the author some suggestions about how s/he might vary constraints and parameters to get a better exhibition, for example optimizing the wall space. Each suggestion is explained in details, so that even inexperienced users can operate without problems.

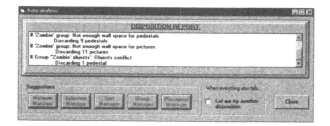

Fig. 11. Self-check results.

5   Conclusions

In this paper we have presented the basic definitions which are exploited in *Matthew*, a user-oriented authoring system, and we have discussed its main characteristics (see [4] for a complete description). *Matthew* is thought for authors who want to set up one or more exhibitions ranging over a set of objects, which are stored in a multimedia database. The author is allowed to select from such a database the objects to be shown, and to impose some constraints. A reasonable, constraint-satisfying exhibition is automatically generated, which the author can change by moving or eliminating some objects, or by reviewing and editing the criteria previously defined.

Matthew may be proficuously used for several purposes. First, while setting up a museum there is no need of physically moving objects, as placement criteria can be varied and tested in a few seconds. Second, not only there is the possibility to virtualize real museums (for example, to realize touch-screen kiosks to be integrated in a real visit), but also virtual exhibitions can be built (for example, to show in a single environment all the paintings of a certain author, which in reality are spread over the world) and widely distributed (CD-ROM's, Internet...) for a massive diffusion of art and culture.

Summarizing, the main features of our work are:

- originality: to the best of our knowledge there seems to be no other software product specifically thought for supporting authors setting up generic exhibitions in any kind of environment;
- a really friendly interface, meant for those who have no computer experience at all;
- a reasonable trade-off between simplicity of use and power;
- a low cost of implementation: a standard Pentium with a CD-ROM drive will suffice. The current version of *Matthew* has been developed using a standard PC 486/100 and 8 MB of RAM;
- no training time needed: anyone can become an author in a blink!

We are currently working to improve the present version of the system, from the point of view of both interface and algorithms. The next step will be to implement the creation of visit paths, by using interactive 3-D rendering. As for this last topic, our work is proceeding along similar lines to [1], [2] and [5].

References

1. Boyle, J., Fothergill, J.E., Gray, P.M.D.: Amaze: a three dimensional graphical user interface for an object oriented database, 2nd International Workshop on Interfaces to Databases, 2:7, 117-131
2. Ciabatti, E., Cignoni, P., Montani, C., Scopigno, R.: Towards a distributed 3D virtual museum, Proceedings of International Conference on Advanced Visual Interfaces (AVI 98), L'Aquila, Italy, 1998
3. Foley, J., Van Dam, A., Feiner, S., Hughes, J.: Computer graphics: principles and practice, Addison-Wesley, 1990
4. Grimaldi, A.: *Matthew*: uno strumento autore per l'allestimento automatico di musei, Master Thesis, Dipartimento di Informatica e Sistemistica, Universita' degli Studi di Roma "La Sapienza", 1998.
5. Massari, A., Saladini, L., Hemmje, M., Sisinni, F.V.: Virgilio: A non-immersive VR system to browse multimedia database, Proceedings of the IEEE International Conference on Multimedia Computing and Systems, IEEE Computer Society Press, Los Alamitos, CA, 573-580
6. TenCORE and PC PILOT: A Comparison of Two Authoring Languages - Part I, Interactive Learning International, 1:2, October - December 1984.
7. Encarnação, J.L., Foley, J.D. (Eds.): Multimedia, Springer-Verlag, Berlin, 1994.
8. AuthorBase. http://wwwetb.nlm.nih.gov/authorb/irx, 1995

Modeling and Retrieving Audiovisual Information
- A Soccer Video Retrieval System -

A. Woudstra[1], D.D. Velthausz[2]*, H.J.G. de Poot[2], F. Moelaert El-Hadidy[2],
W. Jonker[1], M.A.W. Houtsma[2], R.G. Heller[1], J.N.H. Heemskerk[1]

[1] KPN Research
P.O. Box 15000, 9700 CD, Groningen, the Netherlands
Phone: +31-50 -5821124, Fax: +31-50 -3122415
E-mail: {Woudstra, Jonker, Heller, Heemskerk}@research.kpn.com
[2] Telematica Instituut
P.O. Box 589, 7500 AN, Enschede, the Netherlands
Phone: +31-53-4850485, Fax: +31-53-4850400
E-mail: {Velthausz, Poot, Moelaert}@telin.nl

Abstract. This paper describes the results of an ongoing collaborative project between KPN Research and the Telematics Institute on multimedia information handling. The focus of the paper is the modelling and retrieval of audiovisual information. The paper presents a general framework for modeling multimedia information (ADMIRE) and discusses the application of this framework to the specific area of soccer video clips. The core of the paper is the integration of feature extraction and concept inference in a general framework for representing audio visual data. The work on feature extraction is built on existing feature extraction algorithms. The work on concept inference introduces a new approach to assigning semantics to collections of features in order to support concept-based retrieval, rather than feature-based retrieval. Finally, the paper describes our experiences with the implementation of the methods and techniques within the ADMIRE framework using a collection of commercially available tools. The latter is done by implementing a soccer video clip annotation and query tool.

1 Introduction

The development of the WEB has lead to an increasing research effort into methods and techniques for the realization of multimedia applications ([8], [18], [21], [32]), like video-on-demand, tele-shopping, and e-commerce. A major part of this research effort is devoted towards multimedia database management ([1], [4], [16]), driven by the expectation that multimedia database management systems will form the

---

* Contact person for ADMIRE framework

S. Jajodia, M.T. Özsu, and A. Dogac (Eds.): MIS'98, LNCS 1508, pp. 161–173, 1998.

cornerstone of the next generation of multimedia applications, just like relational database management systems are at the heart of current information systems.

Multimedia database research brings together researchers from different disciplines like databases, image processing, information retrieval, and artificial intelligence, and thus covers a wide variety of issues. The research in this paper concentrates on issues related to modeling of audiovisual data to support ad-hoc retrieval of video clips. The motivation for this research is the fact that the amount of video data in Web based information systems is growing so fast that techniques for efficient retrieval are mandatory. Current practice is semi-automated classification and manual annotation of video material after which the video material is stored and can be retrieved based on (keywords from) the classification and annotation scheme being used. This approach has a serious drawback: the retrieval can only be done based on a predefined classification and annotation. So one can not search on issues not covered by the classification and annotations. To overcome this problem there is a need for retrieval based on the content of the video, rather than on annotations. (An analogy can be drawn with text retrieval, where we have seen a shift from retrieval based on classification by means of indices towards full text retrieval [10]). So, what is needed are retrieval techniques that act directly on the video content. These techniques are commonly denoted as content-based retrieval techniques ([9], [11], [20], [28]).

A widely accepted first step towards content-based retrieval is feature extraction. Features are interpretation independent characteristics. Examples are pitch and noise for audio, and color histogram and shape for images. Currently some impressive results have been shown on retrieval of images based on feature extraction ([7], [12], [15], [23], [25]). The approach is purely based on features and does not incorporate any conceptual interpretation of the images. The approach is roughly a query-by-example approach in which the system is asked to retrieve images 'similar' to an example image. Quite a number of features have been identified and a lot of feature detection algorithms already exist ([3], [13], [22]).

However, query-by-example is not always appropriate, especially in the case of video clips. In the Soccer domain, for example, instead of providing the system with an example video shot of a goal, a user simply wants to issue a query like 'show me all goals of this match'. Therefore, a next step is adding semantics to (collections of) features. For example, from a collection of features (e.g. whistle sound in audio, grouped players in video, ball in goal area, etc.) one can infer that a goal has happened. Some simple but effective interpretation techniques are already available, for example, using color histograms of individual video frames for shot detection in videos ([2], [27]). For real content-based retrieval a more fine-grained approach is needed, for example, in the soccer domain one must be able to infer that an object that has a round shape and a black and white color histogram is a ball. Given that a video can be seen as a sequence of frames, many techniques applied to images can be used. An additional difficulty that is introduced by videos is temporal relationships, such a tracking objects through a sequence of frames.

In the this paper we present our approach towards content-based retrieval of video clips based on an extensive modeling of the content of the videos. The main focus of the research is:

- to refine and assess the ADMIRE framework (see below) for modeling audiovisual data for content-based retrieval;
- to develop a concept inference technique and validate it in the context of soccer video clips;
- to investigate which steps to automate and implement a prototype to support that.

Our approach covers both feature extraction and semantic interpretation (we call it 'concept extraction'). As a general representation framework, ADMIRE [29] (see Chapter 2) is used. Roughly ADMIRE distinguishes three levels: the raw data level, the feature level, and the concept level (where interpretations of data objects are given, such as player and ball). In this framework specific techniques for the representation of raw data, features, and concepts can be put, as well as specific techniques for feature extraction and concept inference [24]. Feature extraction and concept inference is given in Chapter 3. The validation of the approach is done by means of the implementation of a soccer video retrieval system [19] described in Chapter 4. Apart from validating the approach the implementation also served as a means to assess the quality of generally available tools for the manipulation of audiovisual data.

2   ADMIRE Model

Audiovisual information consists usually of three types of media: audio, video and text (e.g. subtitles). To disclose this information efficiently we first need to represent it in a model. This model should support the representation of the different types of media in a uniform way. Information should be characterized at different aggregation levels (e.g. frame, shot, coverage). Further, the model should support different types of relationships (i.e. spatial, temporal) and a wide variety of query mechanisms.

Existing, multimedia models focus mostly on a single aspect of multimedia information, like presentation (e.g. PREMO), or exchange of documents, or on a particular format (e.g HyTime). Models that do facilitate content-based information retrieval in general are for example MORE [26], VODAK [14], CORE [31], AIR [15]. These models either do not support a layered definition of information objects (e.g. MORE and VODAK) or can only represent the content of specific unstructured media types (e.g. AIR). The ADMIRE model [29] can be seen as a generalization of the existing models. It resembles the CORE model but offers more flexibility in modeling object relationships. ADMIRE emphasizes on the disclosure of all kinds of forms and types of existing digital information [30]. It uses an object-oriented modeling technique together with a layered definition of information objects. It is suitable for representing multimedia information and thus audiovisual information.

An information object in ADMIRE consists of different properties, *raw data* (a sequence of elementary data units), *format* (a representation of the raw data, e.g. MPEG-1), *attribute* (characterization of the raw data that can not be extracted from the raw data and its format in relation to the external world, e.g. creation date), *feature* (a domain-independent representation of the raw data and format, e.g. color histogram), and *concept* (a domain-dependent and format-independent semantic interpretation of the other property types); *relations* refer to other information objects. Properties are modeled in a three-layer hierarchy, see Fig. 1. The lowest layer is the data layer. It contains the raw data, format and attribute properties. All the properties in this layer are stored as they convey information that cannot be determined differently. The feature and concept layers contain information that can be determined (respectively via feature extraction and concept extraction) using the properties of the lower layers and extraction algorithms (for features) and (domain) knowledge rules for concepts. As opposed to features, concepts are context dependent, different concepts can be inferred from the same lower layers. For example, a 'thumb pointing upwards' has a different interpretation for scuba-divers than for e.g. stock brokers. The context only influences the usefulness of particular features.

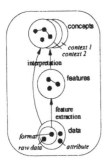

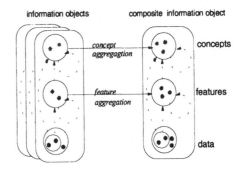

Fig. 1. Information object operations.   **Fig. 2.** Property aggregation operations.

Information in the ADMIRE model can be modeled at multiple levels of granularity, e.g. an individual frame or a whole movie. Through the use of composite relations logical structures between the information objects can be modeled. For example, a video can subsequently be decomposed into a sequence of scenes, shots, and eventually frames. The composite relationships facilitate aggregation of property values, see Fig. 2. In addition to the layout information conveyed in the information object's properties, i.e. the format, the layout structure of a composite information object is represented by the spatial and temporal relations.

An example of a composite information object for audiovisual information is a TV-coverage. Within a TV-coverage we distinguish the following information object classes: *scene* (a sequence of semantic coherent shots), *shot* (continuous recording of audiovisual material), *video shot* (a successive collection of frames, see Fig. 4, *audio track* (shot's audio part), *text title* (e.g. actual score, play time, name of player that received a yellow card), and *frame* (a 2-dimensional image sample). This is presented in Fig. 3.

To model any subpart of an information object we introduce the term 'pseudo' as these objects are not retrievable, only via their accompanying (basic or composite) information objects, see [29]. The data layer of a pseudo information object refers to a subset of the raw data and format of the accompanying retrievable information object. For example, (a pseudo frame object) a rectangle box (e.g. indicating a ball or player) within a frame, see Fig. 4, and (a pseudo video shot object) correlated successive boxes within a video shot, e.g. indicating the ball (labeled with '1' in Fig. 4). Similarly, an audio-track can have accompanying pseudo objects, e.g. that part of the track that indicates the reporter's voice. Notice that a pseudo video shot object is a composite object, i.e. composed of pseudo frame objects, see [30] for detailed description. Although these pseudo information objects are not directly retrievable they are very helpful during the inference of property values of retrievable information objects and provide a flexible way to model relations, see [29].

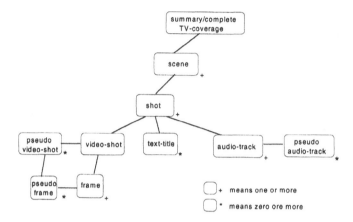

Fig. 3. Hierarchy of information objects within a summary- or complete TV-coverage.

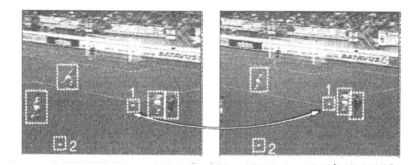

Fig. 4. Example of a video shot information object (IO) consisting of two successive frame IOs. The frame information objects may contain multiple pseudo frame IOs. Corresponding pseudo frame objects, e.g. indicated by '1', form a pseudo video-shot IO.

3 Extraction and Inference

Previous approaches for content-based information retrieval focused on manual attachment or automated properties extraction and identification of information objects. We propose a combination of these. First, we compare these approaches. Manual attachment is good for information reduction, but lacks consistency [33] and details and is labor intensive. Automatic property extraction requires massive common sense knowledge bases (like Cyc [34]), which are slow, cumbersome [17] and fail unique determination of concepts [5]. Semi-automatic systems combine the best of manual and automatic extraction. Humans can give semantic descriptions, annotations [12], while computers are more precise and consistent in measurements and can propagate annotations [6]. Since multimedia information extraction involve technologies from various disciplines (e.g. image process, pattern recognition, AI, neural networks) and most of these technologies are continuously changing and improving, we need an approach that can easily adapt to the future needs. In a fourth approach, sophisticated manual, human resources are used to 'simulate' existing or future algorithms, introducing restrictions to a subset of key-frames and requiring human labeling as error prone as the algorithms. This approach supports the simulation of future capabilities, e.g. when new algorithms become available.

In the soccer prototype the identification of (pseudo) information objects is partly automated. For example, via pair wise comparison of two successive frames, correlated pseudo frame objects (and thus pseudo video shot information objects) can be found, see Fig. 4. Given a pseudo video shot information, additional features are extracted, i.e. motion features. Further, the identification of concepts like goal events, involving the combination of multiple pseudo shot information objects, can be done. These are inferred from the features and attribute data. . This is discussed in the next section. A similar hierarchy exists for the audio track. Another example is the detection of scene breaks by comparing successive shot information objects. These examples illustrate that concept inference is a bottom up approach, see ([30], [24]).

3.1 Property Aggregation

In an information object, features are extracted from data and concepts are inferred from features and attribute data. The properties of composite information object, as presented in Fig. 2, can be determined using the inferred properties of the underlying information objects. This operation is called property aggregation. There are two different ways to derive concepts of a composite information object via features aggregation and concept aggregation. See Fig. 5 for an example.

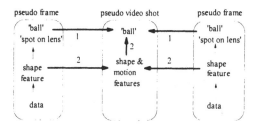

Fig. 5. Example of feature (2) and concept aggregation (1) for two pseudo frames using motion feature information and knowledge that a moving object can not be a fixed spot on the lens.

3.2 Inference Rules for a Soccer Example

Concepts become pronounced at a sufficiently high level of abstraction in the information object hierarchy. Nevertheless, they can not be inferred with absolute certainty. Hence, we incorporate uncertainty in our inference mechanism, discussed in [24]. Take for example the inference of the concept *ball*. Using the shape feature in a frame information object to identify the concept *ball*, may not only identify the ball but also a spot on the camera for example. If the inference takes place on the video shot level, spatial and temporal features, e.g. motion can be combined and inference happens with a higher certainty. The inference of, e.g. the concept *ball*, should thus be delayed. In this manner a *ball* and *spot* can be distinguished, as shown in Fig. 4 where '1' indicates the ball and '2' a spot.

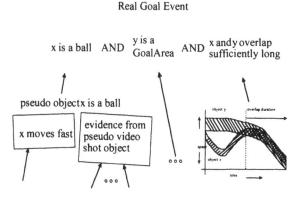

Fig. 6. Schema of the inference of the concept Goal shot.

Object motion can often be told from camera motion (pan, tilt, roll, zoom), after identification of some fixed points, e.g. spots on the soccer field. Having defined a distance measure, e.g. between objects' boundaries, spatio-temporal phenomena like: player *A* getting the ball *B* from player *C* may be inspected. For the soccer prototype a set of key events and key objects where defined for every information (pseudo)object layer in the hierarchy, e.g. at the pseudo frame level and pseudo video shot level *ball* is a supported concept (i.e., inference rules exist for it). At the pseudo video shot level the event *goal shot* is also supported as interaction between the *ball* and the *goal* object. At the audio track level *cheering audience* is a supported pseudo object, etc. An example of the combination of evidence for a *goal shot* is shown in Fig. 6.

4 Implementation

This chapter describes the implementation of the Soccer Video Retrieval System (SVRS). The implementation forms a validation of the information modeling approach described in the previous chapters. In addition, it serves as a means to assess the quality of generally available tools and algorithms for the manipulation of video data. The architecture and the mapping of the information model onto the architecture is described. This architecture provides for storing videos at the raw data, feature and concept levels. In order to extract this data from the raw video material and store it in the multimedia database an *annotation module* was implemented. Retrieving this pre-annotated information is done by means of a *query module*.

4.1 SVRS Architecture

The SVRS is implemented as a client/server application using the Informix Universal Server (IUS) as the object-relational database platform. The clients are implemented on Windows NT 4.0 machines using Delphi and IUS query tools. Communication between the clients and server takes place using ODBC. All Soccer data is stored at the server side. Raw video material is stored in Quicktime format. The clients contain several applications for manipulating the data. The Universal Server is extended with a number of software libraries called DataBlades that provide data storage and management functionality. The SVRS uses DataBlades for video (Informix), image (Excalibur), audio information retrieval (AIR by Musclefish) and text (Excalibur).

The architecture revealed two weaknesses of the currently available multimedia database technology. First, there is the impedance mismatch between the data models at client and server sides. The ADMIRE information model perfectly maps upon an object oriented data model. At the client side an object oriented implementation could be used, while at the server side, the object-relational IUS lacks true object oriented characteristics such as inheritance and encapsulation. It therefore forced us to implement all data types in a relational table format. A second limitation is the lack of support for continuous video streams, which requires either the transmission of complete video clips before playout or the development of add-on streaming functionality. A solution for this problem is a streaming DataBlade within IUS which is currently not available.

4.2   SVRS Annotation Module

As stated in the introduction of this paper, we were interested in tools that support the automatic annotation processes. In our implementation, the annotation process can be seen as a 'human supervised approach'. This differs from the initial approach we proposed in section 0 for simplicity reasons. Although the user is supported by several tools (e.g., feature extraction) still a number of decisions and corrections have to be made manually.

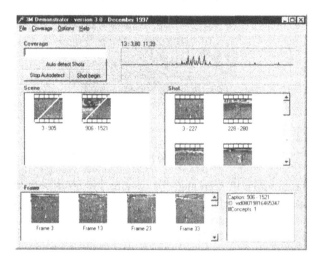

Fig. 7. User interface of the SVRS annotation module, the upper right window shows the color histogram of the current frame.

The level of automation that can be achieved with currently available feature extraction technology in a real-world application is still very basic. The annotation module *automatically* divides videos into frames and supports automatic shot detection based on differences in color histograms of successive frames. This is based on functionality offered by the image DataBlade for extracting and storing a color, shape and texture index of each image. Automatically detected shots can be manually corrected. In addition, some very limited automated detection and tracking of pseudo frame information objects is supported, e.g. the tracking of players and the ball, as illustrated in Fig. 4. Finally, the audio DataBlade is used for indexing and storing sound features of audio fragments. All additional feature and concept annotation has to be done manually. The feature and concept annotations are used for comparison and inference to support retrieval (see below).

4.3   SVRS Query Module

The query module was built to retrieve previously annotated information from the database. Fig. 8 shows a screen-dump of the query module. The query module supports standard functions like viewing video clips (including fast forwarding, rewinding, pause and stop) as well as querying video clips based on annotated (or inferred) concepts.

Fig. 8. User interface of the SVRS query module.

In Fig. 8 the example of searching for exciting moments with the help of audio features is displayed. Exciting moments in the soccer game were manually selected and used to define the distinguishing characteristics of the audio information features such as duration, pitch, tone, and loudness. These patterns were used to automatically search for similar audio tracks in the video clips using the functionality of the AIR DataBlade. The query module returns an ordered list of exciting moments that can directly be displayed on the screen by simple mouse clicks.

The current prototype implementation offers basic support for inference. Some simple rules like a moving round shape with black and white color histogram is a ball are implemented as well as some limited inference on audio as explained above. Improving this inference is one of the major topics we currently work on.

5 Conclusions

In this paper we presented an integrated approach towards the modeling and retrieval of audiovisual information. The approach includes an overall modeling framework (ADMIRE), a formalism for concept representation and inference, as well as an experimental implementation environment with tools supporting modeling, annotation, and retrieval of audiovisual information.

In the introduction we listed the main research issues of the project. As far as the assessment of ADMIRE is concerned we conclude that ADMIRE is a very useful framework for structuring the overall representation of audiovisual information. Especially, the explicit distinction between feature level and concept level offers a strong modeling advantage. Explicit concept modeling and inference allows querying at the conceptual level. The latter is an important improvement over existing approaches, which lack the notion of concept inference and as a result only offer querying at the feature level (mostly by means of query-by-example).

As far as the refinement of ADMIRE is concerned we recall that ADMIRE is a modeling framework. In order to use ADMIRE in the context of a specific application the framework has to be populated by adequate representations at the data, feature, and concept level. In our research we focused on refining ADMIRE by providing a representation formalism for concept modeling and inference. We based our formalism on knowledge representations from artificial intelligence and presented a logic based formalism augmented with an uncertainty model. The formalism supports multi-modal inference, i.e. combining information from different media (e.g. audio and video) to infer context dependent concepts.

Although our experiments with inference are in an early stage, we already conclude that fully automated inference with an acceptable degree of certainty for inferred concepts is limited to very specific and well defined concepts here. In addition, we of course face the same problems as people working on knowledge representation in general.

One of the current shortcomings of the inference model is that it lacks adequate representation of spatio-temporal information. At the moment the way to represent the temporal information to explicitly model dependencies between concepts. We will look for an appropriate temporal logic to have explicit time modeling.

An additional focus of our research is the investigation of the level of automation that can be achieved with currently available techniques. We distinguish two areas: annotation and database support. As far as annotation is concerned, we conclude that fully automated annotation is not feasible, not even at the feature level. Actually only for simple features like color histograms fully automated annotation is feasible, however, for more completes features like shape or object recognition the only feasible way is a human supervised annotation process. At the concept level the situation is even worse, although concept inference can be of help for very simple concepts, also here human supervision is indispensable.

As far as the database support is concerned, we have to conclude that commercially available systems have a long way to go before they can offer integrated support for multimedia data. The main issue being the integration problem. Multimedia data management brings together techniques from various disciplines. What is needed therefore is an open data base management kernel that allows plug-in of the various techniques. This is understood by leading providers of database technology like Oracle, IBM, and Informix. However, their current products are based on traditional database management kernels with add-ons to support multimedia. As a result the kernels do not offer the level of openness to allow tight integration of the various techniques which is an absolute prerequisite to support multi-modal retrieval.

Finally, we mention our future work. The main emphasis will be on concept inference and generalization of results. The work on concept inference will focus on modeling context dependent inference, and spatio-temporal reasoning. The work on generalization will focus on the applicability of the approach in the soccer domain to other (non-sports) domains.

References

1. S. Adali., K.S. Candan, Y. Papakonstantinou, and V.S. Subrahmania, *Query Caching and Optimization in Distributed Media Systems*. In Proc. of SIGMOD'96, Canada, pp137-148.
2. P. Aigraine, P. Joly and V. Longueville, *Medium Knowledge-Based Macro-Segmentation of Video into Sequences*. In Intelligent Multimedia Information Retrieval M. T. Maybury (Ed.) AAAI/MIT Press, 1997, pp 159-173
3. A. Akutsu, Y. Tonomura, Y. Ohba, and H. Hashimoto, *Video Indexing Using Motion Vectors*. In Proc. of SPIE Visual Comm. and Image Processing '92, Boston, Massachusetts, pp343-350, 1992
4. C. Baumgarten, and K. Meyer-Wegener, *Towards a Scalable Networked Retrieval System for Searching Multimedia Databases*. SIGIR'97 Networked Information Retrieval workshop, Philadelphia, July, 1997
5. C.H.C. Leung, J. Hibler, and N. Mwara, Content-based Retrieval in Multimedia Databases, In *Computer Graphics*, Vol. 28 No. 1, February 1994, pp 24-28
6. R.W. Picard and T.P. Minka, Visual texture for annotation, In *Multimedia Systems, Springer Verlag*, Vol. 3, No. 1, 1995, pp 3-13
7. J. C. Fuller Bach, A. Gupta, A. Hampapur, B. Horowitz , R. Humphrey, R Jain and C. Shu, *Virage image search engine: An open framework for image management*. In Proc. of the Symposium on Storage & Retrieval for Image and Video Databases VI, IS&T/SPIE, San Jose, California, Feb. 1996
8. M.G. Brown, J.T. Foote, G.J.F Jones, K. Sparck Jones and S.J. Young, *Automatic Content-based Retrieval of Broadcast News*. In Proceedings of ACM Multimedia, pp 35-43, San Francisco, 1995
9. S.F. Chang, W. Chen, H. Meng, H. Sundaram, and d. Zhong, VideoQ: *An automatic content based video search system using visual cues*. In Proc. of ACM Multimedia '97, Seattle, Washington, Nov. 1997
10. M.W. Davis and W.C. Ogden. *QUILT: Implementing a Large Scale Cross-Language Text Retrieval System*. In Proc. of SIGIR'97, Philadelphia, USA, pp. 91-98, July 1997.
11. M.E. Davis, *Media streams: representing video for retrieval and repurposing*, PhD. Thesis, MIT, 1995
12. M. Flickner, H. Sawhney, W. Niblack, J. Ashley, Q. Huang, B. Dom, M. Gorkani, J. Hafner, D. Lee, D. Petkovic, D. Stelle and P. Yanker. *Query by Image and Video content: The QBIC System*, IEEE Computer, September 1995, pp23-32
13. R.C. Gonzalez, & Woods, R.E. (1992). *Digital Image Processing*. Addison-Wesley
14. Gu J., and E.J. Neuhold, *A data model for multimedia information retrieval*. Proc. of 1st Int. Conf. on Multimedia Modeling, Singapore, 1993, p. 113-127
15. V.N. Gudivada, V.V Raghavan, and K. Vanapipat, *A Unified Approach to data Modelling and Retrieval for a Class of Image database applications*. In Multimedia Database Systems, Issues and Research Directions, Subrahmanian, V.S., S. Jajodia (Eds.), Springer Verlag, pp37-78, 1996
16. W.I. Grosky, *Managing Multimedia Information Database Systems*. In Communications of the ACM, Vol. 40., No. 12, pp 72-80
17. V. Burrill, Group I Report: Authoring Systems, In *Multimedia Systems and Applications*, J.L. Encarnação, J.D. Foley (Eds.), Springer-Verlag, 1994, pp 11-23
18. A.G. Hauptmann, and M. Witbrock. *Informedia: News-on-Demand Multimedia Information Acquisition and Retrieval*. In Intelligent Multimedia Retrieval. Maybary (Ed.), AAAI/MIT Press 1997, pp 215-239

19. J.N.H. Heemskerk, R.G. Heller, W. Jonker, E.J. Sommer & A. Woudstra (1997). *Multi Media Manifestation Part II: Implementation of a Soccer VDS*. KPN Research, R&D-RA-97-1036

20. R. Lienhart, S. Pfeiffer, and W. Effelsberg, *Video Abstracting*. In Communications of the ACM, Vol. 40, No.12, December 1997, pp55-62

21. I. Mani, D. House, M.T. Maybury and M. Green, *Towards Content-Based Browsing of Broadcast News Video*, In Intelligent Multimedia Information Retrieval, M. T. Maybury (Ed.) AAAI/MIT Press, 1997, pp 241-258

22. J.R. Parker, *Algorithms for Image Processing and Computer Vision*. John Wiley & Sons, Inc. 1997

23. A. Pentland, R. Picard, and S. Sclaroff, Photobook: *Tools for Content Based Manipulation of Image Databases*. In International Journal on Computer Vision, Vol. 18, No. 3, 1996, pp 233-154.

24. H.J.G. de Poot, F. Moelaert El-Hadidy and D.D. Velthausz (1997). *Multi Media Manifestation Part I: Modelling a Soccer VDS using ADMIRE*. Telematica Instituut, internal report IRS/97020.

25. R.K. Srihari, *Automatic Indexing and Content-Based Retrieval of Captioned Images*. In Special Issue of Computer, IEEE, September 1995 Content-Based Image Retrieval Systems, pp 49-56

26. K. Tsuda, and K. Yamamoto, M. Hirakawa, and T. Ichikawa, *MORE: An object-oriented data model with a facility for changing object structures*. IEEE on Knowledge and Data Engineering, vol. 3-4, '91, p. 444-460

27. H.J. Zhang, A. Kankanhalli, and S. Smoliar, *Automatic Partitioning of Full Motion Video*. In Multimedia System Vol. 1 No 1., pp 1-28, 1993.

28. H.J. Zhang, C.Y. Low, S.W. Smoliar and J.H. Wu, *Video parsing, retrieval and browsing: an integrated and content-based solution*. In Proc. 3rd ACM Int. Multimedia Conf., San Francisco, USA, '95, p. 15-24

29. D.D. Velthausz, Bal, C.M.R., Eertink, E.H., *A Multimedia Information Object Model for Information Disclosure*. MMM'96 proc. of the Third International Conference on MultiMedia Modelling, Toulouse, France, 12-15 November 1996,pp 289-304

30. D.D. Velthausz, *Cost-effective networked based multimedia information retrieval*. PhD. thesis to be published in 1998.

31. J.K. Wu, A.D. Narasimhalu, B.M. Mehtre, A.P. Lam and Y.J. Gao, *CORE: a content-based retrieval engine for multimedia information systems*. In Multimedia Systems, Vol. 3, No. 1, 1995, p. 25-41

32. E.A. Fox, R.M. Akscyn, R.K. Furuta, and J.L. Leggett (Eds), *Special issue of Communication of the ACM on Digital Libararies*, April 1995.

33. Narisimhalu, Special section on content-based retrieval. In *Multimedia Systems*, Vol. 3., No. 1, 1995, pp 1-2

34. D.B. Lenat, and R.V. Guha, Building Large Knowledge-Based Systems, Representation and Inference in the Cyc Project, Addison-Wesley Publishing Company, 1990

A Flexible Architecture for the Integration of Media Servers and Databases

Henrike Süß

Database Group, Department of Computer Science,
Dresden University of Technology, Germany,
suess@db.inf.tu-dresden.de

Abstract. Information systems in general manage formatted data, and most of them use databases to store them adequately. While these systems work well, there are new requirements now to improve them towards the inclusion of multimedia data, i.e. images, graphics, video, and audio. Usually, multimedia data are stored in specialized servers which can cope with the requirements of real-time storage and delivery. Applications being developed today, however, need the services of both databases and these media servers. This paper presents a flexible architecture for the integration of media servers and databases into a single system.

1 Introduction and Motivation

Today, much work is dedicated to the handling, storing, and transporting of particular continuous-media data. But little work is invested to make the resulting systems interoperable, so that they can be integrated with existing systems or other components. In this paper, an architecture is presented for a Distributed Multimedia Database Management System (DMDBMS) that integrates databases – relational as well as object-oriented – with media servers or media-object stores.

The separate handling of formatted data and media data has several reasons. First, conventional databases often exist already, and they must be used in newly developed multimedia information systems as well, because the risk and the cost of building a completely new system are too high. Second, media data, especially the continuous types, must usually be stored on special hardware or on a separate server, because significant computing power is still required by the data transformations and even by the bandwidth used in delivery. Finally, the handling of media data is essentially different from that of formatted data.

The architecture consists of component systems and services. *Component systems* are conventional databases which store formatted data (FDB) like relational or object-oriented ones, and media servers or media-object stores. A *media server* can manage multimedia data, while a *media-object store* additionally offers database functionality, i.e. persistence, data independence, etc. Media-object stores can also be called *multimedia databases*. *Services* are built on top of these component systems. These services form an integration middleware that is

S. Jajodia, M.T. Özsu, and A. Dogac (Eds.): MIS'98, LNCS 1508, pp. 174–184, 1998.

also called a *Distributed Multimedia Database Management System* (DMDBMS). They are characterized by their interfaces and functionalities. *Applications* can access the DMDBMS through the provided interfaces. *DMDBMS Clients* also use these interfaces. They provide a user interface to the DMDBMS.

The main characteristics of the DMDBMS are (1) the use of homogeneous, yet functionally different interfaces to describe services and component systems, (2) the special handling of media data which concerns search and media data access and (3) the tight coupling of the component systems, so that read and write operations as well as transactions are supported.

2   General Architecture

Interfaces can be found on different levels of the main architecture (Fig. 1):

- for DMDBMS applications,
- between DMDBMS and component systems and
- within the DMDBMS i.e. between the DMDBMS services.

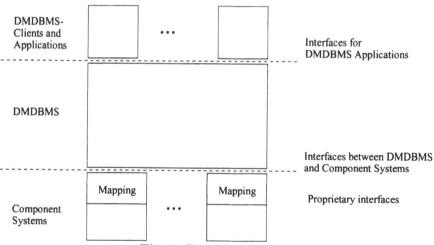

Fig. 1. General architecture

Homogeneity of interfaces is achieved by defining a common syntax for all interfaces. The proprietary interfaces that have similar semantics must be mapped to this syntax. Since component systems and services are quite different, it is useful to have not just one, but several interfaces, which have different functionality. Each interface defines a set of functions, e.g. for boolean queries, fuzzy queries, multimedia access, and transaction management. This set can be organized in a specialization hierarchy to support tailoring and reuse. A component system is described by a set of control interfaces (and protocols) it maps to. A service uses interfaces which are called base interfaces to control or manage other services or component systems, and it offers control interfaces to be used by other services, the DMDBMS clients or applications.

Here, the set of interfaces is first divided into *Access Interfaces* (AIs) and *Interoperability Interfaces* (IIs). Interoperability interfaces are characterized by functions, and by a protocol that specifies allowed sequences of function calls. Access Interfaces are defined by functions only.

The advantages of using homogeneous interfaces are that (1) services can be composed as necessary, (2) services can be changed as long as the interfaces remain the same, (3) component systems can be added easily and (4) software reuse is possible.

3   Interfaces of Component Systems

Conventional database systems in general have an interface **AccessF** to access stored data, an interface **Session** to manage connections, an interface **TransTM** to control internal transactions, and an interface **TransRM** that allows control of transactions from the outside. A media server has at least an interface **AccessMM** to access multimedia data, an interface **Session** to manage connections, and often an interface **Search** for search over multimedia data. A multimedia database system must have **TransTM** and **TransRM** in addition.

Some interfaces, e.g. **Search**, have specializations, because there are many different search methods for multimedia data. On the contrary, the access to multimedia data is rather straightforward: its media-object identifier can be used. This is one reason for separating search from access for multimedia data. The other reason is that search and access are often performed in two consecutive steps: Access to multimedia data requires a protocol and a tight connection, while search does not. Other interfaces, e.g. the transaction interfaces, have a fixed set of functions and no specialization. They stick to the DTP standard as defined by X/Open. The transaction interfaces, **AccessMM**, and **Session** are interoperability interfaces, while the other ones are access interfaces. In order to mark this difference, the interface names are qualified by II (for interoperability interfaces) or AI, respectively. In Table 1 all component-system interfaces are summarized.

II-Session	connection management
AI-Search	search over multimedia objects
II-AccessMM	access to multimedia objects
AI-AccessF	access to formatted data
AI-AccessDev	access for multimedia devices (input devices: camera, ... ; output devices: screen, ...)
II-TransTM	control transactions
II-TransRM	control transactions of resources (e.g. a database system) from the outside

Table 1. Functional interfaces

In the following subsections some interfaces are described.

3.1   II-Session

The two functions needed here are open and close. They help to authorize a user or application and to attach function calls to a session/connection. The protocol has two states: Init(0) and Opened(1). An open call causes the state transition: $0 \rightarrow 1$, the close call reverses it.

3.2   AI-AccessF

The **AI-AccessF** interface can be defined in different ways. First, a generic interface based on standardized languages can be used. These languages are SQL (SQL-2 or SQL-3) for relational database systems and ODL/OQL defined by the ODMG [5](ODMG 1.2 or ODMG 2.0) for object-oriented ones.[1]

- **AI-AccessSQL**
  exec_sql(sql-statement) and
- **AI-AccessODMG**
  exec_odmg(odmg-statement).

Using a generic interface is a general and universal approach. A single interface can be used for all databases with the same data model. It is independent of schema modifications as well as change of user requirements. But there remains the mismatch between relational and object-oriented technology which leads to at least two of these interfaces.

The other approach is to think of **AI-AccessF** as a description of the schema. For an object-oriented database system, the description consists of all methods that offer access to the data. In a relational database system, such a description is provided by an application program that implements access functions. This variant requires a fixed schema and thus bears less flexibility. If users have new requirements, it is necessary to change the mapping, for instance by implementing new methods or functions.

3.3   AI-Search

There are many search methods for multimedia data; a general overview can be found in [11]. Content-based information retrieval or media information retrieval are usually tailored to a certain media type, whereas the attribute-value search based on meta-data is applicable to all media types. Media information retrieval is fuzzy and therefore ranks the results. This yields a list, while attribute-value search leads to boolean retrieval and thus produces a set.

In Table 2, some search methods are described by the types of their input and output values. This is exactly the information needed for the integration into a DMDBMS.

---

[1] The latter, however, is not widely used yet. Up to this date, object-oriented database systems offer many different query and data definition languages and do not even have a common object model.

Input (Search argument)	Output (Search result)	Comment
text_object	list(text_object)	fulltext matching or linguistic similarity
text_object	list(media_object)	media objects must be described textually
type_x_media_object	list(type_x_media_object)	sample object or pattern
type_x_media_object	list(type_y_media_object) with $x \neq y$	
language expression	set(media_object)	media objects must be described by a language expression (for instance through prolog rules)
formatted data	set(media_object)	media objects must have a schema, e.g. attached attributes
keywords	list(media_object)	media objects must be described with keywords

Table 2. Input and output values of search engines

3.4   II-AccessMM

Media server store single media objects. Media objects are addressed by their media-object identifiers. Each media object has a determined media type, i.e. image, graphic, audio, or video. The hierarchy of single media objects is shown in Fig. 2.

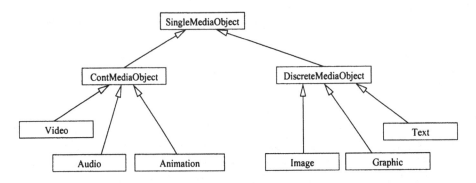

Fig. 2. Hierarchy of Media Objects

The interface AccessMM contains of two parts: management functions which are independent of media objects e.g. to get informations about the media server and methods on media objects. The latter follow a protocol. So some methods on media objects can only be called in a certain state. The states reflect different access modes. All media objects can be downloaded, but only continuous media objects can be streamed. So the states *Unspecified, Opened* and *Data Defined* are appropriate for all media objects, whereas the states *Stream Defined* and *Streaming* are only appropriate for continuous media objects.

A media type dependent set of parameters is used to specify the desired quality of a media object. For example the set of parameters for the media type image consists of image format e.g. gif, part, resolution, color depth, color and dpi. Additionally parameters are necessary that specify the quality of a stream i.e. service type (guaranteed, best effort or statistical), the degree of interactivity, delay and error-rate.

4 Services

In this section several services are introduced. An overview of all services, together with their control interfaces, base interfaces, and base services, is given in Table 3. A *base service* is a service which is used by the service under consideration.

The service that allows to execute distributed transactions is called the *Transaction Coordinator*. It requires all component systems to have an interface **II-TransRM** supporting the two-phase commit protocol.

If a user wishes to integrate two or more conventional database systems, a additional database management system is used to manage the global schema. This service is called *Formatted-data Integration Service*.

If more than one media component system is used, a *Media Manager* has to be employed. A single media component system can be handled through its own client software, but with more than one, a service is needed that negotiates quality of service and controls media transport.

The *Media Naming Service* is responsible for a global naming of media objects, the *Media Integration Service* stores and manages relations between media and formatted data, and the *Media Search Services* use information-retrieval methods to find media objects.

There are two new interfaces related to these services, namely **AI-NameMM** and **AI-IntegratedAccess**. **AI-NameMM** is the interface of the Media Naming Service, **AI-IntegratedAccess** is that of the Media Integration Service.

4.1 Media Search Service

It is not possible to apply one search method to all media servers because (1) search methods supported by media servers are quite different and (2) there is no standardized query language and even no standardized meta-data model for media data.

To make a search possible that produces a list or set of relevant media data stored in different media servers, it is necessary to use an external service. Since meta-data stored in media servers are quite different, an Information Retrieval service called Media Search Service which indexes the media data itself seems most appropriate.

Formatted-data Integration Service	Management of a global schema
Control interface	AI-AccessF
Base interface	AI-AccessF
Base services	none
Media Integration Service	Management of relations between media and data objects
Control interface	AI-IntegratedAccess
Base interface	II-AccessMM, AI-AccessF
Base services	Formatted-data Integration Service, Media Manager, Media Search Service
Media Manager	Negotiation, reservation, and observation of quality; transport of media objects according to that quality
Control interface	II-AccessMM
Base interface	II-AccessMM
Base services	Media Naming Service
Media Naming Service	Global naming of media objects
Control interface	AI-NameMM
Base interface	II-AccessMM
Base services	none
Media Search Service	Information retrieval in media objects
Control interface	AI-Search
Base interface	II-AccessMM
Base services	Media Naming Service
Transaction Coordinator	Control and management of (distributed) transactions
Control interface	II-TransTM
Base interface	II-TransRM
Base services	none

Table 3. Services

The interface **AI-SearchIR** of the Media Search Service has operations *search* and *order*. *Search* determines a list of media objects similar to a given sample media object. The number of media objects in the result list can be limited. The media objects are ordered by degree of similarity within the result list. *Order* sorts a given set of media objects by degree of similarity to the sample media object.

4.2 Media Integration Service

The Media Integration Service manages relations between media and data objects. The relations must be identified by a user and stored persistently. They can be defined in different ways. Here, a relation is defined by a name, a class in the FDB schema, the cardinality (1 or n), and the media type. A data object of the given class, selected by its OID, can reference through this relation one or more media objects of the given type, identified by their media-object identifiers. Based on these relations a virtual schema can be presented to the user. This schema and the Media Search Service can be queried together in one query language. Users are thus provided with the option for fuzzy queries over media objects, too.

The Media Integration Services can also be used to store relations between single media objects i.e. multi-media objects or hyperlinks. A multi-media object describes the spatial arrangement and timing of single media objects. Hyperlinks represent arbitrary connections between media objects.

5 Architectures

A full architecture can be build for a system that includes conventional databases as well as multimedia databases (see Fig. 3). If only one conventional database system is used, the Media Integration Service accesses this component system directly, and the Formatted-data Integration Service can be omitted. If only one multimedia database is used, the Media Manager and the Media Naming Service should be omitted, and the client of the multimedia database system should be used instead. If only media servers and just one conventional database system are used, there is no need for a Transaction Coordinator.

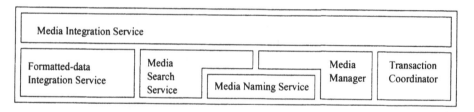

Fig. 3. Full DMDBMS

6 Related Work

Homogeneous interfaces are based on standards. One such standard for databases is the Remote Database Access (RDA) standard, which has been specified by the International Standards Organization (ISO). Is has the status of an international standard since 1993. RDA is a service in layer 7 of the ISO/OSI reference architecture. It is an asymmetrical protocol like the RPC protocol, and it consists of a generic part plus a language-dependent special part for the execution of SQL commands. It is divided into functional units, which are comparable to functional interfaces, i.e. II-Session, II-TransTM, and AI-AccessF (generic using SQL). This standard can be used for session management and access to formatted data.

A lot of work has been done concerning single services and multimedia databases/media servers. The integration of some conventional databases – needed to build the formatted-data integration service – is well examined. An integration based on CORBA is shown in [7,8]. An overview of Quality-of-Service architectures, which can be used for the Media Manager, is given in [2]. At the moment there are many research activities in this area. Transaction Coordinators based on X/Open's DTP standard are already in use, and many conventional database management systems support the XA interface. The Object Transaction Service specified by the OMG as a CORBA service is compatible with this standard, too. Information retrieval of multimedia data is also a current research topic. [3] presents a model and an architecture for distributed information retrieval, which can be used to build a Media Search Service. A lot of research is done in the area of multimedia databases and media servers [12,16,1,10,14,15,9,17].

So far, only a few proposals for systems which include conventional databases and media server can be found.

HERMES [18] and TSIMMIS [6] are based on mediators to integrate different data sources e.g. classical databases and pictorial data. The aim of these projects is the easy integration of data sources in a dynamic system so that all data can be queried together. The data can be read but not modified in such a system. In TSIMMIS and HERMES all data are handled in the same way, so no access methods dedicated to either media data or formatted data are provided. In TSIMMIS media data sources are classified and a static set of meta-data are extracted from media data and exported. The classification and extraction process can be different for all media data sources. So querying does not affect all data sources in the same way. In HERMES software packages e.g. for face recognition can be integrated too, but these services are not coupled to data sources, so calculations must be done at run-time, which can result in long query execution times. An indexing hierarchy cannot be built in advance.

An approach to store multimedia and traditional data in one system is made in Garlic, developed by the IBM Almaden Research Center [4]. It includes heterogeneous data sources such as databases, files, text managers, and image managers. In this project a unified schema based on an extension of the ODMG-93 data model and an object-oriented dialect of SQL are employed. Within Garlic, only internal protocols are used, so it is not an open system. In Garlic special requirements of media data except querying are not addressed. There is no access interface and issues of media data transport are not discussed.

Another approach is the Multiware Database [19]. The federated object-oriented database management system contains objects which describe multimedia documents. An information object contains data that describe content, structure, and synchronization aspects, whereas a presentation object describes features for the presentation. Information objects and presentation objects are related in a one-to-many relationship. Multimedia objects are stored on special servers. Multiware is based on CORBA. All meta-data are stored in a federated (distributed) object-oriented database system. Media servers are used by Multiware, but they are not part of it. The meta-data of a media object are not handled by itself. The presentation features are negotiated via a QoS protocol.

[13] presents an early approach to multimedia databases. An object-oriented data model is introduced that integrates the different conceptual models of the media. Each medium has its own conceptual model and its own database. An object base defines the relations between these media databases. Three Multimedia Database Management Architectures are introduced. A single DBMS architecture manages different media data together with the relations. A primary-secondary architecture consists of two kinds of DBMS. A secondary DBMS manages data of one media type. All secondary DBMSs and the object base are controlled by one primary DBMS. The federated architecture consists of open-member DBMS. These open DBMS can communicate through their external interfaces in order to process queries and updates. The object base can be centralized or decentralized. The primary-secondary architecture comes closest to the architecture discussed above in this paper. Component database systems can be seen as secondary DBMS and the DMDBMS is the primary DBMS. But the description given in [13] is not detailed enough to judge completely.

Commercial objectrelational databases e.g. Informix Universal Server, Oracle 8 or IBM Universal Server enrich the relational data-model with object-oriented concepts. Specifically they allow users the definition of complex data-types and functions on objects of these data-types. But the storage is fixed. It is not possible to add a special storage module for media data. So media objects can be added based on a definition of an appropriate complex data-type, but they are not handled and stored in a specific way according their special requirements e.g. real-time transport.

7 Next Steps

This paper describes work in progress. The specification of the Media Integration Service will be completed. A query language which also supports search based on information retrieval is currently examined. This query language is based on the OQL from ODMG 2.0. A compiler for that language which decomposes queries into three parts (for the FDB schema, the media-data relations, and the IR server) and re-integrates the answers is being developed.

A prototype of a DMDBMS and a DMDBMS client will be implemented based on two component systems: a relational database and a video server.

Later the Media Integration Service will be enhanced to store and manage presentations and hypermedia, too, as mentioned in Sect. 4.2.

References

1. Donald A. Adjeroh and Kingsley C. Nwosu. Multimedia Database Management – Requirements and Issues. *IEEE Multimedia*, 4(3):24–33, 1997.
2. Cristina Aurrecoechea, Andrew Campbell, and Linda Hauw. A Survey of Quality of Service Architectures. Technical report, University of Lancaster, 1995.

3. Christoph Baumgarten and Klaus Meyer-Wegener. Towards a Scalable Networked Retrieval System for Searching Multimedia Databases. In *Proc. ACM SIGIR Workshop on Networked Information Retrieval*, 1997.

4. M.J. Carey et al. Towards Heterogenous Multimedia Information Systems: The Garlic Approach. www, 1995. http://www.almaden.ibm.com/cs/garlic/ridedom95.html.

5. R.G.G. Cattell. *The Object Database Standard: ODMG-93*. Morgan Kaufmann, 1994.

6. Sudarshan Chawathe et al. The tsimmis project: Integration of heterogeneous information sources. In *Proc. of IPSJ Conference*, 1994.

7. Asuman Dogac, Cevdet Dengi, and M. Tamer Özsu. Building interoperable databases on distributed object management platforms, 1996. http://web.cs.ualberta.ca/ ozsu/publications.html.

8. Asuman Dogac et al. METU Interoperable Database System. www, 1995. http://www.srdc.metu.edu.tr/mind/publications.html.

9. D.James Gemmell et al. Multimedia Storage Servers: A Tutorial. *IEEE Computer*, pages 40–49, May 1995.

10. Sreenivas Gollapudi and Aidong Zhang. Netmedia: A Client-Server Distributed Multimedia Database Environment. www, 1996. http://www.cs.buffalo.edu/pub/tech-reports/README.html.

11. John Z. Li, M. Tamer Özsu, and Duane Szafron. Query languages in multimedia database systems. Technical report, Department of Computing Science, The University of Alberta, Canada, 1995.

12. Ulrich Marder and Günter Robbert. The kangaroo project. In *Proceedings of the Third Int. Workshop on Multimedia Information Systems*, 1997.

13. Yoshifumi Masunaga. Multimedia Databases: A formal framework. In *Proceedings of the IEEE Computer Society Symposium on Office Automation*, pages 36–45, 1987.

14. A. Desai Narasimhalu. Multimedia Databases. *Multimedia Systems*, 4(5):226–249, 1996.

15. M. Tamer Özsu, Duane Szafron, Ghada El-Medani, and Chiradeep Vittal. An onject-oriented multimedia database system for a news-on-demand application. *Multimedia Systems*, 3(5):182–203, 1995.

16. Thomas C. Rakow, Wolfgang Klas, and Erich J. Neuhold. Research on Multimedia Database Systems at GMD-IPSI. *IEEE Multimedia Newsletter*, 4(1), 1996.

17. Prashant J. Shenoy, Pawan Goyal, Sriram S. Rao, and Harrick M. Vin. Symphony: An Integrated Multimedia File System. Technical report, Department of Computer Sciences, University of Texas at Austin, 1997.

18. V.S. Subrahmanian et al. HERMES: A Heterogeneous Reasoning and Mediator System. www, 1994. http://www.cs.umd.edu//projects/hermes/overview/paper/index.html.

19. Carlos M. Tobar and Ivan L.M. Ricarte. Multiware Database: A Distributed Object Database System for Multimedia Support. www, 1995. http://www.dca.fee.unicamp.br/ ricarte/Papers/papers.html#iciims96.

Sketch-Based Images Database Retrieval

Stanislaw Matusiak[1], Mohamed Daoudi[1], Thierry Blu[2], Olivier Avaro[3]

[1] Groupe de Recherche Image et Formes ENIC/INT
Cité Scientifique, Rue Guglielmo Marconi
59658 Villeneuve d'Ascq France
e-mail : {matusiak,daoudi}@enic.fr
[2] Swiss Federal Institute of Technology,
DMT/IOA, PO Box 127,
1015 Lausanne, Switzerland
[3] France Telecom CNET DSE/SGV
38-40 rue du Général Leclerc
92794 Issy Moulineaux Cedex 9, FRANCE

Abstract. This paper describes an application allowing content-based retrieval that can thus be considered as an MPEG-7 example application. The application may be called "sketch-based database retrieval" since the user interacts with the database by means of sketches. The user draws its request with a pencil: the request image is then a binary image that comprises a contour on a uniform bottom.

1 Introduction

This paper describes an application allowing content-based retrieval that can thus be considered as an MPEG-7 example application [1]. The application may be called **"sketch-based database retrieval"** since the user interacts with the database by means of sketches. The user draws its request with a pencil: the request image is then a binary image that consists of a contour on a uniform background. Retrieval by content based on the similarity between shapes and user drawn sketches has been addressed by a few authors [2], [3].

The solutions proposed in the literature follow different approaches and emphasize different aspects of the problem. In [2], the correlation between a linear sketch and edges in the image databases is evaluated, and the object is retrieved by shape similarity. High correlation values require that the shape drawn by the user must be close to the shapes in the images which, in practice, is nearly impossible. To model user inaccuracy, the correlation is evaluated with respect to a search area with limited horizontal and vertical shifts. This method allows the retrieval of an image based on a rough user sketch. This method is not invariant with regards to changes in the size, position and orientation of the images from the database, nor of the sketch. In order to incorporate invariance with regards to rigid motion (i.e., rotation and translation) the

S. Jajodia, M.T. Özsu, and A. Dogac (Eds.): MIS'98, LNCS 1508, pp. 185–191, 1998.

methods need to be applied for all possible rotations and translations, and thus reduces the speed of the retrieval. When we consider large image databases, this speed reduction can become considerable.

A shape similarity based on an elastic deformation of user sketches to match image data has been proposed by Del Bimbo [3]. The elastic matching allows to approximate the human perception of similarity but is not rotation invariant, although the algorithm can usually cope with small rotations. In order to have scale invariance, the elastic matching assumes that the user, while making a query, draws an object approximately with the same aspect ratio as that of the objects he wants to retrieve. In general, one estimates that the drawing never corresponds exactly to the searched image.

In this paper, we propose to modelize the user sketch by its Euclidean curvature, which we assume to play an important perceptive role. The paper is organized as follows: Section II explains the preprocessing step of image databases and the modelization of a sketch. Section III describes the Curvature Scale Space (CSS) matching algorithm. Section IV presents a Web interface and some experimental results. Section V contains a summary and the conclusion.

2   The Scale Space Representation

In our approach to compare a sketch to images from a database, we assume that each image is segmented and described by its contour.

Several sources of error are inherent to feature extraction such as, for instance, image acquisition noise, quantization errors, edge detection errors and user drawing errors. The matching process and recognition task can be eased by smoothing, so as to remove the noise and extraneous details as well. However, without a priori knowledge, it is difficult to distinguish between useful structural informations and relevant details in the user sketch. Given that the required scale or scales are not known, one solution is to represent the user sketch and curves at multiple scales so that each structure can be represented at its appropriate scale.

For computation purposes, a curve is parametrized by its arc length parameter. Different curve parametrizations are used to represent a given curve. The normalized arc length parametrization is generally chosen when the descriptors are required to be invariant under similarities.

Lets $\gamma(s)$ a parametrized curve, which is defined by $\gamma = \left\{ (x(s), y(s) \big| s \in [0,1] \right\}$. An evolved γ_σ version of γ $\left\{ \gamma_\sigma \big| \sigma \geq 0 \right\}$ can be computed. This is defined by:

$$\gamma_\sigma = \left\{ (x(s,\sigma), y(s,\sigma) \big| s \in [0,1] \right\}$$

where

$$x(s,\sigma) = x(s) * g(s,\sigma) \qquad y(s,\sigma) = y(s) * g(s,\sigma)$$

where $*$ is the convolution operator and $g(s,\sigma)$ denotes a Gaussian width σ. It can be shown that curvature k on γ_σ is given by [4]:

$$k(s,\sigma) = \frac{x_s(s,\sigma)y_{ss}(s,\sigma) - x_{ss}(s,\sigma)y(s,\sigma)}{\left(x_s(s,\sigma)^2 + y_s(s,\sigma)^2\right)^{3/2}}$$

where

$$x_s(s,\sigma) = \frac{\partial}{\partial u}(x(s)*g(s,\sigma)) = x(s)*g_s(s,\sigma) \qquad y_s(s,\sigma) = y(s)*g_s(s,\sigma)$$

$$x_{ss}(u,\sigma) = \frac{\partial^2}{\partial s^2}(x(s)*g(s,\sigma)) = x(s)*g_{ss}(s,\sigma) \qquad x_s(s,\sigma) = x(s)*g_s(s,\sigma)$$

The Curvature Scale Space (CSS) of γ is defined as the solution to [4]:

$$k(s,\sigma) = 0.$$

The extrema and zeros of the curvature are often used as breakpoints for segmenting the curve into sections corresponding to shape primitives. The zeros of the curvature are its points of inflection. The curvature extrema characterize the shape of these sections.

Fig. 1b shows the CSS of the curve of Fig. 1a. Horizontal lines have been drawn across that image to indicate the values of σ that were used to compute the evolved curves of Fig. 1a.

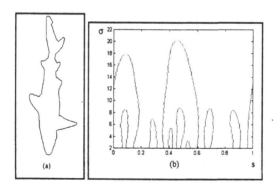

Fig. 1. Curvature Scale Space

The CSS representation has the following properties [4]:
1. Invariance with regards to the similarity group, i.e, the composition of translations, rotations and scale changes.
2. Completeness, which allows the reconstruction of the object.
3. Stability, which gives robustness with regards to small distortions caused by sketch or quantization.

4. Simplicity and real time computation. This property is very important in database applications.

3 Matching Algorithm

Having defined the CSS as an invariant and robust contour representation, we need to define a similarity metric between two CSS.

In [6], it is suggested that a scale-space metric should be invariant to with respect to rotation, translation and zooming, and from this requirement a hyperbolic geometry for linear and nonlinear scale-spaces is derived. Given two points (x_1,σ_1) and (x_2,σ_2), with $\sigma_1 \leq \sigma_2$, their distance is computed along the geodesic curve connecting these points:

$$d\left((x_1,\sigma_1),(x_2,\sigma_2)\right)= \log\left|\frac{\sigma_2}{\sigma_1}\frac{\left(1+\sqrt{1-(\varphi\sigma_1)^2}\right)}{\left(1+\sqrt{1-(\varphi\sigma_1)^2}\right)-\varphi L}\right|$$

where

$$\varphi = \frac{2L}{\sqrt{\left(\sigma_1^2-\sigma_2^2\right)^2+L^2\left(L^2+2\left(\sigma_1^2+\sigma_2^2\right)\right)}}$$

and $L = \|x_1-x_2\|$ is the Euclidean distance.

In this paper, we propose to compute this distance between the CSS maxima. In fact, like Mokhtarian [5], we represent every image in the database just by the location of its CSS contour maxima. For example, the representation for the contour in figure 1 will be as follows:

CSS$_M$={(0.46,20.0),(0.09,17.70),(0.69,8.70),(0.47,8.50),(0.086,8.40),(0.86,8.30),
(0.28,6.8),(0.41,5.10),(0.54,3.20) }.

4 Web Interface and Experimental Results

We use the Vision, Speech, and Signal Processing Surrey University database which contains about 1100 images of marine creatures. Each image shows one distinct species on a uniform background. Every image is processed in order to recover the boundary contour, which is then represented by the maxima of the curvature zero-crossing contours in its CSS.

An example of sketch-based retrieval of marine creatures is shown in Fig. 2 and Fig. 3. In the query, we draw a rough sketch (Fig. 2a and Fig. 3a). The retrieval of images with the highest similarity ranks are shown in Fig. 2b,c,d and Fig 3b,c,d.

The ability to perceive as similar, objects that have undergone a great variation in shape, is typical of human beings. By "robustness" (of the retrieval, with respect to a sketch query) we intend the ability of the system to retrieve objects of the same kind as the sketch, irrespective of shape variations of the database instances.

As we can see in Fig. 2, Fig 3, the obtained results show that the retrieval system is robust to these variations. Moreover, the retrieved images are in different positions and orientations.

Example 1

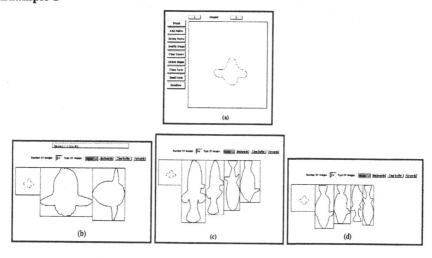

Fig. 2. a) Web interface, example 1 of sketch made by the user; b) and c) ten first's matching images, with sketch in the left

Example 2

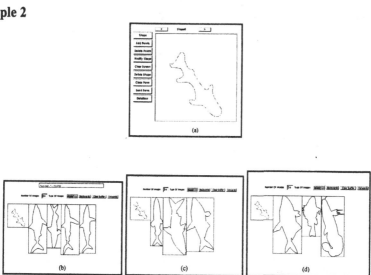

Fig.3. a) Web interface, example 2 of sketch made by the user; b), c) and d) Ten first's matching images, with sketch in the left

4.1 Computational Requirements

It is desirable to have a fast scheme for retrieving images from a database. The retrieval scheme described above, computes sequentially the distance of a given query image with the images in the database.

The CPU time (on SUN SparcStation 5) ranged between 10 and 45s for a query on a database containing 800 images. This time depends on the complexity of the sketch.

For *example 1* we measure the time of calculation in function of number of models in database:

Number of models in the Database	Time of CSS computing	The research in the Database	Total time
800	9,8 sec.	3 sec.	12,8 sec.
700	9,8 sec.	2,5 sec.	12,3 sec
100	9,8 sec.	1,5 sec.	11,3 sec
50	9,8 sec.	0,2 sec.	10 sec

We observe that the time of contour processing (computation of CSS max representation of shape) is the most important in this retrieval system.

5 Conclusions

A sketch(content)-based image database retrieval application has been proposed in this paper. Our experiments show that the Curvature Scale Space is a meaningful sketch representation and corresponds to human perception. It has the advantage of being rotation/translation and scale invariant, and is robust with regards to shape variations.

Acknowledgements

This work has been supported by France Telecom CNET under grant 971B356.

References

1. ISO/IEC JTC1/SC29/WG11 MPEG7/1942 /Bristol : Sketch-Based Database Retrieval. A Demonstration of an MPEG-7 Application. (April 1997)
2. Kyoji Hirata Toshikazu Kato: Query by Visual Example, Content based Image Retrieval. In Advances in Database Technology EDBT'92 Third International Conference on Extending Database Technology, Vienna, Austria, March (1992) Springer-Verlag.

3. Del Bimbo, A., Pala, P.: Visual Image Retrieval by Elastic Matching of User Sketches. IEEE PAMI Vol. 19, pp. 121- 132, No. 2, (1997).
4. Mokhtarian F. , Mackworth A.K.: A Theory of Multiscale, Curvature-Based Shape Representation for Planar Curves. IEEE PAMI, Vol. 14, pp. 789-805, August (1992).
5. Mokhtarian F.,: Silhouette-Based Isolated Object Recognition Through Curvature Scale Space. IEEE PAMI, Vol. 17, No 15, pp. 539-544, (1995).
6. Eberly D. H.,: Geometric Methods for analysis of Ridges in N-Dimensional Images. PhD Thesis, University of North Carolina at Chapel Hill, (1994).

An Integrated Data Model and a Query Language for Content-Based Retrieval of Video

Young-Il Choi[1], Yoo-Mi Park[1], Hun-Soon Lee[2], and Seong-Il Jin[2]

[1] ETRI, Yusong P.O.Box 106, Taejon, Korea, 305-600
{yichoi, parkym}@etri.re.kr
[2] Dept. of Computer Science, Chungnam National University,
Kung-Dong, Yosong-Gu, Taejon, Korea, 305-600

Abstract. As video data have been used in multimedia information systems, the need for the database support that provides an efficient way for users to retrieve video data is growing. In this paper, we propose a video data model that integrates feature based model and annotation based model for the purpose of improving content-based retrieval of video data. The proposed video data can act as a generic video data model for multimedia applications, and support free annotations, image features, and structure information of video data within the same framework. The proposed video query language provides semantics to access arbitrary segments in the video data. It can formalize various kinds of queries based on the video contents.

1 Introduction

With the advancement of computer technology and the establishment of information super highway, the development of multimedia information systems is rapidly progressing. To provide various services such as News on Demand, Digital Library etc., it is necessary to implement video database systems that can accommodate multimedia data such as video. In order to provide content-based retrieval of video data, the video database systems need to be expanded in data model and query language to handle the video data type.

Video data models are classified into two categories: feature-based model and annotation-based model. Feature-based model uses features to represent the contents of video, but it does not provide semantics that describe high level contents of video, such as events. Annotation-based model uses keywords to represent the video contents. It can describe high level contents of video, but the cost for the indexing of the vast video data is too expensive.

For video querying, content-based retrieval of video data requires a powerful query language that permits easy descriptions of video contents and supports semantic data retrieval [1].

In this paper, we propose a video data model that integrates feature-based model and annotation-based model to provide content-based retrieval of video data efficiently. And we present a video query language which can specify various queries based on the video contents. This paper is organized as follows. Section

S. Jajodia, M.T. Özsu, and A. Dogac (Eds.): MIS'98, LNCS 1508, pp. 192–198, 1998.

2 reviews previous works on video database systems. In section 3, we propose a video data model. In section 4, we present a corresponding video query language, and section 5 concludes the work.

2   Related Works

Video objects in OVID [2] correspond to sets of video frame sequences. But, it does not explicitly support modeling of the video structure. OVID provides the user with the SQL-based query language, VideoSQL, to retrieve video objects by specifying some attribute values. It does not, however, contain language expressions for specifying temporal relations between video objects.

VideoSTAR [4] provides generic data model that makes sharing and reusing of video data possible. But, it is somewhat complex, and does not support modeling of the video features. VideoSTAR provides a user query interface that can handle annotations defined in data model, but does not provide explicit query language.

AVIS [5] provides a formal data structure for characterizing video contents. However, the conditions placed on segmenting a video may be too restrictive to capture all events. AVIS provides the user with the SQL-based query language that can specify attribute values, but it does not contain language expressions for video features.

Venus [6] provides video index structure based on video features. As its data model uses video features on the basis of a frame, it requires large memory to index video features. Venus provides a content-based video query language (CVQL) in which objects appearing in video data, and temporal and spatial relationship among objects can be specified. But it is not easy for users to express video contents such as events.

3   Video Data Model

The proposed video data model is shown in Figure 1 using Object Modeling Technique [7]. The intention has been to make the following characteristics included within the same framework.

Generic Data Model The proposed video data model can act as a generic video data model to facilitate sharing of the video stream and the information about the content and structure of video. It can be adopted easily according to the needs of diverse range of applications, and support accessing of the arbitrary segments in the video data according to the video contents

Free Annotations To deal with free annotations, we have adopted ideas from the stratification approach [3]. *Video Clip* represents an arbitrary video segment at which meaningful scene is described. Frame interval of the video is used as its attribute, and *Event* expresses the content of the meaningful scene that is defined through the video clip. The information about who, when, where, and what are described as its attributes in *Event*. Annotations can be shared among *Video Clips*.

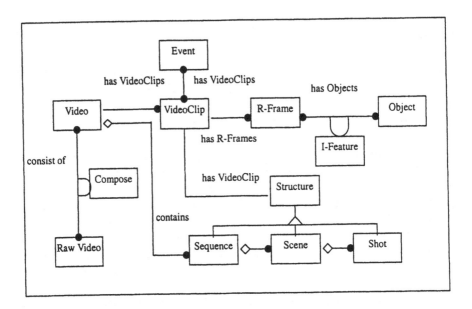

Fig. 1. Proposed Video Data Model

Image Features We include image features in our model on the basis of representative frame. *Representative Frame* is the frame that represents the *Video Clip*. *Object* expresses objects that are shown in representative frames. *Image Feature* defines the relationship between a frame and an object. The object's color, texture, and position information within the representative frame are used as its attributes. The spatial relation between objects can be obtained by the position information, and the temporal relation between video clips can be obtained using the frame interval algebra.

Structure Information of Video A segmentation approach [4] is used to define the video structure that can provide well-defined levels of abstraction for navigation and appreciation of large volumes of video data. *Structure* represents the internal logical structure information of the video. Its frame interval is defined through a *Video Clip*, and its content through an *Event*. It generalizes compositional units of structure such as *Sequence*, *Scene*, and *Shot*. *Sequence* expresses a video segment with which a continuing story in video can be separated. *Scene* describes a video segment which includes an event happening at the same time, and at the same place. *Shot* defines a video segment made from a one-time camera work.

Reuse of Video Stream The same physical video stream can be used in several different videos. *Raw Video* represents the actual video stream that is stored digitally in the storage. Physical characteristics such as video format, frame rate are defined as its attributes. *Video* represents the actual video document recognized by the users. It has bibliographic information such as category, title, director, production, etc., as its attributes. The compositional relationship between *Video* and *Raw Video* is defined through *Composition*.

4   Video Query Language

In order to support content-based retrieval of video data, a query language that can formalize different kinds of queries is important. We propose a video query language that corresponds with the proposed video data model to specify queries based on video contents such as annotations, image features, structure, spatial relations, and temporal relations.

4.1   Syntax of the Proposed Video Query Language

The syntax of the proposed video query language consists of the following three clauses.

FIND	\<Result-Type\>
FROM	\<Video-Expression\>
WHERE	\<Video-Expression\> | \<Object-Expression\> |
	\<Event-Expression\> | \<Image-Feature-Expression\> |
	\<Similarity-Expression\> | \<Spatial-Relation-Expression\> |
	\<Temporal-Relation-Expression\>

In the *FIND* clause, the type of results which users want to retrieve is specified. Classes such as Video, Video Clip etc., and attributes of classes such as Who, What etc., can be used. In the *FROM* clause of a query, we can specify any video stored in the database on which we want to execute a query. In the *WHERE* clause, the qualification of a query is specified. In our video query language, various expressions can be used to describe conditions about contents and features of video. *Similarity Expression* consists of reserved word *Similar-To* and predicates that can specify certainty of similarity. It can take care of fuzzy queries, and visual queries with graphic query interface. *Temporal Relation Expression* consists of reserved word *T-Relation* and a predicate that describes temporal relationship between two events. Seven temporal relations, such as before, meet, during, start, finish, overlap, and equal, are defined. *Spatial Relation Expression* consists of reserved word *S-Relation* and a predicate that describes spatial relationship between two objects. Spatial relation can be classified into the following three categories [8].

positional relation :   left, right, above, below, left-above, left-below,
                          right-above, right-below, center
topological relation :   equal, disjoint, overlap, inside, cover, connect
distance relation :   far, near

4.2 Types of Queries

With the types of results specified in FIND clause, we can afford to define various
types of queries for which applications want to provide.

Video Query A video query is specified using *VideoExpression* in which attributes of Video are used as predicates. To make a storyboard, for example,
a query such as "find all representative frames of the movie 'True Lies'" is expressed as follows.

FIND   R-Frame
FROM   Video
WHERE   Video Category = "Movie", Title = "True Lies"

Object Query Object query is specified using *Object Expression* in which attributes of Object are used as predicates. *Image Feature Expression* can be used
as predicates also.

Event Query Event query is specified using *Event Expression* in which attributes of Event are used as predicates. A query such as "find all the video clips
in which 'Chung Tae-soo' attends the Hanbo Hearing" is expressed as follows.

FIND   Video Clip
FROM   Video Category = "News"
WHERE   Event Title = "Hanbo Hearing", Who = "Chung Tae-Soo"

Temporal Query Temporal query is specified using *Temporal Relation Expression*, and it deals with temporal relations between two events.

Spatial Query Spatial query is specified using *Spatial Relation Expression*,
and it deals with spatial relations between two objects that appear in the same
representative frame. A query such as "find all the video clips in which 'Bill
Clinton' is at the left of 'Kim Young-Sam'" is expressed as follows.

FIND   Video Clip
FROM   Video Category = "News"
WHERE   Object Name = "Bill Clinton"
              S-Relation = "left"
              Object Name = "Kim Young-Sam"

Similarity Query Similarity query is specified using *SimilarityExpression*, and other expressions can be used as predicates also.

Compound Query User can specify a compound query using complex conditions such as the combination of several of the expressions in the proposed video query language.

4.3   Query Processing

The processing of queries is equivalent to converting queries that are expressed with the proposed video query language into the query language provided by commercial database systems.

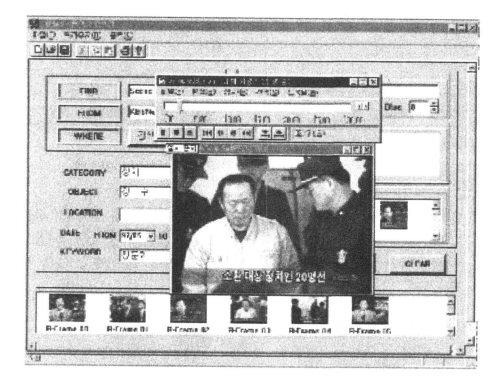

Fig. 2. Graphic Query Interface

A query such as "find all the video clips in which 'Chung Tae-Soo' attends the Hanbo Hearing" is processed as follows.

SELECT	C.of-video.id, C.frame-interval
FROM	Event E, E.has-videoclip C
WHERE	E.title = "Hanbo Hearing" And E.who = "Chung Tae-Soo"
	C.of-video.category = "News" And C.type = "Scene"

We use the Object Query Language (OQL) [9] in order to describe the processing of the query specified in proposed video query language.

5 Conclusion

We propose an integrated video data model and a corresponding video query language for the purpose of improving content based retrieval of video data.

The proposed video data model includes the following characteristics within the same framework: generic data model, reuse of physical video stream, free annotations, image features, and structure information of video. It provides various semantics to access arbitrary segments in the video data, and it can be adapted easily according to the needs of applications. The proposed video query language corresponds with the proposed video data model to specify queries based on video contents using annotations, image features, structure information, spatial relations, and temporal relations.

A prototype video database system has been implemented with commercial database management system. Graphic user interface is provided, through which queries can automatically be converted into the proposed video query language for query processing. Optimization of query processing will be considered in our future work.

References

1. John Z. Li, M. Tamer Oisu, and Duane Szafron, "Querying Languages in Multimedia Database Systems," TR95-12, The university of Alberta, Canada, 1995.
2. E. Oomoto and K. Tanaka, "OVID: Design and Implementation of a Video-Object Database System," IEEE Trans. on Knowledge and Data Engineering, Vol.5, No.4, pp.629-643, 1993.
3. Ron Weiss, Andrzej Duda, and David K. Gifford, "Composition and Search with a Video Algebra," IEEE Multimedia, spring 1995.
4. R. Hjelsvold and R. Midstraum, "Modelling and Querying Video Data," Proc. of the 20th VLDB Conference, Santiago, Chile, pp.686-694, Sep. 1994.
5. S. Adali, K. S. Candan, S. S. Chen, K. Erol, and V. S. Subrahmanian. "Advanced video information system: Data structures and query processing," ACM Multimedia Journal, 1995.
6. Tony C.T.Kuo and Arbee L.P.Chen, "A Content-Based Query Language for Video Databases," In Proc. of IEEE MULTIMEDIA '96, pp.209-214, 1996.
7. J. Rumbaugh et al., "Object-oriented modeling and design," Prentice-Hall International, Inc., 1991.
8. John Z. Li, M. Tamer Oisu, and Duane Szafron, "Modeling video spatial relationships in an object model," TR96-06, The university of Alberta, Canada, 1996.
9. R. Cattell. "The Object Database Standard: ODMG-93 (Release 1.1)," Morgan Kaufmann Publishers, San Francisco, CA, 1994.

Virtual Reality for Image Retrieval

J. Assfalg, A. Del Bimbo, and P. Pala

DSI - University of Florence, Via S.Marta 3, 50139 Firenze, Italy

Abstract. Image database systems have been widely studied in the last years. Having to deal with visual information, a great effort has also been put in designing and implementing user interfaces for the different retrieval engines. Most of those interfaces allow the user to specify the query through visual examples, either by feeding a complete image to the system or by drawing some colour patches on a sketchpad. However, in fields such as education or entertainment, some new user interfaces can be developed exploiting Virtual Reality solutions. Virtual Reality provides us with a wide set of previously unexplored interaction techniques, among which we can choose the ones that are best suited for our purposes.
In the application presented hereafter, while navigating a virtual world, the user is given the opportunity of taking some photographs, which can be used to query a database of images.

1   Introduction

Computer graphics and image processing and management have been for a long time two very distant worlds. With the increasing power of graphics hardware, however, these two worlds are getting closer and closer. The staggering amount of multimedia data is today easily managed even with low cost computers. Therefore, there is an increasing interest in dealing with pictures, either paintings or photographs.

Some common issues are shared by applications dealing either with 2D images or 3D worlds: browsing, visualization, modelling, and others. However, different solutions for these issues are exploited. Most of the differences originate from the fact that images only have two dimensions, while real or virtual worlds have three. The latter case allows the user to change the position and orientation of the viewpoint, in order to get different views of a given scene. Differently, with 2D images she/he will not get any benefit from changing her/his viewpoint with respect to the picture.

Resolution is another interesting topic which applies to both the two-dimensional and three-dimensional worlds: in either case, there is a constant quest for a trade-off between accuracy and the dimension of data. The more an image or model has to be refined, the more data is required. For pixel images multiple resolutions (e.g.: photo CDs) has been the solution, whereas in three-dimensional modelling the solution is levels of detail.

One interesting field where this relationship between 3D and 2D can be exploited is retrieval by content from image databases. In this kind of applications,

S. Jajodia, M.T. Özsu, and A. Dogac (Eds.): MIS'98, LNCS 1508, pp. 199–204, 1998.
© Springer-Verlag Berlin Heidelberg 1998

the main issue is to have access to images, either paintings or photographs, in a large collection, based on their visual content. Visual features, such as colour, shape, texture or any combination of them, far longer than keywords, characterize an image.

Querying by visual example is a paradigm, particularly suited, to express perceptual aspects of low/intermediate features of visual content. This paradigm requires that the user provides a prototype image which is used as a reference example. Several paradigms for querying by visual example are available: *i*) By painting, usually employed in colour-based retrieval. The user sketches colour patches and reproduces salient colours of an image, colour regions, and their spatial arrangement. *ii*) By sketch, commonly used to retrieve images that contain objects with shapes similar to the example. *iii*) By image, indicated for queries based on global colour or texture. A sample image, taken either from the answer to a previous query or from a sample image set, is used as a prototype to retrieve similar images.

In the application presented hereafter, we have created a connection between a three-dimensional virtual world and the two-dimensional space of images. On one side there is navigation in virtual environments, on the other there is image browsing, for which the former provides a new interaction metaphor. While exploring the virtual world, the user is given the opportunity of taking some photographs, thus actively participating in the process of projection of 3D onto 2D. These two-dimensional snapshots are passed to the retrieval engine and matched against the archived images. The user may then extract the content of the retrieved images (colour, texture) and use it to interactively modify the virtual scene. In this way, the two-dimensional data is backprojected to the three-dimensional world, thus closing an ideal loop which connects these two domains.

2   Image Retrieval by Colour Similarity

In our application we concentrated on colour, which is by far a feature which strikes the observer. In this case, the system is required to query the database and retrieve those images whose colour distribution is globally similar to that in a query image.

Image retrieval based on global colour distribution has been proposed in [4], [2], [1], [3]. Different approaches use appropriate transformations to represent colour properties in appropriate colour spaces [7], [5]. In our approach, image chromatic content is expressed through the image colour histogram. The $L^*u^*v^*$ colour space has been used to guarantee that the euclidean distance in the colour space conforms to the perceptive colour distance. The histogram is computed using 128 reference colours which are selected through a uniform tesseletion of the $L^*u^*v^*$ colour space [6]. At archival time the histogram is computed for all the images that have to be indexed. At query time, the histogram of the query image I_Q is matched against the histogram I_D of each image stored in the database using an histogram intersection algorithm.

3   A Simplified Interaction Model

One of the goals of our work has been to develop an interface in which the complexity of the graphics library should not bother the end user. For the development of the graphic environment we have chosen the *OpenGL* library. This library has a fairly complex model for lighting, in which both light sources and materials are defined by a set of attributes. Each of these specifies the colour of a particular component of light or reflectance respectively. These components are *ambient*, *diffuse* and *specular*. To get the resulting colour of a single fragment, light and material components with the same name are multiplied together; the resulting terms are then summed up using a formula which also takes attenuation and other factors into account.

Since a generic user only associates one colour with an object (or one of its parts), we had to hide the complexity of that model and decided that she/he could interactively change only the diffuse component of one object's colour description. The other components, if different from the default values, can be specified by the designer in the *VRML* files describing the 3D models. Thus, in our application, the user may choose the desired colour from a standard colour chooser, as she/he would do in any painting program, and simply apply it to a given object with a single mouse click on it. The same considerations apply for textures.

4   The User Interface

In designing the user interface for our application, we had to take into account the fact that most of the users would be occasional users. Therefore, we decided to adopt one solution in which we could take advantage of possible users' experiences in using WIMP[1] interfaces.

Our application requires support for different functions:

- editing colour, texture and position of objects;
- browsing a virtual environment, with different metaphors possible;
- cutting a portion of the rendered scene;
- browsing a set of retrieved images;
- cutting a portion of a retrieved image.

To ease the interaction with the user, functions have been clustered into groups and tree modes have been introduced to keep these functions separate: *navigation*, *editing* and *selection*. The first group of functions allows navigation of the virtual environment, the second group allows its interactive editing, the last one lets the user cut a portion of the rendered scene. Browsing and cutting of images are performed in a separate window and, therefore, are kept clearly separate from the other functions. These groups are shown in Figure 1, which also shows the possible combinations of the various tasks, thus giving an overview of the rich interactivity of the system.

---

[1] Windows, Icons, Menus, Pointers

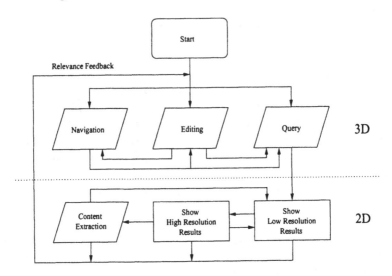

Fig. 1. Diagram showing the possible interaction combinations

The virtual environment is represented in a rectangular region which covers most of the display's surface. Navigation in the three-dimensional space is performed through a *walk* metaphor which lets the user freely move, following the landscape's orography. Some additional interaction schemes such as panning and tilting let the user fine tune the position and orientation of the viewpoint (or camera).

The display includes several buttons through which the operation modes of the interface are selected. On the upper portion, several mode-depending tools are displayed: in *editing* mode they select one of the three submodes (*object*, *colour* and *texture*) and the respective palettes are shown; in *navigation* mode, some buttons are shown which allow the use and definition of bookmarks. When in *editing* mode, the user can interactively edit the three-dimensional scene by either adding, moving or removing objects, or by changing their properties, such as colour and texture.

Finally, the *selection* mode provides the user with a *photographer* interaction metaphor which lets her/him select a rectangular area of the current view. This selection will be fed to the retrieval engine which, once having extracted the interesting features out of it, will run the query and show the results in a separate window.

The results window (Figure 2(d)) shows low resolution thumbnails of the images in the database that match the user's query. The images are listed with ranking scores decreasing from left to right and from top to bottom. Clicking on one of the thumbnails will show the corresponding high resolution image for a detailed analysis. In this condition the user also has the aforementioned ability to extract textures from the displayed image by selecting a rectangular area. These textures can be stored in the system's texture archive and may later be used in editing mode to change some objects' appearance.

5   Examples

During database population the administrator has to cope with both the two-dimensional entities and the three-dimensional ones: Adding items to the system means adding pictures and textures on one side and *VRML* models on the other one. This fact is remarkable since it highlights, once more, the tight relation between the two worlds.

Based on the principles previously expounded, a prototype system has been developed for image retrieval by global colour similarity in which the queries are performed providing the database engine with snapshots of the virtual environment. Initially, the user may choose one of the bookmarked locations as a starting point for the navigation in the virtual environment. This is a good initial state since it provides a new way to start browsing an image database. As a matter of fact, in most interfaces to image databases the user is asked to set up a query from scratch, assuming she/he roughly knows what she/he is looking for. On the contrary, the target user of our application does not necessarily have a precise idea of what she/he is looking for in the database. Therefore, having to formulate a query from scratch would be of no use to her/him.

Indeed, while walking through the virtual world, the user may be struck by a scene, either because of some particular object represented in it, or because of the sensations and emotions it conveys. The user is here given the opportunity to lightly, or even heavily, modify the scene, according to the ideas that are arising in her/his mind. This can be achieved by adding, deleting or moving objects, as well as by changing their colours and textures (Figures 2(a),(b)).

In Figure 2(a) a view of the virtual environment is shown. In Figure 2(b), a texture taken from the default textures set has been applied to one of the trees. A snapshot of the framed scene has been taken (Figure 2(c)). Actually, such a picture may represent the complete scene as well as a small part of it. Thus, the *photograph* has been used as an example for a query to the database system. The search in the archive is based on a global colour similarity criterion that matches the query image against the archived images. For this purpose a colour histogram intersection algorithm [4] has been implemented. The results are shown in a separate window. The thumbnail representation lets the user have an overall view of the response of the system (Figure 2(d)). She/he may then further examine some of the images by requesting their high resolution version.

References

1. C. Faloutsos, M. Flickner, W. Niblack, D. Petkovic, W. Equitz, R. Barber: *Efficient and Effective Querying by Image Content*, Res.Report 9453, IBM Res.Div. Almaden Res.Center, Aug.1993
2. B.V. Funt, G.D. Finlayson: *Color Constant Color Indexing*, IEEE Trans. on Pattern Analysis and Machine Intelligence, Vol. 17, n. 5, May 1995
3. J. Hafner, H.S. Sawhney, W. Equit, M. Flickner, W. Niblack: *Efficient Color Histogram Indexing for Quadratic Form Distance Functions"*, IEEE Trans. on Pattern Analysis and Machine Intelligence, Vol. 17, n. 7, July 1995, pp. 729-736

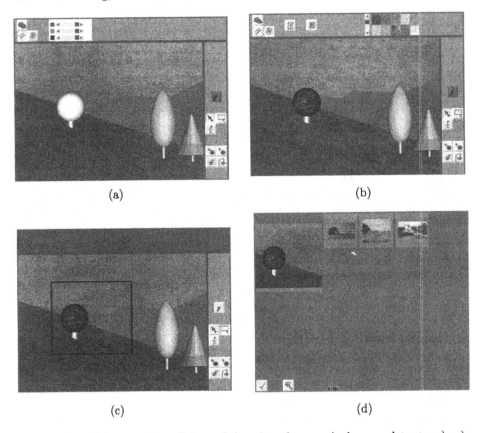

(a)   (b)

(c)   (d)

Fig. 2. a) - b) Interactive editing of the virtual scene (colour and texture); c) snapshot of part of the virtual scene used as a query; d) results for the query.

4. M. J. Swain, D. H. Ballard: *Color Indexing*, International Journal of Computer Vision, 7:1, 11-32 (1991)
5. K.C. Liang, C.C.J. Kuo, *Progressive Image Indexing and Retrieval Based on Embedded Wavelet Coding*, Proc. ICIP'97, Int. Conf. on Image Processing, Vol. I, pp. 572-575.
6. A. Del Bimbo, M. Mugnaini, P. Pala, F. Turco, *Visual Querying by Color Perceptive Regions*, to appear on Pattern Recognition
7. A. Vellaikal, C.C.J. Kuo, *Content-based Retrieval Using Multiresolution Histogram Representation*, Digital Image Storage Archiving Systems, Vol. 2602, Oct. 1995, pp. 312-323.

Trends in Visual Information Retrieval
(Panel Description)

Chahab Nastar

INRIA Rocquencourt, BP 105, F-78153 Le Chesnay, France.

Abstract. Visual information retrieval has been given a lot of attention in the past few years, in conjunction with the raise of multimedia. Vast amounts of multimedia data are today available to the average person with a computer. Video is the dominant modality with respect to bandwidth and complexity. In this paper, we address the research challenges of visual information retrieval.

While traditional information retrieval has addressed retrieval issues for over thirty years, visual information retrieval remains a very difficult task. Luckily, as opposed to classic computer vision, *user interactivity* in at the core of visual information retrieval, and helps to solve several image understanding issues. For instance, deciding for a specific query language - such as the popular query-by-example approach - will lead to retrieving images from an example image, based on pictorial similarity (as a metaphor of content).

Despite many research groups working on the subject, visual information retrieval is still in its infancy today. Many image retrieval systems basically compare color histograms to retrieve similar images. Video indexing systems, on the other hand, heavily focus on shot detection. Obviously, the true challenges of this field go far beyond these issues. Some of them are mentioned hereafter.

- **Testbeds.** There is need for large image and video testbeds that will allow for effective evaluation and comparison of retrieval algorithms.
- **Good applications**. Oddly enough, visual information retrieval has always had great applicative potential, but that potential sometimes did not become reality. General-public applications such as searching the web, or dedicated applications such as medical image retrieval - among others - can be mentioned as promising.
- **User interaction**. User interaction is subjective per definition, since it depends on each user. It is also highly context-dependent. Learning from user interaction has been studied recently; it still needs improving by integrating ideas from information retrieval and machine learning.
- **Use available data**. For many databases, extra information about the images (metadata, keywords) are available and should be combined with image search for improved performance.
- **Semantics vs. features**. The fact that the internal representation of images is based on image features (such as color, texture, shape) is not of direct

S. Jajodia, M.T. Özsu, and A. Dogac (Eds.): MIS'98, LNCS 1508, pp. 205–206, 1998.
© Springer-Verlag Berlin Heidelberg 1998

interest to the end user, who is mainly interested in image semantics. In particular, the user should not have to specify which image feature is relevant for their particular goal. That is up to the computer.

- **Browsing vs. retrieval**. There are currently very few systems that allow for efficient browsing of a database. Instead of smart browsing, most current image retrieval systems will randomly sample the database, while video indexing systems will generally output one or several images per shot. Browsing goes beyond these aspects and integrates retrieval as a special case. As a matter of fact, retrieval assumes the user to know what they are looking for (e.g., "show me more like this" in query-by-example), which is often not the case if the right query image is not available.

- **Open up**. Visual information retrieval is currently mainly addressed by computer vision scientists, who might extract sophisticated information from images, but will generally design poor user interfaces, use basic database models and do little indexing.

In conclusion, visual information retrieval is at the crossroads of several research fields: image processing, pattern recognition, computer vision, databases, information retrieval, information theory, human-computer interaction, cognitive science, psychology, machine learning.

A cooperative effort involving researchers of all these fields is required, and that is probably the biggest challenge.

Author Index

Springer
and the
environment

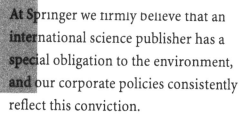

At Springer we firmly believe that an **inter**national science publisher has a **spec**ial obligation to the environment, **and** our corporate policies consistently reflect this conviction.
We also expect our business partners – paper mills, printers, packaging manufacturers, etc. – to commit themselves to using materials and production processes that do not harm the environment. The paper in this book is made from low- or no-chlorine pulp and is acid free, in conformance with international standards for paper permanency.

Springer

Lecture Notes in Computer Science

For information about Vols. 1–1420

please contact your bookseller or Springer-Verlag

Vol. 1460: G. Quirchmayr, E. Schweighofer, T.J.M. Bench-Capon (Eds.), Database and Expert Systems Applications. Proceedings, 1998. XVI, 905 pages. 1998.

Vol. 1461: G. Bilardi, G.F. Italiano, A. Pietracaprina, G. Pucci (Eds.), Algorithms – ESA'98. Proceedings, 1998. XII, 516 pages. 1998.

Vol. 1462: H. Krawczyk (Ed.), Advances in Cryptology - CRYPTO '98. Proceedings, 1998. XII, 519 pages. 1998.

Vol. 1463: N.E. Fuchs (Ed.), Logic Program Synthesis and Transformation. Proceedings, 1997. X, 343 pages. 1998.

Vol. 1464: H.H.S. Ip, A.W.M. Smeulders (Eds.), Multimedia Information Analysis and Retrieval. Proceedings, 1998. VIII, 264 pages. 1998.

Vol. 1465: R. Hirschfeld (Ed.), Financial Cryptography. Proceedings, 1998. VIII, 311 pages. 1998.

Vol. 1466: D. Sangiorgi, R. de Simone (Eds.), CONCUR'98: Concurrency Theory. Proceedings, 1998. XI, 657 pages. 1998.

Vol. 1467: C. Clack, K. Hammond, T. Davie (Eds.), Implementation of Functional Languages. Proceedings, 1997. X, 375 pages. 1998.

Vol. 1468: P. Husbands, J.-A. Meyer (Eds.), Evolutionary Robotics. Proceedings, 1998. VIII, 247 pages. 1998.

Vol. 1469: R. Puigjaner, N.N. Savino, B. Serra (Eds.), Computer Performance Evaluation. Proceedings, 1998. XIII, 376 pages. 1998.

Vol. 1470: D. Pritchard, J. Reeve (Eds.), Euro-Par'98: Parallel Processing. Proceedings, 1998. XXII, 1157 pages. 1998.

Vol. 1471: J. Dix, L. Moniz Pereira, T.C. Przymusinski (Eds.), Logic Programming and Knowledge Representation. Proceedings, 1997. IX, 246 pages. 1998. (Subseries LNAI).

Vol. 1473: X. Leroy, A. Ohori (Eds.), Types in Compilation. Proceedings, 1998. VIII, 299 pages. 1998.

Vol. 1474: F. Mueller, A. Bestavros (Eds.), Languages, Compilers, and Tools for Embedded Systems. Proceedings, 1998. XIV, 261 pages. 1998.

Vol. 1475: W. Litwin, T. Morzy, G. Vossen (Eds.), Advances in Databases and Information Systems. Proceedings, 1998. XIV, 369 pages. 1998.

Vol. 1476: J. Calmet, J. Plaza (Eds.), Artificial Intelligence and Symbolic Computation. Proceedings, 1998. XI, 309 pages. 1998. (Subseries LNAI).

Vol. 1477: K. Rothermel, F. Hohl (Eds.), Mobile Agents. Proceedings, 1998. VIII, 285 pages. 1998.

Vol. 1478: M. Sipper, D. Mange, A. Pérez-Uribe (Eds.), Evolvable Systems: From Biology to Hardware. Proceedings, 1998. IX, 382 pages. 1998.

Vol. 1479: J. Grundy, M. Newey (Eds.), Theorem Proving in Higher Order Logics. Proceedings, 1998. VIII, 497 pages. 1998.

Vol. 1480: F. Giunchiglia (Ed.), Artificial Intelligence: Methodology, Systems, and Applications. Proceedings, 1998. IX, 502 pages. 1998. (Subseries LNAI).

Vol. 1481: E.V. Munson, C. Nicholas, D. Wood (Eds.), Principles of Digital Document Processing. Proceedings, 1998. VII, 152 pages. 1998.

Vol. 1482: R.W. Hartenstein, A. Keevallik (Eds.), Field-Programmable Logic and Applications. Proceedings, 1998. XI, 533 pages. 1998.

Vol. 1483: T. Plagemann, V. Goebel (Eds.), Interactive Distributed Multimedia Systems and Telecommunication Services. Proceedings, 1998. XV, 326 pages. 1998.

Vol. 1484: H. Coelho (Ed.), Progress in Artificial Intelligence - IBERAMIA 98. Proceedings, 1998. XIII, 421 pages. 1998. (Subseries LNAI).

Vol. 1485: J.-J. Quisquater, Y. Deswarte, C. Meadows, D. Gollmann (Eds.), Computer Security – ESORICS 98. Proceedings, 1998. X, 377 pages. 1998.

Vol. 1486: A.P. Ravn, H. Rischel (Eds.), Formal Techniques in Real-Time and Fault-Tolerant Systems. Proceedings, 1998. VIII, 339 pages. 1998.

Vol. 1487: V. Gruhn (Ed.), Software Process Technology. Proceedings, 1998. VIII, 157 pages. 1998.

Vol. 1488: B. Smyth, P. Cunningham (Eds.), Advances in Case-Based Reasoning. Proceedings, 1998. XI, 482 pages. 1998. (Subseries LNAI).

Vol. 1490: C. Palamidessi, H. Glaser, K. Meinke (Eds.), Principles of Declarative Programming. Proceedings, 1998. XI, 497 pages. 1998.

Vol. 1493: J.P. Bowen, A. Fett, M.G. Hinchey (Eds.), ZUM '98: The Z Formal Specification Notation. Proceedings, 1998. XV, 417 pages. 1998.

Vol. 1495: T. Andreasen, H. Christiansen, H.L. Larsen (Eds.), Flexible Query Answering Systems. IX, 393 pages. 1998. (Subseries LNAI).

Vol. 1497: V. Alexandrov, J. Dongarra (Eds.), Recent Advances in Parallel Virtual Machine and Message Passing Interface. Proceedings, 1998. XII, 412 pages. 1998.

Vol. 1498: A.E. Eiben, T. Bäck, M. Schoenauer, H.-P. Schwefel (Eds.), Parallel Problem Solving from Nature – PPSN V. Proceedings, 1998. XXIII, 1041 pages. 1998.

Vol. 1499: S. Kutten (Ed.), Distributed Computing. Proceedings, 1998. XII, 419 pages. 1998.

Vol. 1501: M.M. Richter, C.H. Smith, R. Wiehagen, T. Zeugmann (Eds.), Algorithmic Learning Theory. Proceedings, 1998. XI, 439 pages. 1998. (Subseries LNAI).

Vol. 1503: G. Levi (Ed.), Static Analysis. Proceedings, 1998. IX, 383 pages. 1998.

Vol. 1504: O. Herzog, A. Günter (Eds.), KI-98: Advances in Artificial Intelligence. Proceedings, 1998. XI, 355 pages. 1998. (Subseries LNAI).

Vol. 1508: S. Jajodia, M.T. Özsu, A. Dogac (Eds.), Advances in Multimedia Information Systems. Proceedings, 1998. VIII, 207 pages. 1998.

Vol. 1510: J.M. Zytkow, M. Quafafou (Eds.), Principles of Data Mining and Knowledge Discovery. Proceedings, 1998. XI, 482 pages. 1998. (Subseries LNAI).

Vol. 1513: C. Nikolaou, C. Stephanidis (Eds.), Research and Advanced Technology for Digital Libraries. Proceedings, 1998. XV, 912 pages. 1998.

Vol. 1514: K. Ohta,, D. Pei (Eds.), Advances in Cryptology – ASIACRYPT'98. Proceedings, 1998. XII, 436 pages. 1998.

Vol. 1516: W. Ehrenberger (Ed.), Computer Safety, Reliability and Security. Proceedings, 1998. XVI, 392 pages. 1998.